CLOSELY WATCHED FILMS

Closely Watched Films

An Introduction to the Art
of Narrative Film Technique

Marilyn Fabe

UNIVERSITY OF CALIFORNIA PRESS Berkeley Los Angeles London

University of California Press
Berkeley and Los Angeles, California

University of California Press, Ltd.
London, England

Portions of chapters 3, 8, and 9 have been previously
published in a series of Film Study Extract Booklets,
Macmillan Films Inc., Mount Vernon, N.Y., 1975.

Library of Congress Cataloging-in-Publication Data

Fabe, Marilyn.
    Closely watched films : an introduction to the art of
narrative film technique / Marilyn Fabe.
        p.   cm.
    Includes bibliographical references and index.
    ISBN 0-520-23862-1 (cloth : alk. paper)
    ISBN 0-520-23891-5 (pbk. : alk. paper)
    1. Motion pictures—Evaluation.   2. Motion
pictures—Aesthetics.   3. Motion pictures.
I. Title.
    PN1995.9.E9F17   2004
    791.43'015—dc22   2004000202

Manufactured in the United States of America

13   12   11   10   09   08   07   06   05   04
10   9   8   7   6   5   4   3   2   1

The paper used in this publication meets the minimum
requirements of ANSI/NISO Z39.48–1992 (R 1997)
(Permanence of Paper).

For Tom and Daniel

Contents

Illustrations

Acknowledgments

First I would like to thank Cass Canfield, Jr., who suggested that I turn my lectures from Film 50, an introductory film course for University of California students and the Berkeley community, into a book. He provided valuable feedback, encouragement, and editorial suggestions. I am also indebted to Edith Kramer, director of the University of California, Berkeley's Pacific Film Archive, and the staff of the Pacific Film Archive Theater for providing the perfect place to teach Film 50. While digital video makes teaching films more convenient, there is nothing like showing an archival 35mm print perfectly projected on a big screen to inspire audiences to appreciate film art. My efforts to expand lecture notes into a book benefited from the help of members of my Berkeley writing group, which over the years has included Elizabeth Abel, Janet Adelman, Gayle Greene, Jodi Halpern, Claire Kahane, Mardi Louisell, Wendy Martin, and Madelon Sprengnether. I also received valuable feedback from the members of the Townsend Center Working Group in Psychobiography, including Jacquelynn Baas, Ramsay Breslin, Liz Cara, Alan Elms, Candace Falk, Lorraine Kahn, Mac Runyan, Reit Samuels, Adrian Walker, and Stephen Walrod.

Madelon Sprengnether was the book's muse. Her kind enthusiasm and brilliant editorial advice kept up my morale and gave me the determination to keep writing. Brenda Webster was a major impetus in convincing me to undertake the project. Margaret Schaefer and Claire Ka-hane, close friends who date back to my graduate-school days in the En-glish Department at Berkeley, read the book from end to end several times, suggesting ways to make it better, clearer, and more coherent. I am solely responsible for the defects that remain.

I am grateful to the group major in film at Berkeley for giving me the opportunity to teach film since 1976. Working with the bright and chal-lenging film majors at Berkeley nourished my enthusiasm for learning about and teaching film. Conversations with faculty colleagues and grad-uate students at Berkeley have greatly enriched my perspectives on film and have helped inform my ideas. These include Mark Berger, Seymour Chatman, Carol Clover, Anton Kaes, Russell Merritt, Gabriel Moses, Anne Nesbet, Bill Nestrick, B. Ruby Rich, Mark Sandberg, Kaja Silver-man, Maria St. John, and Linda Williams. At the University of Califor-nia Press, I am grateful to Jim Clark for his enthusiasm about the book, Mari Coates for helping me to get the book ready to launch, Rachel Berchten for guiding it through the production process, and Laura Schattschneider for the intelligence and grace with which she copyedited the manuscript.

My son, Daniel Schmidt, an undergraduate at Berkeley while I was writing *Closely Watched Films*, was my ideal audience. Daniel provided me with both generous encouragement and astute criticism of various chapters. Finally I would like to thank my husband, Tom Schmidt, who gave me ideas, editorial advice, technological support and much, much more. The book is dedicated to Tom and Daniel.

Introduction

How do films work? How do they tell a story? How do they move us and make us think? This book argues that shot-by-shot analysis is the best way for film students to learn about and appreciate the filmmaker's art. Having taught film studies for many years, I have learned that viewers trained in close analysis of single film sequences are better able to see and appreciate the rich visual and aural complexity of the film medium. Close analysis unlocks the secrets of how film images, combined with sound, can have such a profound effect on our minds and emotions. Through detailed examinations of passages from classic and near-classic films, I hope to provide nonspecialist readers with the analytic tools and background in film theory that will help them see more in every film they watch. As their knowledge of the vast possibilities of the film medium thus increases, so will their enthusiasm for the films they already love.

The book focuses on exemplary works of fourteen film directors whose careers, put together, span the history of the narrative film, beginning with D. W. Griffith and ending with Mike Figgis. Rather than discussing many films in a general way, I discuss a few films in detail, singling out particular sequences from each that either best illustrate what is special or significant about its director's style or help to illuminate a significant theoretical or aesthetic concern. I begin with a study of directors who worked before synchronized sound came to the screen, focusing in chapters 1 through 3 on exemplary films by D. W. Griffith, Sergei Eisenstein, F. W. Murnau, and Charles Chaplin. Because silent-era filmmakers did not have the option of using the spoken word to express their ideas, they *had* to convey their ideas through pictures. As a result, contemporary directors are still inspired by the visual richness and emotional intensity of their films.

Because silent film directors were working with few precedents, their works convey a doing-it-for-the-first-time exuberance and vitality that encourage us to look at film techniques freshly. Just knowing that a certain kind of camera movement, point-of-view shot, or method of juxtaposing two shots was being used in an innovative way helps students to think about and better appreciate the effects of formal elements of film art.

An analysis of one short sequence from Griffith's *The Birth of a Nation* offers a crash course in the foundations of narrative film art, introducing readers in a clear and precise way to essentially all the basic narrative techniques we see in mainstream films today. I purposefully chose this controversial film to begin this book because its racist content illustrates the way in which narrative film technique is never neutral or innocent: every nuance of a narrative film can convey an ideology. The close analysis of sequences from classic silent films, moreover, makes it possible to clarify and test out theoretical ideas about the medium by prominent film theorists whose ideas are still influential today. An examination of a few sequences in Sergei Eisenstein's *The Battleship Potemkin*, for instance, illustrates why prominent Soviet film directors believed that editing was the foundation of film art. The analysis of just one shot in Charles Chaplin's *The Adventurer* provides a vivid and concrete means to introduce students to the French film theorist André Bazin's realist aesthetic. A study of the techniques used to create the dream sequence in F. W. Murnau's *The Last Laugh* clarifies what is meant by the term "expressionism" in film art. By illustrating the above perspectives on the film medium with strikingly effective examples from silent films, I offer readers a solid foundation on which to appreciate the transformative effect on film art occasioned by the introduction of synchronized sound.

In chapter 4, a discussion of Howard Hawks's *His Girl Friday* (1940), a film made thirteen years after the introduction of talking pictures, introduces readers to the impact of synchronized sound on the art of the motion picture. Included in this chapter is an account of the debate between early and modern sound theorists—those who thought the talking film meant the death of cinema as a visual art and those who thought that the sound film was a rebirth of the medium, opening it up to new potentials of expressiveness. The analysis of a sequence from *His Girl Friday* demonstrates how even a film dominated by talk can still be highly cinematic. *His Girl Friday* also offers the occasion to introduce some of the conventions of classical Hollywood cinema. It is important to identify and define these conventions, not just because they are fascinating in their own right, but because readers versed in them will better appreciate the aesthetic breakthroughs of directors who worked outside the classical model or modified it to open up new channels for expressiveness in film form. This is exactly what Orson Welles did in *Citizen Kane* (1941), discussed in chapter 5, and this and the two following chapters introduce a series of breakthroughs made in film narrative in the 1940s and 1950s. By the time we get to *Citizen Kane*, readers are well equipped to appreciate Welles's narrative innovations (and why many critics and historians still consider *Citizen Kane* one of the greatest films ever made). Likewise, chapter 6, on Vittorio De Sica's *The Bicycle Thief* (1948), demonstrates what was new and vital about Italian neorealism. In chapter 7, I introduce readers to auteur theory and demonstrate what was groundbreaking about François Truffaut's *The 400 Blows* (1959), the film that ushered in the French New Wave.

No introductory text on the art of narrative film is complete without a chapter on Alfred Hitchcock. In chapter 8, I build upon my discussion of auteur theory in chapter 7, and take a close look at Hitchcock's *Notorious* (1946). A thematic and stylistic analysis of this film demonstrates why Hitchcock is considered a serious artist, and not just a master of suspense. The chapter begins with a broad overview of Hitchcock's career in order to illustrate auteur theory's claim that the greatest directors will always draw upon personal themes and obsessions to mark their films with a distinctive cinematic style, no matter what genre they are working within, and even when they are adapting material written by someone else.

A discussion of Federico Fellini's *8 1/2* (1963) in chapter 9 introduces readers to the European art film, which brought the complex narrative forms and self-reflection of literary modernism to film. The close analysis of one sequence from *8 1/2* opens up the secrets of its strangely disorienting but highly expressive techniques and leads viewers to a deeper understanding and appreciation of this extraordinary, difficult film. In chapter 10 I discuss the American art films of Woody Allen. Unlike many of the European art films, Woody Allen's films do not need anyone to explain their meaning or to help viewers follow the plot. They are easy to "get" and enjoy on first viewing. Yet close analysis of Woody Allen's technique in *Annie Hall* (1977) is revelatory. Allen's style is just as fractured, achronological, free associative, and self-reflecting as Fellini's in *8 1/2*, a film Allen was obviously influenced by. I discuss Woody Allen as a postmodern artist whose works incorporate and reconceive modernist techniques to question the stability of our identity and the meaningfulness of life.

In chapter 11, I move away from film as an expression of a director's philosophy to discuss film as a political instrument. My chapter on Spike Lee's *Do the Right Thing* (1989) shows how Lee plays with and against film stereotypes of African Americans to convey a serious political message, drawing on some of the dialectical methods used by Sergei Eisenstein to offer a complex, sophisticated meditation on the tragedy of racism in America. In chapter 12, a discussion of Patricia Rozema's *I've Heard the Mermaids Singing* (1986), I begin with an overview of feminist approaches to the representation of women in films directed by male directors. Then I look closely at the style and techniques used in Rozema's film to address the question of how representations of women in film differ when a woman with a feminist consciousness writes and directs. The book concludes with an epilogue discussing Mike Figgis's *Timecode* (2000), the first American studio film shot entirely in digital video. *Timecode* enables us to speculate about possible new directions in narrative film just as we enter the age of digital media.

Closely Watched Films guides readers through significant works of narrative film art and introduces them to theoretical perspectives on how cinematic techniques create and heighten a film's narrative, emotional, and ideological effects. The title of the book alludes to *Closely Watched Trains*—the famous film by Czechoslovakian director Jiři Menzel. It is also the title of a book devoted to Czechoslovakian cinema by Antonin Liehm. I too have chosen this title, because it so perfectly expresses my enthusiasm for teaching students how to do close analyses of films, shot by shot, thereby opening their eyes to a more informed understanding of the art and experience of film. My purpose is not to issue the last word on the meaning or effect of a film sequence, but to engage readers in the process of looking at films closely. Indeed, because the films I discuss in this book are available on video and DVD, readers are encouraged to use these media to follow along with my analysis of the sequences I have chosen and to test their readings against mine. Above all, I encourage my readers to see and hear more in every film they encounter and to appreciate the heightened intellectual and emotional pleasures that come from closely watched films.

1

The Beginnings of Film Narrative

D. W. Griffith's *The Birth of a Nation*

D. W. GRIFFITH'S BACKGROUND AND EARLY CAREER

D. W. Griffith, arguably the most influential pioneer in the art of the narrative film, was born on a farm near La Grange, Kentucky in 1875, ten years after the Civil War. He came from a family of wealth on his mother's side. His father, known as "Roaring Jake" and "Thunder Jake" for his oratory skills, achieved glory on the battlefield as a colonel in the Civil War. But Griffith's father was also a wanderer and a gambler who left his family in debt when he died. Hence, after Griffith's mother moved the family to St. Louis, Griffith took a number of jobs to help his mother financially and never finished high school. A job at a bookstore sparked a passion for literature, and his prime ambition in life was to be a writer.[1]

He was also, at an early age, intrigued by the theater. His eventual career as an actor, he claimed, was the result of advice he received from a stage manager who told him that a good playwright had to be an actor first. Although his literary success was limited (he produced one play and published one poem),[2] his success as an actor was more considerable. After playing bit parts in repertory companies in St. Louis, he went on tour with various productions all over the country, often playing leading roles and receiving good notices. Eventually he settled in San Francisco where he gained steady employment and acted in better quality

1

plays. He was on tour in Minnesota when the San Francisco earthquake and fire of 1906 occurred. Rather than returning to the devastated city, he decided to try his fortunes as a playwright and actor in New York, where his career took an unexpected turn.

Married and short of cash, he took the advice of a colleague and approached a movie production company, the Edison Studio, for work as a scriptwriter. His scripts were too complex and expensive to produce, but film companies were eager to use stage actors because of the prestige they brought to film from the theater. Thus Griffith was hired not to write for films but to act in them. After playing a lumberjack in an Edison film directed by Edwin S. Porter, *Rescued from an Eagle's Nest* (1908), he got work, again as an actor, for a rival studio, the American Mutoscope and Biograph Company. He came at an auspicious moment. The company was flooded by the demand for short fiction films and, after a brief time acting, he was offered the opportunity to direct. Between 1908 and 1913 Griffith directed over 450 short films for the Biograph Company, molding the film medium into a sophisticated instrument for creating dramatic and suspenseful film narratives.

In order to appreciate the significance of Griffith's contribution to the creation of narrative film art, it is necessary to recall the state of the fiction film when Griffith began making movies in 1908. Film viewing by then was no longer a novelty but a regular mode of entertainment. People saw movies in small storefront theaters called nickelodeons because the price of admission was usually a nickel. Audiences saw anywhere from fifteen- to sixty-minute programs of short, mostly fiction films, lasting up to ten minutes each. But these films did not tell stories very well. They comprised a series of loosely spliced scenes or tableaus, shot with a static camera in long takes (sometimes lasting up to ninety seconds) with the camera remaining at a fixed distance from the action. The scenes proceeded in a strict chronological order, and the temporal and spatial relations between the shots were often ambiguous or unclear. The most common type of shot was the long shot, in which the human figure fills only a small portion of the lower quadrant of the frame, much as the human figure appears in the proscenium of stage dramas. In a theater, however, even though the actors may appear tiny, especially to spectators in the last row of the balcony, their words loom large, conveying dramatic excitement through the expressiveness of the human voice. This resource, of course, was not possible in the then-silent medium of film, which relied on static printed title cards to convey exposition or dialogue. Griffith found ways to compensate for the lack of spoken words, increasing the drama and emotional power of his fiction films in three ways. First, he paid close attention to elements of the filmic mise-en-scène. Second, he photographed his scenes in more imaginative ways. Third, he added complexity to his narratives through editing.[3]

GRIFFITH'S REFINEMENT OF NARRATIVE FILM TECHNIQUES

MISE-EN-SCÈNE

The term *mise-en-scène* denotes all the elements of film direction that overlap with the art of theater. Thus a film's mise-en-scène involves the director's choice of actors and how they are directed, the way the scene is lit, the choice of setting or set design, props, costumes, and make-up. Since Griffith was an actor before he came to film, it is not surprising that he carried over his experience from the stage to the screen. Griffith, more than other contemporary filmmakers, took the time to cast actors who looked the part and carefully rehearsed the players before shooting the scenes (a practice rare in early filmmaking). He also chose costumes, props, and settings with an eye to providing narrative information that would enhance the film's dramatic effect. Griffith realized, moreover, that blatantly artificial painted background details, common in early films, would undermine the realism of filmed fictions. In a pre-Griffith film such as *The Great Train Robbery* (1903), for example, a fairly realistic rendering of a railroad telegraph office is marred by a painted clock on the wall, its hands perpetually set at nine o'clock. Griffith insisted on the construction of authentic-looking three-dimensional props and sets for his films. He also brought increased realism to the screen by directing the players to act in a restrained, natural, less flamboyantly theatrical style.

THE ENFRAMED IMAGE

Griffith did more than improve the mise-en-scène of early cinema. Early on he began to shape and arrange the profilmic elements of the mise-en-scène into an emotionally charged picture language by exploiting the dramatic potential of techniques specific to the film medium. The term profilmic refers to the objects placed in front of the camera to be photographed—the actors, sets, props, etc. It is a critically useful term because it calls attention to the difference between objects that exist in the world before they are photographed and these same objects once they have been enframed on celluloid. The choices the director makes in framing the images, whether they are in long shot or close-up, shot from a high or low angle, shot with a moving or static camera, or even how they are composed within the frame, can add powerful dramatic effects to the filmed action.

Griffith was especially sensitive to the impact of the close-up, a shot in which the head and shoulders of a character fill the screen. As noted above, in most film dramas prior to Griffith, the camera stayed back, showing all of the action in long or full shots. By moving the camera closer to a character at crucial moments of emotional significance in the narrative, Griffith made it possible for spectators to better observe and hence to relate empathetically to the expressions on the character's face, thereby increasing their emotional involvement in the story. Griffith did not limit his close-ups to the human face. His insertion of close-up details of a significant prop such as a gun or a flower also enabled him to direct the spectator's attention to objects that were crucial to the dramatic unfolding of the plot. In most narrative films before Griffith viewers had to pick out the significant details of the action from a mass of superfluous and contingent visual information. Griffith performs this job for us. By deciding when to insert a close-up of an actor's face or a detail of the film's mise-en-scène, he determines what viewers focus their attention on, as well as the most dramatic moment for a plot revelation. In addition, close-ups of objects in Griffith's films are often imbued with subtle symbolic resonance.

Griffith also understood the dramatic power of pulling the camera back, far away from the action. Extreme long shots, in which a small human figure is dominated by the landscape, can make characters seem vulnerable to larger forces beyond their control. Also, by incorporating spectacular panoramic shots of landscapes into his films—waterfalls, snowstorms, massive battle scenes—he enhanced his narratives with a grandeur and scope that far exceeded what was possible in even the most extravagantly produced stage dramas. Further, as we shall see in the analysis of a sequence from *The Birth of a Nation,* these panoramic landscape shots, like Griffith's close-ups of objects, often functioned symbolically in the narrative.

Griffith did not "invent" the use of the close-up in film, nor was he the first to use extreme long shots. A close-up had appeared in one of Edison's very first films, *Fred Ott's Sneeze,* made in 1888, and the pioneering films of the Lumière brothers in 1895 included panoramic scenes taken in extreme long shot. Not until Griffith came along, however, were shots taken from various distances from the camera systematically combined into sequential wholes to produce dramatic narrative effects. Karel Reisz in *The Technique of Film Editing* succinctly sums up Griffith's achievement:

> Griffith's fundamental discovery . . . lies in his realisation that a film sequence must be made up of incomplete shots whose order and selection are governed by dramatic necessity. Where Porter's camera had impartially recorded the action from a distance (i.e., in long shot), Griffith demonstrated that the camera could play a positive part in telling the story. By splitting an event into short fragments and recording each from the most suitable camera position, he could vary the emphasis from shot to shot and thereby control the dramatic intensity of the events as the story progressed.[4]

EDITING

Once Griffith had taken the first crucial steps of breaking a scene down into numerous shots (instead of photographing the action in one lengthy, static long shot), he was faced with the problem of reconnecting the shots smoothly, so that what was in reality a discontinuous sequence of separate shots would appear to the viewer to be a smooth and continuous action taking place in a unified time and space. He wanted spectators to maintain the illusion of watching a seamless flow of reality and not become distracted or disoriented by jerky edits that called attention to the film medium. In order to accomplish this effect, Griffith systematically developed the editing device known as the "match" or the match cut.[5]

The match cut, which has become a standard convention in the cinema, refers to any element in conjoined shots that smooths the transition from one shot to the next, so that viewers do not notice the cut or lose their orientation in relation to the screen space. In a movement match, for example, if a gesture of a character raising a hand to her face is begun in a long shot, the gesture must be smoothly continued in the subsequent close-up shot so that the viewer focuses on the gesture. The seemingly continuous gesture thus masks the fact that there has been a cut. In a direction match, the direction in which a person or object is moving is kept consistent across the splice. That is, in a chase sequence, a character moving across the screen from left to right must continue in the same direction from shot to shot. If the character exits screen right at the end of a shot, he or she must enter from screen left in the subsequent shot. If the character were instead to exit frame right and enter the next shot from frame right, it would appear that she had turned around and reversed direction.

To help maintain the spectator's orientation in a coherent screen space, Griffith made systematic use of the eye-line match. If he had established that Person A was positioned to the right of Person B, but then wanted to move the camera closer to photograph each of the characters separately for greater dramatic emphasis, he was careful to match the directions of the two characters' eye lines (or glances) so that they would seem to converge. Person A would look screen left, while person B would look screen right. If the actors both looked off in the same direction (let's say they both looked screen right), viewers would no longer have the impression that the two were facing each other and would lose their orientation in screen space. By carefully matching his shots in the ways described above, Griffith succeeded in breaking down the action of his narratives into a number of separate shots, creating dramatic emphasis, without drawing attention to the medium or confusing his audience.[6]

Griffith also refined the use of transitional editing devices such as fade-ins and fade-outs and iris-ins and iris-outs to heighten the impact of his narratives. In a fade-in, a shot begins in darkness and gradually brightens until the image appears fully exposed. In a fade-out, the opposite occurs: the image slowly fades to black. In an iris-in, a black screen opens from darkness in an expanding circle of light. An iris-out reverses the process. These optical devices allowed Griffith control over the pacing of the narrative (a fade or iris effect could be rapid, or very slow and drawn out), and heightened its dramatic effect. When a sad or ominous action ends with a shot that fades to black, for example, the effect is to make the action seem all the more troubling. Griffith also used these transitional devices to signal that time has elapsed from the end of one sequence to the beginning of the next. While these editing devices do call attention to the medium, they quickly became familiar conventions, and audiences were not distracted by their artificiality.

More significant than Griffith's refinement of methods for smooth continuities and his use of creative transitions to signal time ellipses was his creative development of associative editing techniques. These are editing devices that cue viewers to mentally construe the screen action in a way that greatly increases their mental participation in the story. Griffith especially made dramatic use of the point-of-view or POV shot. A POV shot follows a shot in which a character looks pointedly at something offscreen, revealing, from the character's point of view, what the character sees. Through the technique of the POV shot, viewers are mentally lifted out of their theater seats and put in the place of a character up on the screen, seeing the action as if through that character's eyes. The POV shot is often followed by a reaction shot, a shot in which the camera captures the character's reaction to what was seen in the POV shot. The combination of a POV shot followed by a reaction shot is especially powerful because it gives us two ways of identifying with on-screen characters. First we identify with them because we are seeing through their eyes, and then we identify with the reactions we see on their faces. Especially powerful effects can be created when the reaction of the character is unexpected. (For example, a character might see something horrifying, and smile.)[7]

The associative editing technique for which Griffith is best known is the cross-cut. A cross-cut is an alternation (a cutting back and forth) from one line of action to another, giving the impression that two or more spatially separated but plot-related events are occurring simultaneously. Although crosscutting appears in rudimentary form in a few early narrative films, the standard narrative practice when Griffith began directing in 1908 was to follow the actions of one character or a set of characters in an uninterrupted linear chronology. Griffith soon realized that more narrative excitement could be generated if he systematically intercut or alternated between two or more narrative threads happening simultaneously, thus thickening his plots by giving the spectator greater knowledge than the characters have. At the climax of *The Lonely Villa* (1909), for example, Griffith intercut three spatially separate simultaneous actions: (1) Shots of a mother and her three little girls alone in their isolated country house because the father has been called away on business; (2) shots of three male intruders trying to break into the house; and (3) shots of the father, who, after telephoning home, frantically rushes to the rescue in a borrowed gypsy wagon. Here the crosscutting of the three actions creates tremendous excitement, pace, and suspense, generating the question: Will the father get home before the intruders get to his wife and children? So much tension is built up by the crosscutting that, when the father arrives in the nick of time, the relief is enormous, even to audiences today. This crosscutting device became famous as the Griffith last-minute rescue, a convention that made failed last-minute rescues (the hero does not make it in time to prevent disaster) all the more devastating. Through constant experimentation with this technique, Griffith honed it into an increasingly powerful and complex narrative tool. Griffith became so excited by the potentials of crosscutting that in *Intolerance* (1916), the film he made after *The Birth of a Nation*, he told four separate stories, each taking place in different historical periods. At the end of the film, for a grand finale, he cut back and forth between the climaxes of the various tales.

THE NARRATOR'S POINT OF VIEW

Griffith's attention to details of mise-en-scène, his cinematography, and his editing innovations not only enabled him to increase the dramatic power of his fictions, they also made it possible for him to fulfill another important storytelling role—the imparting of the narrator's point of view or commentary on the action. Narratives in any medium are rarely innocent. There is always some point to any story. But film narratives, because of their photographic realism, appear on the surface to be presenting events objectively or neutrally. Apparently unaware of the rhetorical power of his own pioneering film techniques, Griffith believed that the historical events he retold in his blockbuster feature film *The Birth of a Nation* were objectively rendered—the unvarnished truth. In an interview that came out shortly after the release of *The Birth of a Nation* he predicted that "in less than ten years . . . the children in the public schools will be taught practically everything by moving pictures. . . . There will be no opinions expressed. You will merely be present at the making of history."[8] But a close analysis of Griffith's techniques in *The Birth of a Nation* demonstrates his skill in imbuing both his narrative actions and historical reenactments with strong moral and political implications. Implicitly and explicitly, Griffith's opinions on "history," many of them repugnant, are expressed throughout this controversial film.

It is one of the sad ironies of film history that Griffith's artistic skill and mastery of his medium was first fully realized in a film that expressed a racist Southerner's view of the Civil War and the Reconstruction period. *The Birth of a Nation* was an adaptation of a play by the white supremacist Thomas Dixon, Jr., which was based on two of his novels, *The Leopard's Spots* (1902) and *The Clansman* (1905). The hero of *The Birth of a Nation* is Ben Cameron (played by Henry B. Walthall), the founder of the Ku Klux Klan, the terrorist organization Griffith celebrates in the film for restoring white supremacy during the post–Civil War era. Griffith depicts black men who are not faithful Uncle Toms as dangerous, power-hungry rapists who equate political equality with the freedom to sexually possess white women. According to this logic, the violent overthrow of black power by the Klan at the end of the film is morally justified. Because Griffith not only told a story in *The Birth of a Nation,* but also conveyed strong ideological and political beliefs, the film provides vivid examples of how, consciously or unconsciously, a director can imbue a story with the director's beliefs and attitudes. To see in detail how Griffith's techniques function both dramatically and ideologically, we shall take a close look at a twenty-shot sequence from the film.

The sequence under analysis relates the action just before Gus (Walter Long), a renegade ex-slave who has joined the Northern army, proposes "marriage" to Flora (Mae Marsh), the little pet sister of Ben Cameron. I put marriage in quotes because even though Gus's request seems innocent enough if you just consider the title card—"I'm a Captain now and I want to marry"—the visual subtext of the film suggests something else. Flora reacts to the proposal by running away in terror. When Gus pursues her, she flings herself from a cliff to her death. When her brother discovers her broken body, the strong implication is that Gus has raped and murdered her. As if this had actually been the case, Ben uses his sister's blood in a ceremonial ritual to spur on the Ku Klux Klan to a mission of vengeance against the newly empowered blacks, a mission that begins with the lynching of Gus and ends in the violent suppression of black power in the South. If we look carefully at just twenty-one shots from the Gus stalks Flora sequence, the incidents that lead up to Flora's fatal encounter with Gus, it will become evident why, despite the seeming innocence, even respectability, of Gus's proposal, audiences know it is not marriage Gus is after.

SEQUENCE ANALYSIS: "GUS STALKS FLORA" IN *THE BIRTH OF A NATION*

Shot 1 of the sequence is a fade-in to a long shot of Flora, who has left the safety of her home to fetch water from the spring for her mother. She enters from screen left into a small clearing in a heavily forested landscape. Although the spring water she seeks would supposedly be within walking distance from her house, in this shot she seems suddenly transported to a very remote place.[9] As far as the eye can see, there are no signs of civilization, only huge towering trees. The landscape illustrates how well Griffith understood the potential symbolic resonance of the background or setting against which a dramatic sequence is staged in a film. The forest through which Flora passes on her way to the spring evokes an archetypal dream landscape, the woods of fairy tales and myths where innocent little girls carrying buckets or baskets are likely to meet up with big bad wolves.

Flora appears in a long shot, her body tiny in relation to the vastness of the forest. Here the long shot of Flora functions dramatically to increase our sense of her smallness and vulnerability. The way in which

Figure 1. The long shot of Flora functions dramatically to increase our sense of her smallness and vulnerability. The dark shadow at the base of the frame functions as foreshadowing. (*The Birth of a Nation*, 1915, Film Preservation Associates.)

Flora is lit, the light coming from behind her, creates a halo effect around her head. This technique, referred to as "angel lighting," adds to our sense of her innocence. A dark shadow cutting a diagonal wedge at the base of the frame into which she is headed functions as an ominous (and literal) foreshadowing of the doom she will meet as the result of her entry into the forest. (See figure 1.)

At this point Griffith might well have continued to follow Flora on her journey to the spring. But at the moment she enters the shadowy portion of the image and before she exits the frame, he interrupts her action with a cross-cut to Gus (shot 2) standing by a fence and seeming to peer after her. The cross-cut to Gus sets up dramatic irony, giving the viewer information that the protagonist, Flora, does not have—that Gus is following her into the woods. Thus, in shot 3, when Griffith cuts back to Flora heading deeper into the forest, blissfully unaware of the threat that we know has materialized, he increases our anxiety for her well-being. A cross-cut back to Gus (shot 4), however, dispels some of the anxiety. Gus seems to have had second thoughts about pursuing Flora and turns back.

The first two shots of Gus in this sequence provide another example of Griffith's sensitivity to the symbolic potential of a film's setting or mise-en-scène. It is significant that in these two shots Gus shares the frame equally with a slatted fence which juts out diagonally on the left side of the screen. (See figure 2.) In a film obsessed with the threat of breached boundaries between blacks and whites, the image of a fence appearing large in the frame as a black man is about to pursue a young white woman into a forest is anything but accidental. Gus is shown to hesitate at the fence, as if the fence represents a kind of societal superego. He hesitates, however, very reluctantly looking back in the direction of Flora even as he seems to turn away from his pursuit. As a result, the question is raised in the viewer's mind: Will Gus's internal restraints be sufficient to keep him from pursuing Flora in a society where restraints have recently been weakened? Griffith has already established that societal restraints have been undermined by the reckless policies of Reconstruction, "the vicious doctrines spread by the carpetbaggers" mentioned earlier in a title, and by a law that has recently passed guaranteeing blacks "Equal Marriage." Here Griffith gives us a powerful dose of his ideology (that Reconstructionist policies are reckless and dangerous) through an image of Gus's reluctance to stop at the fence—without the need for a title.

In shot 5 Griffith cuts back to Flora, who has arrived at her destination: the spring where she is to fetch water for her mother. Here we see Flora in a full shot bending down to fill her bucket. Shot 6 is a close-up of the bucket being filled with spring water. Griffith then cuts back to a full shot of Flora as she finishes her task and wipes her wet hands on her dress. Griffith could easily have conveyed the same narrative information in one shot, but he chooses to present it in three separate shots joined together through match cuts on Flora's movements.

It is interesting to speculate why Griffith took the trouble to insert the detail of Flora's bucket being filled with water rather than presenting the action in one long shot. For part of the answer we need only consider the techniques of nineteenth-century novelists such as Charles Dickens, whose literary techniques Griffith often drew upon for inspiration in the construction of his films.[10] Dickens is renowned for the care he took to render his fictional world in minute detail, in order to enhance the reader's impression that it was real. By focusing on the detail of the bucket being filled, Griffith too adds verisimilitude to his fictional world. The close-up of the bucket also gives the action dramatic emphasis. Fetching water at the spring was Flora's goal, her reason for the journey through the forest. By giving emphasis to this action through the close-up, Griffith

Figure 2. In a film obsessed with the threat of boundary breakdowns between blacks and whites, the image of a fence appearing large in the frame as a black man is about to pursue a young white woman is anything but accidental. (*The Birth of a Nation,* 1915, Film Preservation Associates.)

allows the viewer to breathe a sigh of relief. Flora's task is done. Nothing has happened to her. She can now return home.

But there is, I think, one more effect of Griffith's close-up here. The close shot of the bucket dipping into the water emphasizes the symbolic resonance of the spring. Springs, with their pure water, are often associated with virgins, but in myths and fairy tales, springs are also associated with the violation of virgins. Ingmar Bergman's film *Virgin Spring,* for example, is based on a legend in which a young girl on her way to church is accosted deep in a forest by roaming vagabonds who rape and murder her. At the very spot in the forest where her violation occurred, a spring miraculously appears. Because of the archetypal associations of springs with both virgins and the violation of virgins, Griffith's close-up heightens the sexual foreboding and anxiety that already infuse this sequence. Adding to this effect is the female imagery suggested by the close-up—a circular orifice in the midst of heavy foliage.

In shot 8 Griffith crosscuts from Flora back to Gus. Gus now appears in the same forest location where Flora appeared in shot one. Here Griffith indicates through the location match that Gus has not turned back. He is following Flora. Because we have seen Gus turning back from his pursuit of Flora in shot 4, this shot comes as a shock, illustrating how good Griffith was at manipulating audience emotions through the careful ordering or editing of his shots. He is playing with our expectations: first teasing us to think the danger to Flora has diminished, only to surprise us now with the information that Gus has moved beyond the fence and is still on her trail.

Our knowledge that Gus is in pursuit makes the next series of shots (shots 11 through 15) all the more alarming. Flora, rather than going straight home after filling the bucket with water, becomes distracted by a squirrel in a tree. Griffith conveys the depth of her distraction by cutting from shots of Flora gazing screen right to POV shots of a close-up of a squirrel from Flora's perspective. The squirrel appears surrounded by an iris, or circular matte, also signifying that we are seeing it through Flora's eyes. Griffith then cuts back to reaction shots of Flora from a reverse angle, capturing her fascination and delight in observing the forest creature.

Aside from making us worry that Flora is so involved with the squirrel that she will be taken unaware by Gus, Griffith's cuts between the squirrel and reaction shots of Flora have other narrative functions. Flora's interest in the squirrel provides a vivid visual means of characterization. Small animals like squirrels convey a sense of harmlessness, helplessness, and innocence, and these characteristics spill over onto Flora by association. If Griffith had depicted her as fascinated instead by the sight of a spider eating a fly or two moles mating, the effect would be quite different. Finally, and most crucially, cutting back and forth between Flora and the squirrel artificially prolongs the moment before the dreaded outcome we all fear, when Gus reveals his presence to Flora. Literary critics refer to this technique of delaying a denouement as "retardation." Here, the 13 shots this sequence devotes to Flora interacting with the squirrel enable the tension to build, in the cinematic equivalent of foreplay.

The rhythmic alternation between shots of Flora and the squirrel is suddenly interrupted by shot 16, a cross-cut to Gus emerging, as if from out of a cave, from the murky depths of the forest. Tangled, dead branches fill the top third of the frame. Gus stares intently, crouched and predatory, creating the impression that he is more a wild beast than a man. This shot comes as a shock not only because of the sudden appearance of Gus, but also because the film's mise-en-scène has totally changed. Up

Figure 3. Griffith was intuitively aware that as an image gets bigger on the screen, the intensity of its emotional effect grows proportionately. (*The Birth of a Nation,* 1915, Film Preservation Associates.)

to this point we have been in a sunny forest filled with leafy foliage. But now, Gus appears surrounded by darkness with an eerily illuminated tangle of dead white branches framing his head, a skeletal configuration associating Gus with death. While Gus's facial expression is neutral (he's not foaming at the mouth or gnashing his teeth like a stage villain), the black-and-white color symbolism and nightmarish setting in which he is placed tell us all we need to know about his evil nature.

Shot 17, a POV shot, reveals the not-unexpected object of Gus's intent stare—Flora, who is rocking back and forth on a log, still fascinated with the squirrel. The camera has moved even closer to her now, framing her in medium shot, conveying the impression that Gus is moving in on her. Like the squirrel, she too appears in an iris, but now we know that the watcher is not a benign child gazing at a cute forest creature, but an evil stalker staring at a cute little girl. In a foreshadowing of her doom, the screen has darkened within the circular iris that surrounds her. Shot 18 is a POV shot of the squirrel from Flora's perspective, followed by shot 19, a reaction shot of Flora who continues to rock on the

Figure 4. Because we know we are looking at Flora through Gus's eyes, her actions become sexualized. (*The Birth of a Nation,* 1915, Film Preservation Associates.)

log and look up at the squirrel in innocent delight. Shot 20 is the most ominous in the sequence. The camera has moved up to a big close up of Gus. Just his face fills the left half of the frame; on the right are the dead tangled skeletal branches. (See figure 3.) Griffith was intuitively aware that as an image gets bigger on the screen, the intensity of its emotional effect grows proportionately. When a character is sympathetic, a big close-up can increase our feeling of intimacy and deepen our identification with the character. When a character is unsympathetic, the big close-up has the opposite effect, making the character seem threatening and intrusive because it is "in our face."

The intense effect of the big close-up in shot 20 heightens the effect of shot 21. Here Flora appears as in shot 19, from Gus's point of view in a medium shot. She is laughing and blowing kisses at the squirrel. (See figure 4.) If we were to see this shot in almost any other context it would connote innocence and joy. But because we know we are looking at Flora from Gus's perspective her actions take on new significance. She not only seems terribly vulnerable because we know she is being watched by someone with evil designs, but her actions of blowing kisses and rocking on the log become sexualized. (A student once suggested that Flora's rocking was masturbatory, a thought that would not have occurred to him, I suspect, if this shot had appeared in another context.) Through the use of the POV shot here, Griffith places the spectator inside Gus's subjectivity and invites us to participate in a perverse excitement.

This perverse excitement is all the more heightened, we might speculate, because, as Christian Metz observes in *The Imaginary Signifier,* his influential psychoanalytic investigation into the pleasure and fascination of cinema, we are all voyeurs when we go to the movies.[11] Whether or not the cinematic scenario involves explicitly sexual scenes, an important part of the excitement and appeal of most narrative films is the illusion that we are secret observers looking into private lives and worlds. We can watch a film's characters in their most private moments to our heart's content, while they remain unaware that they are being observed. Griffith gives us the double pleasure of spying on Gus (who is hidden in the dark like the film spectator), while Gus is spying on Flora. Perhaps the moviegoer's secret kinship with Gus's voyeurism accounts for the extra appeal, the *frisson,* of these eye-line shots of Flora.

ART AND IDEOLOGY: RACIST REPRESENTATION IN *THE BIRTH OF A NATION*

Few moviegoers, I suspect, would openly acknowledge a kinship with Gus. In fact, as the analysis of the above shots has demonstrated, everything about the way Griffith has portrayed Gus cinematically makes us disavow any association with him. His animal-like gestures and the symbolic suggestiveness of the mise-en-scène make him an image of pure evil, reflecting Dixon's racist view that African Americans are less than human.[12] In contrast, Griffith portrays Flora's brother Ben Cameron (who tries to rescue Flora from Gus but arrives too late) and his Ku Klux Klan followers as forces of transcendental purity and goodness. At the end of the film, they swoop down dressed in white to rescue Southern womanhood from armed and dangerous black men whose goal, like Gus's, is presented as blatantly sexual. In the final climactic shots of the film, images of rioting blacks are crosscut with images of the Ku Klux Klan, dressed in white and riding in orderly formations. The drastic contrast Griffith sets up between the way the white heroes and the black villains are depicted seems laughable today, so blatantly does it expose the racist ideology at the heart of this film. But this example, as well as the sequence of shots depicting Gus as an evil beast-like predator of Flora, serves, nevertheless, as a clear illustration of how a film director can, in the direction of the actor's performance, choice of mise-en-scène, framing of the shots, and editing patterns, project into seemingly neutral photographic representations deeply held cultural and psychological fantasies.

There has been a good deal of critical controversy over how much of the racism in *The Birth of a Nation* was Griffith's and how much was just a reflection of Dixon's beliefs. But placing the blame for the racist representations on one or the other of these two men ignores the pervasive racism in American society in 1915. The film came out during a backlash against progress toward racial equality in this country. Jim Crow laws had recently been instituted in the South, and for the first time in history, black and white government workers were segregated under Woodrow Wilson's administration. As the film historian Russell Merritt observes, in both of the novels on which *The Birth of a Nation* was based, Dixon "rode the back of current fears spawned by the large immigration of Southern Negroes to Northern cities, the waves of immigrants pouring in from Eastern Europe, and the abiding popularity of alarmist social theories."[13] *The Birth of a Nation,* which was a phenomenal box-office success, would never have become the enormously popular film that it did unless it struck a chord with members of the dominant white society who flocked to see it, and who were all too eager to accept Griffith's filmed "history" as truth.

Apparently even Woodrow Wilson, then President of the United States and former political scientist and historian, accepted Griffith's biased account of Reconstruction as factual. After seeing the film at a special screening at the White House arranged by Thomas Dixon, an old college friend of Wilson's, Wilson was reported to have exclaimed: "It is like writing history with Lightning. And my only regret is that it is all so terribly true."[14] Later, the White House denied that it had sanctioned the film, but most historians accept that Wilson did respond to the film with these approving words when he first saw it.[15]

Griffith, it must also be remembered, was born in the South only ten years after the Civil War, and was the son of a Confederate colonel. Thus, he grew up incorporating a set of widespread cultural assumptions and beliefs which the historian Everett Carter calls the "plantation illusion." Carter argues that the plantation illusion "is based primarily upon a belief in a golden age of the antebellum South, an age in which feudal agrarianism provided the good life for wealthy, leisured, kindly, aristocratic owner and loyal, happy, obedient slave."[16] This mythic garden of civilization (epitomized in *The Birth of a Nation* by Dr. Cameron's idyllic plantation), was destroyed in the Civil War by a supposedly envious, vengeful, hypocritical North who punished and humiliated the South by giving the former slaves political power. Carter understands the plantation illusion's insistence on the black man, and especially the mulatto, as a sexual predator of white women, a theme which obsessively runs throughout *The Birth of a Nation*, as a key component of plantation illusion mythology.[17] In fact, the real predators were white males with power over women slaves. By projecting[18] their lawless sexuality onto black men, whom they can then hate, revile, and punish with impunity, white men are able to protect the illusion that they are pure, lawful and restrained. Interestingly in this regard, Gus and Silas Lynch, both lawless men who lust after white women, are played by white actors wearing unconvincing blackface. Scratch the black façade and underneath the leering exteriors of the film's prime villains are white men.[19]

The study of Griffith's pioneering techniques in *The Birth of a Nation* illuminates his achievement in molding the film medium into a vehicle for transforming ideologically and psychologically charged fantasies into dramatic fictions that seemed stunningly real. Not everyone, of course, bought into the truth of the film's representations. The NAACP declared in its annual report the year the film was released that "Every resource of a magnificent new art has been employed with an undeniable attempt to picture Negroes in the worst possible light."[20] *The Birth of a Nation* sparked riots and protests against its racist representations in many cities, and the film was refused license for exhibition in Connecticut, Illinois, Kansas, Massachusetts, Minnesota, New Jersey, Wisconsin, and Ohio.[21] At the same time, the huge box-office success of the film in 1915, and the conviction held by many, including the president of the United States, that Griffith's film presented an objective, truthful rendering of Reconstruction, serve as an early warning for viewers. We should never trust film as a transparent reflection of events in the external world and we should especially mistrust the idea that film can objectively re-enact the past. *The Birth of a Nation* is clearly not history but a cultural illusion written with lightning, the lightning of the powerful picture language of film articulated by its first master.

2

The Art of Montage
Sergei Eisenstein's *The Battleship Potemkin*

EISENSTEIN'S BACKGROUND

In 1925, ten years after *The Birth of a Nation* established the potency of Griffith's narrative techniques, the Soviet filmmaker Sergei Eisenstein's *The Battleship Potemkin* dazzled film audiences around the world. "This is not a picture—" the film critic of Germany's leading newspaper, the *Berliner Tageblatt*, wrote, "it is a reality. Eisenstein has created the most powerful and artistic film in the whole world."[1] The film is still acclaimed today: it is included in almost every introductory course in film history and aesthetics. Interestingly, the German film critic praises *Potemkin* for being profoundly real ("This is not a picture—it is a reality") and at the same time for being powerfully artistic. The film, which recounts a historical incident in the city of Odessa in 1905, primarily featured the people of Odessa (as opposed to professional actors) and was shot on location. Both of these factors partially account for the film's reality effect. But, paradoxically, it is the artfulness of Eisenstein's techniques, in particular the editing of his shots, that gives the filmed action such a felt sense of reality. Eisenstein, who was a theorist as well as a filmmaker, explored entirely new principles of film art which took the form well beyond the conventions of realism that Griffith had pioneered. The result, ironically, is that despite *Potemkin*'s artistic stylization of reality, never before had a film been experienced as so "real."

Since Eisenstein's innovative film style was heavily influenced by cultural currents that emerged after the Russian Revolution in 1917, I will begin with some background on Eisenstein's life and the effect of the Russian Revolution on his ideas about film form. Eisenstein was born in 1898 in Riga, Latvia, into a prosperous middle-class Russian family.[2] His father was a civil engineer. Despite his son's fascination with and aptitude for the arts, especially drawing, Eisenstein's father insisted that he enroll in the Institute of Civil Engineering to study engineering and architecture. But while Eisenstein was immersed in studying for an engineering degree in Saint Petersburg, the world was changing around him. The growing unrest of the Russian people forced Czar Nicholas to abdicate the throne on March 15, 1917. The Provisional Government of Kerensky was formed, only to be overthrown by the Bolsheviks, the revolutionary Socialist party headed by Lenin. In 1918, when civil war broke out, Eisenstein enlisted in the Red Army and never returned to his engineering studies. (His father joined the counterrevolutionary White Russians). The Russian Revolution thus liberated not only Russia from the Czars but Eisenstein from engineering and the influence of his father. "If it had not been for the Revolution," Eisenstein wrote, "I should never have broken with the tradition passed down from father to son of becoming an engineer. The germ was there, but only the Revolution gave me . . . the freedom to take my fate into my own hands."[3]

Once in the Red Army, Eisenstein first worked as an engineer, but was eventually transferred to a theatrical unit, where he designed propaganda posters and directed amateur productions at the front to help keep up the morale of the Red Army. In the autumn of 1920, once the Red Army had won the civil war and the power of the Bolsheviks was consolidated, Eisenstein arrived in Moscow and joined the avant-garde Proletkult, or workers' theater, as a scenic director and began his career in the arts, first in the theater and then in film.

INFLUENCE OF THE RUSSIAN REVOLUTION ON SOVIET FILM ART

Despite the severe shortage of food, shelter, and money, the postwar period of the 1920s was a time of intense creative activity in the new Soviet Union. The revolution had killed the past, and artists were seeking radical new means of creative expression. The innovations Eisenstein brought to cinematic art were very much a product of his being an artist in the heady, idealistic first days of the revolution when the Soviet Union, for a short time, encouraged its artists to create original and vital new art forms in the service of the new society.

Lenin pronounced the cinema the most influential of all the arts. Film, he believed, should do more than entertain: the powerful picture language of the new medium could instruct the illiterate masses in the history and theory of socialism. Moving pictures, moreover, could be used to mold and reinforce the values of the people so that the Bolshevik revolution would prosper. On August 27, 1919, Lenin nationalized the film industry, and established state film workshops to undertake a systematic, theoretical study of film art. The goal of these workshops was to determine the best methods for shaping the film medium into a powerful tool of instruction and propaganda.

As they began to study film systematically in these workshops, Soviet film pioneers were deeply impressed by the emotional effects generated by D. W. Griffith's narrative techniques—his use of the close-up, his innovative camera movements, and the way he changed camera angles. They were especially excited by his crosscutting and editing rhythms. The Soviet pioneers were influenced most by Griffith's *Intolerance* (1919), the next film Griffith made after *The Birth of a Nation*. "All that is best in the Soviet film," Eisenstein later acknowledged, "has its origins in *Intolerance*."[4] On the foundation of Griffith's achievement, Soviet filmmakers sought to establish general principles about film art which they could apply to their project of creating powerful political propaganda that would entertain, inspire, and instruct the masses.

The most influential of the state-run film schools was Lev Kuleshov's workshop. Kuleshov conducted experiments which seemed to prove that film art did not begin when the cameraman photographed an action (enframed the image) but when the individual shots took on new meanings as they were arranged in editing. A famous Kuleshov experiment, for example, purported to prove that it was the editing or arrangement of shots that creates meaning in the mind of the spectator, above and beyond the meaning of the content of each individual shot. In the experiment, a close-up of the prerevolutionary cinema matinee idol Mosjukhin was juxtaposed in turn with shots of a plate of soup on the table, a coffin containing a dead woman, and a little girl playing with a toy bear. According to an account by the Soviet director V. I. Pudovkin, who attended Kuleshov's workshop, "When we showed the three combinations to an audience which had not been let into the secret the result was terrific. The public raved about the acting of the artist. They pointed out the heavy pensiveness of his mood over the forgotten soup, were touched and moved by the deep sorrow with which he looked on the dead woman, and admired the light, happy smile with which he surveyed the girl at play. But we knew that in all three cases the face was exactly the same."[5]

Kuleshov concluded from this and similar experiments that "an actor's play reaches the spectator just as the editor requires it to, because the spectator himself completes the connected shots and sees in it what has been suggested to him by the montage."[6] Kuleshov's experiments and the example of Griffith's powerful shot juxtapositions suggested to the Soviet filmmakers and theoreticians that editing was the foundation of film art. They termed the process of creative, artful arrangement of shots "montage," in order to distinguish it from the simple process of editing or splicing shots together simply to obtain narrative continuity. While few filmmakers today would accept the proposition that editing counts for everything in the art of making films, Soviet filmmakers were inspired by their fascination with the effects achieved through editing to create works that opened up new channels of expression for film art.

Like Pudovkin, Eisenstein attended Kuleshov's workshop, where he studied for three months in 1923, but originally he applied the principles of montage not to film but to the stage. Eisenstein's revolutionary ideas for the theater inspired many of his innovations in film art. The Proletkult theater where Eisenstein worked after the end of the Civil War was dedicated to promoting culture among the workers and encouraging them to seek artistic self-expression. But, as I noted above, the revolution had drastically changed Russian society's attitude toward art. The basic precept of the Proletkult theater was that bourgeois culture must be forced to give way to a new, purely proletarian culture. The purpose of art under the new revolutionary order was not to provide intellectual or aesthetic pleasure to the privileged few, but to educate the workers and reinforce their dedication to the values of socialism. The function of art was also seen as an energizer, a force that would pump up the people with the psychic wherewithal necessary for the hard work of building a socialist society.

In this context, the traditional, realistic theater (the theater of Chekhov and Ibsen) that created the illusion that the spectator was looking in on a slice of real life with the fourth wall removed, would not do. Realistic theater, it was believed, encouraged viewers to become too vicariously involved with the fictional action, a process that, it was thought, siphoned off their revolutionary energies. Eisenstein, who had been brought up on (and loved) the traditional theater, quickly realized that it was inappropriate for the new society. "What diabolical mechanism lies hidden in this art that I serve!" he wrote. "It's not merely a cheat and a swindle. It's poison—a dreadful, terrifying poison. For, if you can get your enjoyment through fantasy, who is going to make the effort any more to find in real experiences what can be had without moving from the theatre seat?"[7]

Heavily influenced by the famed avant-garde theater director Vsevolod Meyerhold, Eisenstein enthusiastically developed original theatrical methods for conveying revolutionary themes. He sought a means to intensely affect the audience in a different way from that by which audiences are affected in the traditional theater, that is, not through the fantasy immersion in a realistic theatrical world where meaning and emotion are communicated primarily through the word. He thought theater should be based on what he called a "montage of attractions," which would take theater back to its primitive roots in spectacle or circus entertainment. Eisenstein envisioned a political theater in which spectators could be pleasured and thrilled by wondrous circus attractions and spectacles, while at the same time they were instructed in correct political views and values through carefully constructed political satires.

Eisenstein's theatrical productions were performed not on a traditional stage but in an area resembling a circus arena, with most of the players wearing masks. While the actors enacted political satires, acrobats performed. At one point in Eisenstein's production of Ostrovsky's *Even a Wise Man Stumbles* a player exited on a tightrope above the audience's head. Caps exploded under the audience's seats. As chaotic as it all seemed, there was a method to the madness. The caps were to keep everyone awake and alert. The acrobatics and circus performances both entertained the audience and mirrored and reinforced the emotions and ideas conveyed by the actors. As Eisenstein writes, "A gesture expands into gymnastics, rage [of an actor] is expressed through a somersault [performed by an acrobat], exaltation through a *salto-mortale*. . . . The grotesque of this style permitted leaps from one type of expression to another, as well as unexpected intertwinings of the two expressions."[8]

Eisenstein abandoned the traditional form of the nineteenth-century realistic theater for a theater based on attractions—spectacles and sights—in which the audience's attention is pulled back and forth between two or more simultaneous scenes, so that the meaning of one spills over into and reinforces the meaning of the other. As we shall see, Eisenstein would exploit more fully the methods of his montage of attractions when he moved beyond theater to film. The influence of his theatrical experiments

is evident in his most famous and successful film, *The Battleship Potemkin,* and especially in the style of the famous sequence in which the citizens of Odessa are massacred on the Odessa Steps.

The Battleship Potemkin, Eisenstein's second film, was commissioned
by the government of the Soviet Union to commemorate the twentieth
anniversary of the uprisings in Russia in 1905, a year of general strikes
and demonstrations against the government of Czar Nicholas II. The government retaliated by killing hundreds of demonstrators, but the revolutionary spirit was never completely quelled. The 1905 unrest, including the takeover of the armored cruiser Potemkin in the port of Odessa
by revolutionary soldiers, was understood by Bolsheviks as a precursor
to their 1917 revolution.

Originally Eisenstein had planned a monumental eight-part work to
capture all aspects of the uprisings of 1905, from the Russo-Japanese
War to the armed uprisings in Moscow. In the original script, only forty-
two shots had been planned to cover the Potemkin mutiny off the shore
of Odessa. But when Eisenstein saw the dazzling white flight of marble
steps leading down to Odessa's harbor, he saw a spectacular stage upon
which to film a massacre of unarmed citizens who supported the mutiny,
even though this event never actually occurred.[9] Eisenstein reconceived
the entire film. It would now center on just one revolutionary episode
from the many uprisings of 1905—the mutiny of the sailors on the armored cruiser Potemkin. This one incident, culminating in the fictional
bloody massacre on the Odessa Steps, would epitomize the age-old oppression of the Russian people by the corrupt Czarist regime and dramatize the necessity of revolt.

SEQUENCE ANALYSIS: "THE ODESSA STEPS" IN *THE BATTLESHIP POTEMKIN*

In the Odessa Steps sequence a crowd of friendly citizens has gathered
on the steps leading down to the port of Odessa to celebrate the victory
of the mutinous sailors over the Czarist officers on the battleship
Potemkin, which is now waving the red flag of revolution offshore. Suddenly, from out of nowhere, lines of government soldiers appear at the
top of the steps, and begin firing into the crowd. The action of this scene
alone is an attraction or spectacle. As filmmakers have always known,
violent images have an irresistible attraction for spectators, for the same
reason that people find it hard not to look when driving by a highway
disaster. But Eisenstein's choice to stage a massacre on the Odessa Steps,
combined with his revolutionary editing techniques, resulted in an un-

precedentedly horrifying and stunning spectacle, charged with political meaning.

Eisenstein's idea of staging a massacre on the Odessa Steps was truly inspired. While being caught in the line of fire is bad enough, the stuff of nightmares, the last place one would want to be if this were actually to happen would be on a lengthy flight of stairs. Steps are always a precarious place to be under any circumstances, because they threaten us with loss of balance. Much of the action at the beginning of the Odessa Steps sequence involves images of people losing their balance, tripping, and falling as they desperately try to flee the gunfire. Eisenstein even strapped a camera to an acrobat and had him do a flip to obtain topsy-turvy footage that approximated the point of view of someone falling headfirst downstairs.

Eisenstein intensifies the spectator's horror (and fascination) at witnessing this spectacle by focusing on the very people who would have the most difficulty escaping from danger on stairs. Thus the first person we see fleeing is a man without legs. We watch him desperately thrusting himself down the stairs supported only by his arms. Soon after, a one-legged man on crutches appears, who negotiates the steps with even more difficulty than the legless man. In quick succession, interspersed with long shots of the crowds of people fleeing en masse, we see a woman with a sick child, a group of elderly men and women, and, toward the end of the sequence, and most pathetically of all, a young mother who has somehow found herself stranded on the steps with an infant in an unwieldy baby carriage. She is horribly caught between the murderous soldiers above and the endless flight of steps below.

Eisenstein compels us to watch in shock and fascination as terrible fates befall the citizens of Odessa. The sick child is shot by the soldiers and falls, his body splayed on the steps. His mother, in her own state of panic, at first does not notice and keeps running. Suddenly aware that her son has fallen behind, she starts back up the stairs to find him. She watches in agony as fleeing citizens trample his body. She picks up the body of her desperately hurt child, but, instead of fleeing, she continues her ascent up the stairs, to confront the soldiers with what they have done. After a suspenseful build-up, as the mother approaches closer and closer to the soldiers, appealing to them not to shoot because her child is ill, mother and child are brutally shot down, as are a group of elderly citizens who have followed the mother up the stairs to join in her appeal to the soldiers. The young mother trapped on the huge flight of stairs with the baby carriage is shot in the stomach. In an almost unbearable irony the mother unwittingly becomes the cause of her infant's demise. Her body, as it falls, pushes the carriage with her infant off the landing sending the helpless baby rolling down the huge flight of steps to certain death. At the bottom of the steps murderous Cossacks on horseback armed with swords cut off the escape routes of those who have survived to reach the bottom. A woman wearing a pince-nez is shot in the right eye. Blood spurts from underneath the shattered lens.

Images such as these are a far cry from Eisenstein's comedic circus attractions, but they serve the same function—to keep the spectator's eyes cemented to the screen. This mise-en-scène of horror leaves an even stronger impression on our psyches and nervous systems because of the way Eisenstein breaks down the action of the massacre into separate shots and joins them together using innovative methods of montage.

Eisenstein, as we have seen, owed much to Griffith's contributions to the development of film as a narrative art, but he both developed Griffith's ideas further and broke Griffith's rules to obtain startlingly new cinematic effects. The Soviet filmmakers learned from their close study of Griffith's methods that if a film narrative was to be dramatically effective it had to free itself from the model of filming a dramatic action from a fixed distance as if the camera were a spectator watching the action in a theater. As I remarked earlier, by fragmenting the proscenium space that early cinema had left whole, Griffith gave varying dramatic emphasis to the action as the story demanded. In the sequence we analyzed from *The Birth of a Nation,* for example, Griffith breaks down the action of Flora filling the bucket with spring water into three separate shots, emphasizing, through the use of an inserted close-up, the action of her dipping the bucket into the spring. The close-up gives the moviegoer a privileged intimacy with the action in a manner that would be impossible for the spectator in the theater. In the same sequence, Griffith reconnected the discontinuous shots by matching Flora's movement from shot to shot. Match cutting was important to Griffith because he wanted the viewer to remain mentally immersed in the dramatic action, in a state of mind that would be disrupted if the viewer were to become aware of the medium through jerky or mismatched shots. Later theorists refer to deliberately mismatched shots as "jump cuts." By matching the movements of Flora in long shot with her movements in close-up as she fills the bucket, Griffith gives the film audience a closer, more dramatically satisfying view of the action while still maintaining the illusion that we are watching an unmediated reality in a coherent screen space. Griffith's goal was to offer the moviegoer an experience similar to that of watching realistic theater, with the advantage of having an even better view of the action.

Since, as we have seen, realistic theater was precisely the kind of theater Eisenstein had renounced, he did not feel constrained by the rules of editing that would maintain the viewer's illusions of a coherent, seemingly real space. In fact, he was adamantly opposed to films that slavishly tried to maintain the illusionism of realistic theater by smoothly joining shots. Eisenstein held that proper film continuity should not proceed smoothly, but through a series of shocks. Whenever possible, he tried to create some kind of visual conflict or discontinuity between two shots, with the goal of creating a jolt in the spectator's psyche. The visual explosions on the screen were intended to create a continual source of stimulants or shocks to keep the audience wide awake, a practice having the same goal as his theater of attractions, or his ploy of exploding caps under the audience's seats. In his essay "The Cinematographic Principle and the Ideogram," Eisenstein compares the process of montage to the explosions of an internal combustion engine, in which each explosion drives the machine forward. "[S]imilarly," he writes, "the dynamics of montage serve as impulses driving forward the total film." [10]

Eisenstein's belief that films should be constructed through a series of shocks or conflicts, he claimed, was inspired by Hegel's concept of dialectics, on which Marx's theories of revolution were based. [11] The dialectical method, according to Hegel, is the principle behind change, a universal law of thesis, antithesis, and synthesis, of contradiction and reconciliation, that governed all matter and history. The Bolshevik revolution itself was seen as a clash of dialectical opposites, between the workers and the property-owning establishment, resulting in the synthesis of the new workers' state. Eisenstein felt that a work of art would have more power if it was structured according to these same dialectical principles, involving a continual clash of opposites. Hence, he imbued his films with conflict, starting at the most fundamental graphic level.

Eisenstein created optical conflicts by juxtaposing shots whose graphic elements visually contrasted. For example, he followed an extreme long shot of the citizens of Odessa running down the stairs (figure 5) with an extreme close-up of the legs of a man on the verge of falling (figure 6). Griffith deliberately avoided such a practice, cutting gradually from long shot to medium shot to close-up, fearing that abrupt changes in the size of the image would unsettle the viewer and call attention to the film's editing, disturbing the spectator's immersion in the story. Eisenstein, who was striving to move his audiences without letting them relax into illusion, was indifferent to such considerations. Eisenstein created visual conflicts in numerous other ways: He edited pieces of film so that the directional movements within juxtaposed shots clashed. That is, a shot of a crowd running in the direction of screen left would clash in the next shot with an image of the crowd running in the direction of screen right. A shot lit somberly would be juxtaposed with a shot lit brightly. An image of organized, purposeful movement would contrast in the next shot with an image of irregular, chaotic movement. (See figures 7 and 8.) A shot compositionally designed to emphasize vertical vectors or lines would be juxtaposed with a shot organized horizontally. Diagonal lines tending toward the left would clash in the next shot with diagonal lines tending right.

In an essay entitled "The Structure of Film," Eisenstein discusses the importance of his "montage of conflict" as a vital element in the construction of a portion of the Odessa Steps massacre. Here he explains how his formal choices add to the impact of the film's content:

> In the first place, noticing *the frenzied condition of the people and masses that are portrayed,* let us go on to find what we are looking for in structural and compositional indications.
> Let us concentrate on the line of *movement.*
> There is, before all else, a chaotic *close-up* rush of figures. And then, as chaotic, a rush of figures in *long-shot.*
> Then the chaos of movement changes to a design: the *rhythmic* descending feet of the soldiers.
> Tempo increases. Rhythm accelerates.
> In this acceleration of *downward* rushing movement there is a suddenly upsetting opposite movement—*upward:* the *break-neck* movement of the *mass* downward leaps over into a *slowly solemn* movement upward of the mother's *lone* figure, carrying her dead son.
> Mass. Break-neck speed. Downward.
> And then suddenly: A lone figure. Slow solemnity. Upward.
> But—this is only for an instant. Once more we experience a returning leap to the downward movement.
> Rhythm accelerates. Tempo increases.[12]

The clashing movements and rhythms of the montage pieces keep the spectator disturbed and off balance, just like a fleeing citizen of Odessa.

Eisenstein believed so strongly in the power of graphic conflict to add visual excitement and drama to his films that he even composed his individual shots with intraframe contrasts in mind. That is, he created conflicts not just between juxtaposed shots but within each individual shot as well. A famous example of intraframe graphic conflict occurs

Figure 5. An extreme long shot of the people running down the Odessa Steps.
(*The Battleship Potemkin*, 1925, Sovexport Films.)

Figure 6. A big close-up of a pair of legs creates a visual conflict with the previous shot
(figure 5). (*The Battleship Potemkin*, 1925, Sovexport Films.)

Figure 7. The purposeful, organized movement of the soldiers. (*The Battleship Potemkin*, 1925, Sovexport Films.)

Figure 8. The chaotic, disorganized movements of the victims, in studied juxtaposition with figure 7. (*The Battleship Potemkin*, 1925, Sovexport Films.)

Figure 9. The line of a boy's body creates a graphic conflict with the line of the steps. (*The Battleship Potemkin,* 1925, Sovexport Films.)

when the sick child is shot by the soldiers. His fallen body is positioned in such a way that it lies perpendicular to the line of the steps, the line of the boy's body creating a graphic conflict with the line of the steps. (See figure 9.) While Griffith composed his shots primarily according to the meaning each shot conveyed through the action within the shot, Eisenstein believed that emotional effects derived not just from the content of the shot but also from the way the shot was graphically composed.

Eisenstein's insistence on the importance of exposing the viewer to a constant barrage of graphic conflicts and visual shocks, and his disdain for the rules of smooth editing continuities established by Griffith, enabled him to achieve striking narrative effects. At the beginning of the Odessa Steps massacre we see a young woman with dark bobbed hair react to what we later realize is her first sight of the soldiers marching in rank and firing on the crowd. Here, Eisenstein does not express the woman's shocked reaction simply by photographing her facial expression and gestures, as Griffith would have done. Rather he presents the woman's reaction in a series of four close-ups, jerkily edited together through obviously mismatched jump cuts, each lasting a fraction of a second. Thus, the woman's shock is suggested not primarily through the expression on her face, but through the jolts created by the unconventional jump cuts.

The shots of the woman are all the more disconcerting because Eisenstein has broken another rule of standard film continuity: He has reversed the order of cause and effect. Rather than showing us shots of the soldiers firing and then the woman reacting, Eisenstein shows us the terrified reaction before he reveals the cause. There is something particularly unsettling when we see someone react in horror before we know what the source of the horror is. It sends our imaginations into high gear as we try to fathom the reason for the reaction. We do not see the cause of the woman's panic for two more shots, both of which focus on another terrible image: the legless man in desperate flight down the steps. The mechanized line of armed soldiers, when they do appear, are even more terrible because the woman's and man's horrified reactions to the soldiers spill over onto our perception of their image. Eisenstein, influenced by the experiments in Kuleshov's workshop, was acutely aware of how viewers' mental processes can heighten the emotional power of film.

The power of the Odessa Steps sequence is further heightened because Eisenstein's editing technique deliberately disorients the spectator in screen space, departing from the methods Griffith developed to provide viewers with a clear, coherent spatial orientation. In Griffith's representation of Civil War battle scenes in *The Birth of a Nation,* for example, Griffith begins his sequences with establishing shots, extreme long shots of the battles which provide the spectators with a panoramic view of the entire scene. Thus, when Griffith cut to closer shots of the action for dramatic emphasis, the viewer had a clear mental picture of offscreen space. Though the battle scene shots are filled with chaotic action, the viewer's orientation in screen space is kept intact. The soldiers from the South are always on screen left, while the soldiers from the North are always on screen right. This kind of careful attention to the viewer's orientation in screen space is entirely lacking in the Odessa Steps sequence. In the first place, we are never given an establishing shot of the Odessa Steps in their entirety. Mostly we experience the steps in fragmented pieces: shots of masses of people rushing down the steps interspersed with close shots of individuals and shots of the faceless soldiers relentlessly advancing and firing their guns. We are never given a clear sense of where anyone is in relation to anyone else.

By refusing to orient the spectator in a coherent screen space, Eisenstein adds greatly to the affective power of the scene. The lack of spatial orientation on the Odessa Steps works because it compels spectators to experience something of the same mental confusion and loss of bearings that the people on the steps suffer. The quick pace of the editing, which jerks the spectator's attention from place to place, likewise mirrors the wild way one's attention would jump from one perception to another when one is in a state of anxiety or panic. In this way, through his editing technique, Eisenstein transfers the panic of the people on the steps to the spectator.

Eisenstein takes as many liberties with his presentation of time as he does with his presentation of space in the Odessa Steps sequence, again creating powerful effects. In an actual count, the Odessa Steps number 120 steps, and, one might estimate that if people were being fired at, they would vacate the steps in well under a minute of actual time. Eisenstein extends the time to over five excruciating minutes. The primary way he extends time is through the repetition of some of the same shots. When one closely observes the sequence, one notices that some of the shots of the people fleeing en masse, as well as shots of the soldiers firing, are in fact repeats of the same shots. Because we are not given an establishing shot of the Odessa Steps and have no idea of their extent, Eisenstein can draw out the duration of the action as long as he wishes through shot repetition and continual crosscutting. In any case, Eisenstein was not striving to give us a literal, realistic picture of the massacre on the steps. Through his innovative, time-expanding film technique, he conveys the subjective reality of what it would feel like to be trapped in a traumatic situation that seemingly goes on forever. In the Odessa Steps sequence Eisenstein creates the time-space continuum of a nightmare from which there is no waking.

The horror on the Odessa Steps culminates when the mother with the infant in the baby carriage is shot. Here Eisenstein plays simultaneously on two primal fears: the fear of an infant being abandoned by a mother and the fear of a mother who realizes she is helpless to protect her infant. Eisenstein drastically expands the screen time given to this moment to etch it forever in our memories. He draws out the mother's agony by devoting 10 shots to her slow and painful death, as her body takes an unnaturally extended time to fall to the ground.

These shots do not happen in quick jump cuts which flash before our eyes, but in shots of agonizingly long duration, some of which last up to seven or eight seconds, forcing us to ponder and dwell on the mother's suffering, which is also emphasized by extreme close-up shots of her face and hands. Eisenstein further extends the duration of the mother's death by cutting away from shots of her as she dies to other actions. He cuts to mounted Cossacks at the bottom of the steps slashing out at the fleeing populace, to images of the soldiers continuing their deadly march down the steps, to long shots of masses of citizens fleeing the troops. Four times Eisenstein cuts to the wheels of the baby carriage teetering on the edge of the steps to prolong the suspense of whether or not it will be pushed over the edge by the body of the dying mother.

BEYOND REALISM

A stunning illustration of Eisenstein's willingness to forego realistic representation in order to heighten the emotional and visual impact of an event occurs in the sequence in which another mother carries her wounded child up the steps to confront the armed soldiers. Eisenstein shoots the scene from behind the mother as she gets dangerously close to the soldiers, who appear at the top of the frame. The steps are dissected by a path of bright light on either side of which are strewn the bodies of the slaughtered people of Odessa. The path of light lends a mysterious religious quality to the image, as if it were lighting the mother's way toward martyrdom. As the woman ascends, her body casts a shadow into the path of light. (See figure 10.) The very next shot is taken from a reverse angle. Now the camera is looking down at the mother and child from behind the soldiers who are offscreen but whose elongated shadows loom menacingly in front of them on the steps. (See figure 11.) The effect here is compositionally brilliant, symbolically rich (the mother is walking into the shadow of death), but logically impossible. The two shots, arguably two of the most memorable in the film, directly contradict one another from the standpoint of realism. For the mother to cast a shadow before her in the first shot and then, an instant later, walk into the shadows cast by the soldiers, the sun would have had to have spun around 180 degrees in the sky. These two most mismatched of shots illustrate once more that Eisenstein was not interested in achieving realistic effects in his films. He conceived his films as made up of autonomous attractions, highly charged moments fascinating in and of themselves, with an undercurrent of pathos for polemical intent.

A final example of Eisenstein's departure from realistic representation to achieve a heightened emotional effect occurs near the conclusion of the Odessa Steps sequence. A sleeping marble lion suddenly rises up. According to Eisenstein, the image of the lion leaping up was intended to

Figure 10. As a woman carrying a sick child ascends the steps, her body casts a shadow into the path of light before her. (*The Battleship Potemkin*, 1925, Sovexport Films.)

Figure 11. In this shot, the soldiers' bodies cast their shadows on the woman and child. (*The Battleship Potemkin*, 1925, Sovexport Films.)

make literal the metaphor that even stone is moved to protest the outrageous oppression of the Czarist regime. Eisenstein achieved this effect by editing together shots of three marble lions—one asleep, one awakening, and one fully aroused, which in actuality were nowhere near the vicinity of the Odessa Steps. His cameraman Eduard Tisse discovered them at the Alupka Palace in the Crimea. Yet this animated stone lion, created from a composite of film fragments, lives in the memory of those who see the film as an outraged witness to the Odessa Steps massacre. Such is the power of associative montage.[13]

The wonderful irony of *Potemkin*'s place in film history is that even though Eisenstein did not strive to create a mimetic illusion of reality, his film was nevertheless experienced as stunningly real. Jay Leyda in *Kino*, his history of the Russian and Soviet film, writes that "One of the curious effects of the film has been to replace the facts of the Potemkin Mutiny with the film's artistic 'revision' of those events, in all subsequent references, even by historians, to this episode."[14] "Absolute realism," Eisenstein wrote, "is by no means the correct form of perception."[15] His films teach us that a film can come across as even more authentic when a director departs from the conventions of realistic representation. Eisenstein's *Potemkin* may not have sparked political revolutions around the world, as the filmmaker had hoped, but its methods of montage revolutionized film art.

3

Expressionism and Realism in Film Form

F. W. Murnau's *The Last Laugh* and
Charles Chaplin's *The Adventurer*

EXPRESSIONISM AND FILM ART: F. W. MURNAU

At the same time that Eisenstein was experimenting with the capacity of editing or montage to give heightened emotional and political impact to his filmed narratives, the German filmmaker F. W. Murnau was concentrating on the potentials of the enframed image, the way specific photographic effects could add psychological expressiveness to the profilmic action. (As discussed in chapter 1, the term *profilmic* refers to the characters, settings, props and other aspects of the film's mise-en-scène before they are captured or enframed on celluloid.) Like many of his contemporaries working in the German film industry in the 1910s and 1920s, Murnau was influenced by Expressionism, the art movement that dominated German painting, literature, theatrical production and acting in the early twentieth century.[1]

In *The Haunted Screen,* a book on German Expressionism in the cinema, Lotte Eisner draws upon the writings of Kasimir Edschmid to define the essence of Expressionism in art:

> Expressionism, Edschmid declared, is a reaction against the atom-splitting of Impressionism, which reflects the iridescent ambiguities, disquieting diversity, and ephemeral hues of nature. At the same time Expressionism sets itself against Naturalism with its mania for recording mere facts, and its

Figure 12. The objects of the natural world have become threatening, unnatural. (*The Cabinet of Dr. Caligari,* 1920, Film Preservation Associates.)

paltry aim of photographing nature or daily life. The world is there for all to see; it would be absurd to reproduce it purely and simply as it is.[2]

The Expressionist artists sought to abstract, distort, and hence transcend the look of everyday reality in order to represent the world—not objectively, but as the artist sees or experiences it. Given the historical context out of which German expressionism emerged—the horrible carnage of World War I, Germany's humiliating defeat, the social instability of the Weimar Republic, and spiraling inflation—it is not surprising that many German artists of this period imbued their vision of the world with feelings of angst, doom, and paranoia.

Cinema's capacity to mechanically reproduce images of the physical world—its ability to faithfully record "mere facts"—might seem to disqualify it as a medium for Expressionism. But German filmmakers nevertheless managed to incorporate the visual motifs and themes of Expressionism into their works. Robert Weine's *The Cabinet of Dr. Caligari* (1919) accomplished this goal by photographing its action against a background of recognizably painted Expressionist sets that weirdly distort

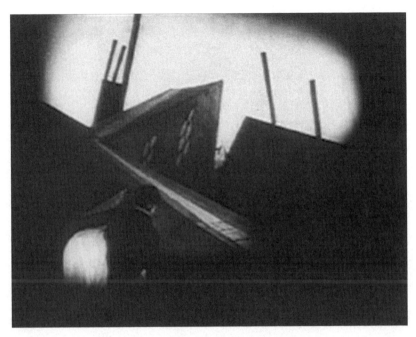

Figure 13. Buildings lean, bend, or rear themselves straight up, against the usual lines. The everyday artifacts that form the world we make to shelter and comfort us have been transformed into the unstable, unbalanced, unsound. (*The Cabinet of Dr. Caligari,* 1920, Film Preservation Associates.)

the natural world into forms that externalize the tortured inner world of the film's disturbed narrator. The artists who designed the sets for *Caligari* (Hermann Warm, Walter Reimann, and Walter Röhrig) were practicing expressionist artists and involved with the publication of the magazine *Der Sturm,* which was dedicated to disseminating Expressionist art.

In describing the sets of *The Cabinet of Dr. Caligari,* William Nestrick conveys the visual impact of the stylized sets by focusing on their radical transformation of the natural and man-made world (figures 12 and 13).

> In the foreground and background of the shots of Caligari's tent, there are short trees or bushes; similar ones appear in the graveyard, around the bridge in the chase after Cesare, and about the path where Cesare finally collapses. They are recognizable representations of nature, but they have become unnatural. They violate principles of growth; on the hillside, they do not grow in the position in which trees usually grow. Most are denuded of leaves, and where they have leaves, the leaves look like spears. They threaten, they point, they seem to cut even as they themselves are cut . . .

Something has also happened to the architectural world. Buildings lean, bend, or rear themselves straight up (against the usual lines). Everywhere the right angle is rejected, the very angle that, in the simplest structures, makes for stability, balance, soundness. . . . Everyday artifacts, the world we make to shelter and comfort us, have been transformed into the unstable, unbalanced, unsound.[3]

For Murnau, *Caligari* was both an inspiration and a dead end as a model for cinematic art. It was an inspiration because it abandoned the slavish imitation of a real, objectively perceived world to present a subjective vision. At the end of the film, which is narrated as an extended flashback, it is revealed that the distorted look of the world was a function of the narrator's mentally unbalanced mind. *Caligari* was a dead end because it projected the character's vision primarily through the film's mise-en-scène, that is, its two-dimensional painted sets, a means borrowed from the theater. Hence, it did not fully exploit the expressive possibilities inherent in the cinematic medium.

EXPRESSIONIST TECHNIQUES IN *THE LAST LAUGH*

In his groundbreaking film *The Last Laugh (Der letzte Mann)* (1924), Murnau achieved expressionistic distortions of the cinematic world not by photographing painted expressionist sets, but by capitalizing on the expressive capacities of the cinematic apparatus: extreme camera angles, special optical effects, and exuberant camera movements.[4] The film vividly portrays the emotional deterioration of an aging doorman (Emil Jannings) at a luxury hotel in a big city when he is demoted from his proud station at the entrance to the hotel to the position of lavatory attendant in the basement below. His downfall comes when the manager of the hotel observes that he is no longer equal to the task of lifting a patron's heavy trunk. The change is tragic for the old man because his self-esteem derives from the impressive doorman's uniform he wears, which makes him the idol of his working-class neighbors. Without his uniform, he becomes the object of mockery and scorn. In *The Last Laugh*, the doorman moves through a convincingly real mise-en-scène (in contrast to the obviously artificial sets of *Caligari*). However, the film is richly emotionally expressive because of the way Murnau's photographic techniques (his use of close-ups, camera angles, moving cameras, superimpositions, distorting lenses—all the transformative effects of the enframed image) convey the doorman's inner states of mind.[5]

Murnau was one of the first filmmakers to exploit systematically the

Figure 14. Murnau films Jannings in close-ups and from slightly below, emphasizing his feelings of pride and self-importance. (*The Last Laugh*, 1924, Friedrich Wilhelm Murnau Stiftung.)

expressive possibilities of camera angle. He realized that, in general, if the subject is seen from a high angle (that is, the camera is shooting from above and thus down at the subject) the character will appear humbled or diminished. If, on the contrary, the subject is seen from below (that is, the camera is looking up at the subject), the character will appear imposing and confident. At the beginning of the film, before he is demoted from his position of doorman, Murnau films Jannings in close-ups and slightly from below, emphasizing his feelings of pride and self-importance. (See figure 14.) When he is obliged to unload a heavy trunk from a carriage, we see him looking up at the intimidating object. Murnau photographs him from a high angle (the camera shooting down at him) to emphasize his feelings of diminishment. (See figure 15.) Then we see the trunk, from his point of view. Shot from a low angle, it seems all the more burdensome. Finally the camera shoots down at the doorman to emphasize his struggle to lift it off the carriage.

In order to project the inner feelings of the doorman, Murnau often presents his world not as it is but as he sees it, distorted by his anxious

Figure 15. Jannings photographed in long shot from a high angle, looking up at an intimidating heavy trunk. The angle and shot type emphasize his feeling of diminishment. (*The Last Laugh,* 1924, Friedrich Wilhelm Murnau Stiftung.)

mental state. On his way home, after he has lost his job as a doorman, a building sways precariously as if it is about to fall on him and crush him. In this mind's-eye image Murnau has found a concise visual means to express the inner devastation of a man who is crushed by the loss of his job and with it, his status in the world. So as not to lose his status with his neighbors, he steals his old uniform from the hotel and continues to wear it home from work. As he is about to leave for work in the morning wearing his stolen uniform, he encounters a woman on the landing outside his door. She gazes at him admiringly. But when we see her face from the doorman's point of view, it appears grotesquely stretched out and elongated, like a face in a distorting fun-house mirror. This distorted image conveys the doorman's fear of his neighbor. Vulnerable because of the loss of his job, he at last begins to penetrate the falseness of his neighbor's adulation to see the awful truth. Her adoring manner is based not on real affection but on her inflated conception of his importance. The grotesquely distorted image of the woman's fawning posture makes her adoration seem strangely menacing, as if hinting

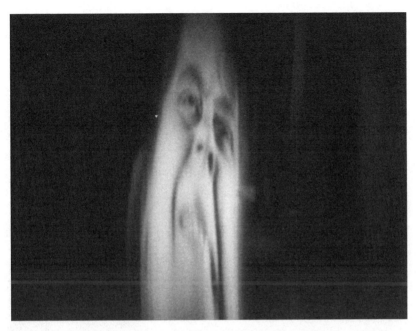

Figure 16. From the doorman's point of view, the neighbor woman's face is grotesquely stretched out and elongated, conveying the doorman's fear of her wrath once she finds out that he is a false idol. (*The Last Laugh*, 1924, Friedrich Wilhelm Murnau Stiftung.)

at the rage and contempt she will feel when she discovers he is a false idol. (See figure 16.)

Murnau, in collaboration with his cameraman Karl Freund and his screenwriter Carl Mayer, added a new dimension to the expressiveness of cinema by "unchaining" the camera. When *The Last Laugh* was made, most directors shot their actions with a static camera, employing camera movement only to make action scenes more exciting. In Griffith's last-minute rescues, for example, a moving camera was sometimes mounted on a truck which drove alongside or in front of the rescue vehicle (horses, trains, carriages, etc.) to lend kinetic dynamism to the shot. Eisenstein mounted a camera on tracks that extended the length of the Odessa Steps so that he could intensify the effect of the spectacle of the fleeing citizens by following their movement down the stairs with his camera.

In *The Last Laugh*, the camera is in motion from the beginning to the end of the film, often adding a subtle psychological dimension to the action. The film begins with a stunning moving camera shot: The camera descends in an elevator, and when the door to the lift opens, it heads out the door through a vast, luxurious hotel lobby, taking the spectator along for the ride. (This shot was obtained by strapping the camera on the chest of the cameraman, who then rode out into the lobby on a bicycle.) The camera then takes us through a revolving door to the front of the hotel where the doorman is on duty. Here the camera movement is more than just a virtuoso display of film technique. The dynamic movement through the hotel lobby emphasizes the spaciousness of the hotel and thereby magnifies our sense of its grandeur. When the camera movement finally ends on the doorman, we understand in a flash the grandiose self-importance he absorbs from his association with such a place. Robert Herlth, one of the set designers for *The Last Laugh*, writes: "we had not 'unchained' the camera for merely technical reasons. On the contrary, we had found a new and more exact way of isolating the image, and of intensifying dramatic incident."[6]

A subtle example of the use of the moving camera to intensify a dramatic incident occurs when the doorman returns to work the day after losing his job but still wearing his old uniform. He has gotten drunk at the wedding party of his niece the night before and has apparently forgotten about his demotion to bathroom attendant. As he approaches the hotel, we see through his point of view an image of the doorman who has replaced him standing at his post in front of the hotel. The shot begins as a long shot of the new doorman and is slightly out of focus. The camera then begins to move in closer and closer to the new man until the lens is sharply focused on the face of the doorman's replacement. The slow camera movement and the gradual sharpening of the image perfectly convey the old doorman's reluctant but dawning recognition that he has been supplanted.

When another neighbor woman[7] discovers the doorman at his lowly new post as bathroom attendant, the moment is given striking dramatic emphasis by a camera movement. We see a shot of the old man taken from outside the bathroom as he timidly opens the lavatory door and peers out to determine who has come to see him. At this point there is a POV shot of the neighbor woman (who has come to bring him lunch) looking back at him. As she opens her mouth to scream the camera lunges toward her until we see her face in an extreme close-up, framing only her eyes and nose. In contrast to the shot described above, in which the camera movement signifies a slow dawning of realization, here the lunge of the camera re-creates the feeling of an unexpected shock—both the woman's shock at seeing her idol so fallen and the ex-doorman's shock at being discovered.

Murnau also uses the moving camera to transfer viscerally to the viewer the doorman's drunken dizziness on the morning after the wedding party. As he sits down in a chair, he begins to start reeling through space. This effect was achieved by placing Jannings on a turntable device that swung back and forth, and then following his movement with the camera. Then we see a POV shot of the room spinning around. Here the cameraman Freund staggered about the room like a drunken man with the camera affixed to his chest. In both shots, the drunken man's vertigo is transferred onto the viewer.

Shortly thereafter, the ex-doorman falls asleep and dreams he still has his old job at the hotel. In his dream he effortlessly lifts an enormous trunk from the top of a hearselike coach and parades with it into the hotel lobby. To the enthusiastic applause of hotel staff and patrons, he repeatedly tosses the trunk into the air and catches it with one hand. The dream is obviously a wish-fulfilling denial of reality. The previous day he had desperately tried to convince the manager of the hotel that he still had the strength to be a doorman by lifting a heavy trunk in the manager's office. The trunk overpowered him, sealing his fate as a lavatory attendant.

Camera movement plays a large part in drawing the audience into the experience of the old man's drunken dream. The camera swishes erratically over the faces of the hotel patrons applauding the old man's prowess with the trunk. At first this shot seems to be a subjective shot: that is, the admiring faces of the patrons are apparently seen from the point of view of the dreamer. But, suddenly, the camera pulls back to capture the dreamer objectively. Here the shift from a subjective to an objective perspective within one shot cinematically re-creates the experience common in dreams that one is simultaneously experiencing an event and watching oneself having the experience. The unpleasant tilting and jiggling of the camera, combined with the manic grandiosity of the content of the dream, has an irritating and disquieting effect, reminding the viewer that the doorman's glorious comeback is only a drunken fantasy.

The dream sequence described above is further enhanced by another special photographic effect, the use of multiple superimposed images to approximate the common dream phenomenon that Freud referred to as "condensation," the merging of two separate people or places into one composite image. Here Murnau superimposes images of the hotel dining room upon images of the doorman's tenement neighborhood. (See figure 17.) The fusion of these separate places into one space underlines the fact that the old man's prestige at work is vital to his well-being at home.

As the dream fades out, a momentary superimposition of dream im-

Figure 17. Multiple superimposed images approximate the common dream phenomenon Freud referred to as "condensation." Here, images of the hotel dining room merge with images of the doorman's tenement neighborhood. (*The Last Laugh,* 1924, Friedrich Wilhelm Murnau Stiftung.)

ages over a shot of the old man dozing visually conveys the semiconscious state between sleep and waking, when the aura of the dream persists even as the real world intrudes. These images abruptly disappear when the neighbor woman who subsequently discovers the doorman at work enters his room and shuts the window, suggesting that the sound of her action finally arouses him from sleep. This is one of many ways in which Murnau uses a visual device to bring sound to the silent medium of film. So adept was Murnau at conveying everything that needed to be conveyed through images—even sounds—that he was able to construct an utterly compelling ninety-minute story about the mental deterioration of an old man using only one written title.[8]

EXPRESSIVE MISE-EN-SCÈNE IN *THE LAST LAUGH*

While I have been primarily emphasizing the way Murnau uses photographic effects, that is, cinema-specific means, to project the subjectivity

Figure 18. The grandeur of the city created through special effects—the use of model shots and forced perspective. (*The Last Laugh,* 1924, Friedrich Wilhelm Murnau Stiftung.)

of his character, no assessment of the visual power of *The Last Laugh* would be complete without a discussion of the film's mise-en-scène. The look of *The Last Laugh* set a new standard of lighting and art design for film, and is still impressive today. Especially striking is the design of the grand hotel situated in the center of a large bustling city. Murnau had to make the hotel especially grand because the grandeur of the hotel and the city had to be commensurate with the size of the old man's over-inflated ego. So glorious are the hotel and city in *The Last Laugh* that shortly after the film appeared in America Murnau received a telegram from someone in Hollywood who deplored the fact that America had no city to compare with the grandeur of the one in *The Last Laugh.*[9] Yet the magnificent city and hotel were the creation of set designers and everything was constructed on the back lot of the studio. The splendor of the city was created through special effects—the use of model shots and forced perspectives. In her book on Murnau, Eisner includes an account by one of the set designers, Robert Herlth, to explain how it was done (see figure 18).

> The view, or rather "background," seen from the revolving [hotel] door was managed by means of a perspective shot of a sloping street 15 metres high in the foreground diminishing to 5 in the "distance." The street ran between model sky scrapers as much as 17 metres high. . . . To make the "perspective" work we had big buses and Mercedes cars in the foreground; in the middle ground middle sized cars; and in the background small ones, with behind them again children's toy cars. Farthest away of all, in front of the shops, we had crowds of "people" cut out and painted and moved across the screen on a conveyor belt.[10]

The look of the city is also enhanced by Murnau's carefully controlled, non-naturalistic use of light, which conveys subtle nuances of *Stimmung*, or mood, that coincide with the doorman's mental state throughout the film. The use of the expressive, unchained camera and special photographic effects, combined with stunning sets and lighting techniques, all in the service of telling a complex story focusing on interior feelings rather than exterior actions, made *The Last Laugh* seem to many film theorists and critics of the time the ultimate example of film as high art, equal or superior in its evocative power to drama and literature.

THE ARTFUL ARTLESSNESS OF CHARLES CHAPLIN AND ANDRÉ BAZIN'S REALIST AESTHETIC

Charles Chaplin was a very different kind of director from F. W. Murnau or Sergei Eisenstein, and his films make an instructive contrast with theirs. In the twelve films Chaplin made for the Mutual Film Corporation between 1916 and 1917, which include *The Rink*, *Easy Street*, *The Adventurer*, *The Pawnshop*, and *One A.M.*, there are little or no photographic or editing pyrotechnics. The majority of the shots are static long shots or medium shots with only occasional close-ups for dramatic emphasis. The editing is mostly invisible, because the shots are linked together to convey the narrative smoothly, not to make a comment, create a striking visual contrast, or to distort real time and space for dramatic effect. The lighting is universally high key,[11] and the camera, if it moves at all, usually does so just slightly, to reframe the action. There are no expressive camera angles or camera movements, no superimposition of images, no distorting optical effects, nor any fancy forced-perspective sets. Yet, despite their lack of obviously artful cinematic techniques, these early films are considered by many critics to be minor masterpieces. They are watched today with as much pleasure as when they first appeared.

The French film theorist André Bazin revolutionized film theory in the

1940s and 1950s in a series of essays that tried to account theoretically for the power of filmmakers like Chaplin, whose films do not employ complicated film techniques but are nevertheless powerful and compelling to watch. Bazin referred to these directors as "realists."[12] A theory of film aesthetics, Bazin believed, must take into account the uncanny realism of the photographic image, the basic unit of cinematography. In an essay entitled "The Ontology of the Photographic Image," which first appeared in 1945, Bazin claims that the photographic image is more like a thumbprint or a death mask than a statue or a painting, because the object captured by the camera's lens literally leaves its imprint on the work of art. That is, the impression on the celluloid emulsion is the direct effect of light beams that bounced off the subject when the shutter of the camera was opened. According to Bazin, photography finally satisfies the human demand, based on an unconscious desire for immortality, for a process which can permanently fix, order, and possess the natural world by literally capturing its image through an impersonal, scientific process. Rather than deploring photography's ability to mechanically reproduce images of the world, or seeing this capacity as a limitation to be overcome by the artist, Bazin celebrates it: "All the arts depend on the presence of man," Bazin proclaims, "Only photography derives an advantage from his absence."[13]

Bazin was arguing against the conception of film art put forth by many prominent film aestheticians. Rudolph Arnheim, for example, in his influential book *Film as Art*, first published in 1933, argues that the very differences between the film image and the everyday ways we see things "provide film with its artistic resources."[14] Arnheim believes that unless the film image is molded and distorted for expressive effect by means unique and specific to the cinematic apparatus, film will be seen as a slavish reproducer of reality, or worse, degenerate into an unimaginatively photographed theater. In contrast, Bazin saw the camera's ability to mechanically capture images of the world as a huge advantage, and put its capacity to capture and record the world realistically at the center of his film aesthetics rather than considering it as a limitation to be overcome.[15]

Bazin does not claim that photography is all science and no art. Obviously someone has to choose an image and frame it. But, because the recording or capturing of the photographic image is so complete and total, in contrast to the sloppy, partial, biased way in which the human eye processes the world, photography makes it possible for reality to reveal itself in an extraordinarily vivid and profound new way. Bazin writes:

"Only the impassive lens, stripping its object of all those ways of seeing it, those piled-up preconceptions, that spiritual dust and grime with which my eyes have covered it, is able to present it in all its virginal purity to my attention and consequently to my love."[16] The imposition of "artistic" cinematic techniques, according to Bazin, got in the way of what was truly special about the film medium: the camera's unprecedented ability simply to observe.

Bazin felt filmmakers associated with the Soviet school of montage, for all their clever and ingenious experiments with film editing, perverted film art, because rather than allowing the medium its unique revelatory dimension, their studied shot juxtapositions forced the photographed images to take on a predigested significance. Bazin goes so far as to argue that there is a fascist dimension to montage style because, like a dictator, the director controls everything the viewer sees by chopping up the world into fragments and recombining them in a tendentious way.

Arguing against those Soviet filmmakers who believed that editing is the foundation of film art, Bazin cites examples in which heavy editing or montage would simply be the wrong approach to certain subject matters. He points to Robert Flaherty's documentary on Eskimo culture, *Nanook of the North* (1922), in which Nanook harpoons a seal. To present a powerful and convincing record of this event, Bazin argues, Flaherty had to show Nanook and the seal together, in the same frame, during the entire act of harpooning, in one long take, without editing. If he had broken the scene down into numerous short shots culminating when Nanook drags the harpooned seal out of the water, the scene would lack credibility. We might even suspect that the event was faked. By avoiding excessive editing, and hence capturing the entire action of Nanook's struggle to harpoon the seal in long takes, Flaherty not only makes the scene more believable, he presents the action in real time, thereby creating a dramatic tension that fancy editing would destroy. Bazin writes: "Montage could suggest the time involved. Flaherty however confines himself to showing the actual waiting period; the length of the hunt is the very substance of the image, its true object. Thus in the film this episode requires one set-up."[17]

Bazin, to be sure, did not advocate that films be shot using no techniques at all. He did not want cinema to return to the days before Griffith established the conventions of film as a narrative art. He was aware that the close-up was needed to emphasize what otherwise would not be noticed, and that crosscutting heightened the drama of the story. He simply called into question the belief that fancy montage and manipulation of the film image through dramatic lighting, acute camera angles, distorting lenses, superimpositions, and flamboyant camera movements were the *only* ways to achieve film art. He suggested that a more self-effacing directorial style, in which the art seems—but not necessarily is—artless, results in a work that is truer to the intrinsic qualities of the film medium.

Bazin favored films created in what has come to be called realist style. Here, I want to emphasize, I am talking about formal realism, the *style* in which the film is shot, as opposed to the realism of the content of the images. *The Battleship Potemkin,* for example, is considered a realist film due to its location shooting and use of nonprofessional actors, but in style it is an expressionist film (as I use the term expressionist in this book) because of the expressive function of its complicated montage. In a realist film the emotional content comes primarily from the profilmic event. In an expressionist film the emotion is conveyed primarily through the director's artful use of film techniques.

Films shot in the realist style favor long takes that sometimes last up to and over sixty seconds, in contrast to the montage style of directors such as Eisenstein, Vertov, and Pudovkin in the 1920s, whose shots average from three to four seconds each and often last less than a fraction of a second. Realist films use lots of camera movements (panning, tracking, reframing), not to create the dramatic and expressive effects of the German expressionist's "unchained camera," but simply to preserve the spatial and temporal unity of a scene so that the actors' performances could been seen intact. They also feature depth-of-focus photography, which frees the viewer's attention to move between the foreground, middle ground, and background of a shot, without forcing any particular object upon the viewer's attention. As mentioned above, realist films strive for invisible editing, which moves the narrative forward through smooth, unobtrusive match cuts, not cuts that deliberately call attention to themselves because their juxtaposition makes some kind of political point or creates an impact through graphic conflict. They use close-ups and extreme close-ups sparingly, preferring to employ the medium shot. In realist compositions, objects spill over the edges of the frame, calling attention to offscreen space. Realist directors conceive of the frame as a window that only temporarily hides a part of the world, as opposed to a picture frame whose lines demarcate the limits of a carefully composed, patently artistic composition.

A realist aesthetic of film art goes a long way toward explaining the appeal of Chaplin's films, which have many of the traits associated with realist style. Since Chaplin was a great comic actor, and his performance is the main attraction in his films, Chaplin wanted spectators to focus on him and his comic actions, not on the artistic capacity of the film medium. Much of the art of a Chaplin film resides in the careful shaping and structuring of the profilmic event, the complex comic actions that Chaplin devised and performed for the camera to record. If Chaplin's performances were presented in montage style, in a series of short shots, we would lose all appreciation for his extraordinary comic timing, which must be seen in long, uninterrupted shots to be fully appreciated.

An outstanding feature of Chaplin's silent comedies is that they can be enjoyed over and over (and I know this is true because I teach his films repeatedly) without becoming stale or boring. This is owing mostly to the brilliance of Chaplin's comic ideas and his comic choreography. Watching him move offers some of the same pleasure we receive from ballet. But the realist style in which Chaplin's films are photographed contributes to their pleasure as well. Because so much of the action is captured in long, medium, or full shot, in long takes, the grace and precision of Chaplin's comic choreography remains intact. So much is going on within every shot, moreover, that there is always something new for the spectator to observe in subsequent screenings.

REALIST TECHNIQUE IN CHARLES CHAPLIN'S *THE ADVENTURER*

A close look at one shot in Chaplin's popular short film *The Adventurer* (1917) demonstrates the virtues of a self-effacing realist style. The shot under analysis is photographed in one long take that lasts forty-seven seconds with no cuts. In *The Adventurer* Chaplin plays an escaped convict (whom I will subsequently refer to as Charlie). After escaping prison guards by jumping into the ocean and swimming away, Charlie rescues a lovely young girl (Edna Purviance), her mother (Marta Golden), and the girl's oversized, jealous bully of a suitor (Eric Campbell) from drowning. The shot under analysis occurs just after Purviance, who has asked her rescuer to be a guest in her house, invites him out onto the veranda to meet her party guests. The shot begins with her introducing Charlie to some ladies. Rather than bowing, Charlie curtsies,[18] first with one leg behind him and then the other. The girl then formally introduces him to Campbell. Charlie politely offers to shake hands, but Campbell puts his hands behind him and turns his back on Charlie with disdain. Then, as Charlie politely bows to the girl, he jabs his lit cigar into Campbell's hand. Campbell lets out a howl and Charlie looks surprised, giving the girl a puzzled look, as if to say, "What's with him?" As Charlie converses with the girl, Campbell retaliates by giving Charlie a back-kick. Charlie deftly diverts the girl's attention and back-kicks back. This is apparently so satisfying that Charlie does it again. At this moment the girl's mother enters the space between Charlie and Campbell. Campbell, whose back is still turned and who assumes that Charlie (who has just kicked him twice) is still there, returns a particularly vicious kick, which of course lands on the mother's rear end just as she bows deeply in her greeting to Charlie. She is outraged. The bully is mortified. Chaplin looks scandalized. Eyeing Campbell with a look of moral disapproval, he escorts the girl into the house. The mother fearfully backs away from the bully as he bows deeply to apologize, giving Charlie a perfect target for one last kick. In this sequence, we get the double pleasure of seeing the revered mother (an archetypal mother-in-law figure) unceremoniously kicked in the rear and seeing Charlie's rival caught in an embarrassing act of aggression against the mother of the girl he is courting. Chaplin also deliciously turns a convention of polite society (bowing) into an opportunity for aggression. Campbell's extended rear end in the last moment of the scene seems to be asking for it.

The comic success of this sequence is enhanced because we see it in one unbroken take. It is amusing to see all the kicking going on while the other guests on the veranda are engaged in polite party conversation and somehow do not seem to notice. (See figure 19.) These actions could not have been conveyed as convincingly if the action had been heavily edited. We need to see the sequence in its entirety to believe it. When the mother moves into Charlie's space, the rhythm of the previous kicks sets up the expectation that she will receive the kick that Charlie has coming, an expectation which is all the more satisfying when it occurs because it is expected. The split-second timing of the mother's movement is essential to the comic effect of the action which, again, must occur in real time (as opposed to the artificial time created through editing) in order to be as convincing and funny as it is.

It is much more difficult to sustain a complicated comic action that goes on for 47 seconds than it is to divide the action up into units of short shots and edit the shots together. Because Chaplin for the most part (and I will discuss some of the exceptions later) refused to rely on editing or camera tricks in the creation of his comic actions, it often took him retake after retake to get everything to go exactly right. The cost of these retakes added up: *The Adventurer* and certain other of his Mutual films cost, on average, $100,000 each to make. At the time they were made, this was an extraordinary amount of money for a two-reeler (a

Figure 19. The comic success of this sequence is enhanced by our seeing it in long shot and in one unbroken take. (*The Adventurer,* 1917, Film Preservation Associates.)

film lasting about twenty minutes), especially when we recall that D. W. Griffith had shot his three-hour blockbuster epic *The Birth of a Nation* just two years earlier for only $115,000. Chaplin's films were so expensive to make because achieving the right effect in long unbroken shots cost far more than achieving effects through fancy editing.[19]

THE ROLE OF THE FILM MEDIUM IN CHAPLIN'S "REALIST" FILM ART

Although Chaplin's films look artless in the sense that they do not call attention to the film medium, the film medium does in fact play a large role in the success of Chaplin's comic art. Chaplin, Bazin observes, was a clown of great genius, as evident from his fame as a music-hall performer, but he needed the medium of the cinema to "free comedy completely from the limits of space and time imposed by the stage or the circus arena."[20]

In order to appreciate the role of the cinematic medium in the success of Chaplin's films we need only consider why Chaplin's filmed performances would not work equally well if performed on the stage. First and most obviously, the film medium permits Chaplin's performances to be seen from the perfect angle and in a much more vivid, intimate way than if we were to see him acting in the theater. The medium shots and medium-close shots which Chaplin frequently employs allow us to see subtle facial expressions that even people in the first row at a theater might miss. The cinematic medium also allowed Chaplin to exercise his talents for comic improvisation in a vastly larger arena than the stage could offer. Because the camera can go anywhere, all the world became his stage. Thus in the first sequence of *The Adventurer*, in which Charlie is hunted by prison guards, Chaplin exploits the seaside caves and cliffs as spectacular "settings" for chase sequences. Charlie avoids capture by running up and down steep cliffs, kicking prison guards over the edges of cliffs, and disappearing into seaside caves. Even the ocean is enlisted for a laugh when a giant wave helps him escape by engulfing the boat of his pursuers.

Although the appeal of Chaplin's films derives from the appeal of Chaplin's persona and the brilliant comic performances of his supporting cast, the gags and comic sequences are all the more amusing because they occur within a narrative context which heightens their comic effects. Chaplin's films gain immeasurably from the use of techniques Griffith pioneered to heighten the dramatic effects of stories told on film. In *The Adventurer*, Chaplin makes excellent use of crosscutting to create comic angst when he cuts between a scene which portrays Charlie's first meeting with the girl's father (Henry Bergman), who, a title tells us, is Judge Brown (most likely the man who sent Charlie to prison), and a scene in which the girl's jealous suitor has found a newspaper with the convict's picture on the front page under a "Wanted" headline. Through the technique of crosscutting the audience becomes painfully aware, before Charlie does, that he is on the cusp of being discovered, even as he is passing himself off to the judge as Commodore Slick, who heard the cries of the judge's distressed family from his yacht.

Also borrowing from Griffith's narrative techniques, Chaplin varies his shot types for dramatic emphasis and edits them together smoothly so that the audience remains unaware of the cutting. Most of his shots are long, full, or medium long shots, but occasionally he uses close-ups to create a joke. In *The Adventurer*, for example, when Charlie wakes up in bed in the girl's house, the camera frames him in a tight medium shot. First he notices he is wearing striped pajamas and then he notices the bars at the back of his bed (an unfortunate detail of the headboard). We know from his expression that he thinks for a moment he is back in

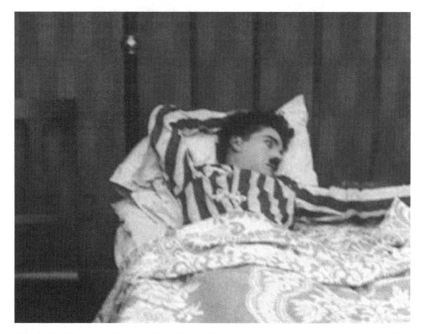

Figure 20. The gag in this shot (that Charlie thinks he is back in prison) only works thanks to the tight framing of the shot. (*The Adventurer,* 1917, Film Preservation Associates.)

jail. (See figure 20.) If this shot were less tightly framed, it would be too obvious that Charlie was in a bedroom, not a prison, and the sight gag would not work.

Perhaps the most important function of the editing in *The Adventurer* is to give a quick comic pace to the action. Every shot lasts just long enough for the spectator to get the point, and not an instant more. The cutting, that is, functions to eliminate all dead time, or any action that is neither vital to the plot nor funny. A particularly good example of this occurs soon after Charlie has escaped from the prison guards by swimming out to sea. Having found a safe haven on the shore, he hears a cry for help and immediately jumps back into the water. This shot is followed by a shot of the drowning mother. Immediately, Charlie swims into the shot. The time it took him to swim out to the mother after he jumped into the water is eliminated through editing. On the stage, such elimination of dead time is impossible because the action, by necessity, takes place in real time and space.

While the editing pace of *The Adventurer* is not as fast and furious as the editing pace of *The Battleship Potemkin,* it does accelerate substantially at the end of the film, in a final chase scene in which the convict desperately tries to evade capture by the police. Here, the pace of the action is also quickened by the use of accelerated or fast-motion photography (achieved by photographing the action at a lower number of frames per second than the projection speed), another effect specific to the cinema.

Finally, the editing in *The Adventurer* creates surreal effects impossible to achieve on the stage. The objects of Chaplin's comic universe are often like objects in a dream, in that they magically seem to materialize when needed. Thus a boat that does not appear on the beach in previous shots suddenly appears when the prison guards need to pursue the convict, who has escaped into the ocean. Similarly, the newspaper picture of the convict materializes out of nowhere. The table on which it appears had only a fruit bowl on it in the previous shots. Just as unexpectedly, a pen becomes available for Charlie to alter his "Wanted" picture to make it resemble his rival. These sudden and surprising appearances of objects also resemble Warner Brothers cartoons in which the dynamite, the bomb, or box of matches is always conveniently at hand, even in the most remote settings. Such effects are possible only in the film medium and would be impossible to achieve on the stage. The dream logic of Chaplin's films lowers the threshold of our willing suspension of belief, making us more receptive to the anarchic humor of Chaplin's absurd comic world.

While Chaplin for the most part created his comedy without camera tricks, he does rely on them in a few additional places in *The Adventurer*. In the opening sequence of the film, he combines accelerated motion with reverse action when Charlie miraculously escapes the prison guards by sliding *up* a hill. This was accomplished by shooting him sliding down the hill but then printing the action in reverse. Other of his camera tricks are more subtle. A gag in which ice cream goes down his pants, for example, would have been impossible to achieve without the help of a stop-motion camera trick. First we see Charlie awkwardly balancing a big scoop of ice cream on his spoon (so he can drink the melted ice cream remaining in his bowl) and then the ice cream falls down his pants. Since it is not easy to guide a scoop of ice cream into one's pants, that is, to make the ice cream land in exactly the right place and still make it look like an accident, the camera was turned off just as the ice cream was about to fall from the spoon. The ice cream was then placed at the right place on Charlie's pants, and the camera was turned back on. When the action is projected on the screen it looks as if the ice cream has plopped from his spoon into his pants.

As the above discussion demonstrates, a good deal of film art went into the making of *The Adventurer.* Chaplin's films are by no means artless— they just look that way. Only by looking very closely does one become aware of the cinematic techniques that heighten the comic effects. The realist style which Bazin preferred (and which he created a theoretical system to justify) does not call for a renunciation of the use of film techniques; Bazin just preferred that the film techniques that are used do not call attention to themselves. The artfulness of films like *The Battleship Potemkin* and *The Last Laugh* cry out for our admiration and attention. Bazin called for a self-effacing style that downplays the use of film techniques and foregrounds the profilmic event, celebrating rather than denigrating film as a medium of mechanical reproduction.

While some filmmakers have veered off toward a stark aesthetic realism (Nagisa Oshima, Yasujiro Ozu, and Jim Jarmusch in *Stranger than Paradise* [1984] come immediately to mind), whereas others (Oliver Stone in *JFK* [1991] and *Natural Born Killers* [1994], Francis Coppola in *Apocalypse Now* [1979], and, more recently, Darren Aronofsky in *Requiem for a Dream* [2000]) use the film medium in a highly expressionist way, the two aesthetics are blended in most contemporary films. The expressionist and realist theories of what constitutes film art offer two compelling ways of looking at the potentials of the film medium. Fortunately, the use of one approach does not exclude the other, so we need not make a choice between them.

4

The Conversion to Sound
and the Classical Hollywood Film
Howard Hawks's *His Girl Friday*

EARLY VERSUS MODERN SOUND THEORY

By the end of 1929, the conversion of the motion picture industry to sound was all but complete in the United States. Nearly every theater had installed sound equipment. So much did the public love the novelty of the sound film that the best-made silent film could not compete at the box office with the worst, most clumsily crafted "talkie." But many film directors, film theorists, and aestheticians believed that the image defined the essence of cinema and was the feature that distinguished it from literature and theater. They felt that the addition of synchronized sound (especially in the form of spoken speech) to film was a disaster that would destroy the cinema as a unique art form. Subsequently, I refer to this group as the early sound theorists. Music, in the form of live accompaniment by a piano, organ, or even a full-scale symphony orchestra, had always been a part of the cinematic experience, so the early sound theorists did not object to the synchronized addition of music, or even to the addition of sound effects. Their enemy was the spoken word.

Béla Balázs, a passionate proponent of the primacy of the image in film, argued that spoken words are less expressive than the gestures and facial expressions that accompany them and that constitute the real language of the cinema. "The silent film is free of the isolating walls of language difference," he writes. "If we look at and understand each other's faces and gestures, we not only understand, we also learn to feel each other's emotions."[1] The inclusion of the spoken word in film, Balázs feared, would desensitize audiences to the deeper communicative force of the purely visual image. In a similar vein, the art historian and film theoretician Rudolph Arnheim argued that because the image already speaks, there is no need for literal voices. "In the universal silence of the image, the fragments of a broken vase could 'talk' exactly the way a character talked to his neighbor."[2] Arnheim went so far as to call for the return of the silent film to restore the golden age of the image.

Other early film theorists who were also filmmakers, such as Sergei Eisenstein, V. I. Pudovkin, René Clair, and Alberto Cavalcanti, struck a compromise. They deplored films that employed sound in a slavish, unimaginative way, by matching every sound to its on-screen source. Nevertheless, they admitted that the addition of music, sound effects, and even the spoken word could potentially enhance the power of the film image if (and this is a big "if") most of the sounds were nonsynchronous, that is, detached from their on-screen source. An even better way to add sound was to use it in counterpoint to the image, creating a clash, a felt disparity, between what was seen and what was heard.

In his book on film art and aesthetics, the French director René Clair points to an example of the effective use of nonsynchronous sound in an early American film musical *The Broadway Melody* (1929). As the camera holds on the anguished face of Bessie Love, whose lover has just departed, the offscreen sound of his car door shutting and the car driving away is heard on the sound track. The combination of the actress's face and the sounds made by the departing car create a far more poignant expression of sorrow, Clair argues, than if the director had cut to the images of the lover shutting the car door and driving away that would have been necessary if the film were silent. "Even in the dialogues of the talking picture," Clair writes, "it seems that at the moment a sentence is spoken it is often more interesting to see the face of the listener than that of the speaker." He concludes that "It is the alternate use of the image of a subject and the sound produced by this subject—and not their simultaneous use—that creates the best effects in the sound and talking picture."[3]

The great Soviet filmmakers Sergei Eisenstein, V. I. Pudovkin and Grigori Alexandrov suggested another compromise. They signed a manifesto in 1929 championing the contrapuntal use of sound as a way to extend the culture of montage which they had painstakingly pioneered.[4] This manifesto argued that just as the creative juxtaposition of images the Soviets favored in their experiments with editing can instill a new idea in the viewer's mind, so could the creative clash or contrapuntal use of sound and image.

In his pioneering work on film aesthetics, *Film Technique and Film Acting*, the Soviet film theorist V. I. Pudovkin gives an example from his own film *Deserter* (1933) of how the use of contrapuntal sound can powerfully convey an idea through a montage of sound and image. The sequence he describes involves a workers' demonstration in Hamburg. The workers set out with great purposefulness, but are brutally beaten back by the police. The conventional way to create a score for the sequence, Pudovkin explains, would be to match the mood of the image to the mood of the music: cheerful march music to accompany the optimism at the beginning stages of the demonstration, ominous music when the police appear, and music of despair when the demonstration is defeated. But this is not how the sound is in fact structured in the film. Instead, Pudovkin tells us, the score was written, played, and recorded so that the music gradually grew in power, with a note of stern and confident victory constantly running through it, and uninterruptedly rising in strength from beginning to end. "As the workers lose ground to the police, the insistent victory of the music grows; yet again, when the workers are defeated and disbanded, the music becomes yet more powerful still in its spirit of victorious exaltation."[5] As a result, at the moment that the workers are most beaten back, the music is most triumphant. By this contrapuntal clash of sound and image (triumphant music is juxtaposed with defeated workers), Pudovkin was able to convey in a subtle, but strongly emotional manner an ideological point: History is on the side of the workers, so that even in defeat lies a hidden victory. Physical losses only strengthen moral resolve.

One theorist who did not deplore the coming of sound was André Bazin, who had no difficulty integrating sound, and especially the spoken word, into his realist theory of film. Bazin, as was discussed in chapter 3, celebrated film for its ability to mechanically record images of the world. Hence for Bazin, sound was the natural extension of film's inherent realism. While many early sound theorists saw the silent films of the late 1920s, just before the coming of sound, as the golden age of film, Bazin saw the silent film even at its most artistic as incomplete, missing one of reality's most important elements: sound.[6]

In *The Technique of Film Editing*, Karel Reisz points out that not only does the addition of synchronized sound make the cinema more realistic in Bazin's terms (that is, closer to our everyday experience of the world), it also permitted much greater economy in storytelling as well as more complex stories. A well-written line of dialogue can convey information which the silent filmmaker could only express in an intertitle or through an often torturously ingenious series of explanatory images, both of which techniques awkwardly slow down the story.[7] Sometimes a word can be worth a thousand pictures.

Reisz, who occupies a position somewhere between early and modern sound theory, concedes that even films that rely heavily on dialogue can still be good films. "Any theory which rules out films like *The Little Foxes, Citizen Kane* or the early Marx Brothers comedies, must be suspect from the beginning," he writes. But he insists, nevertheless, that good films must "make their essential impression by the images."[8] In *Introduction to Film Art,* David Bordwell and Kristen Thompson, modern sound theorists, challenge even that position, insisting that the elements of sound and image in the cinema are equal and complementary. Synchronized speech in a film not only conveys concepts and ideas that would be cumbersome to express in silent film, but the quality of the speech—its pitch, volume, degree of nasality, whether or not the voice has an accent—can strongly affect the way we perceive the speaker, adding layers and nuances of meaning and expressiveness impossible to convey through gestures or facial expressions alone.[9] The image of a beautiful woman, for example, can be shattered by the quality of her voice. This happens famously in *Singin' in the Rain* (1952) when the glamorous silent film star Lina La Mont (Jean Hagen) utters her first screechy words with a pronounced Brooklyn accent. The sound of her voice makes her suddenly no longer appear beautiful. Michel Chion, the ultimate modern sound theorist, goes so far as to argue in *Audio-Vision: Sound on Screen* that sound is in fact *more* important than the image in determining the effect of a film. He argues that sound influences our perception of images. According to Chion, we notice different things in the same image when it is accompanied by different sounds, and sounds can make us notice otherwise insignificant elements of an image.[10]

The arguments of the modern sound theorists, who insist that synchronized sound was good for film, help explain why a film like Howard Hawks's *His Girl Friday* (1940), a film that talks its head off, is still quintessentially filmic. Although the film was an adaptation of a Broadway play, and a great deal of our pleasure in the film derives from the clever, fast-paced dialogue, it is anything but filmed theater. A close analysis of just a few sequences from *His Girl Friday* proves the argument of modern sound film theorists that the addition of sound to film, even in films dominated by talk, expands the aesthetic possibilities and emotional power of the film medium.

The plot of *His Girl Friday* involves a battle of the sexes between Walter Burns (Cary Grant), the editor of a major metropolitan newspaper, and Hildy Johnson (Rosalind Russell), his ex-wife and ex-employee (she was his ace reporter), who divorced Walter because he always put the newspaper before her. At the beginning of the film Hildy comes to Walter's office with a new fiancé in tow to inform him that she is getting married and will be leaving the newspaper business forever in exchange for a more conventional life as a wife and mother. An analysis of a very talky short sequence from the beginning of *His Girl Friday* demonstrates how Hawks's dialogue works brilliantly in tandem with his images, to the benefit of both.

SEQUENCE ANALYSES: SOUND AND IMAGE IN *HIS GIRL FRIDAY*

The first shot of the film is a lateral tracking shot nearly encompassing the length of the entire newsroom that is reminiscent of the "unchained" camera movement that opened *The Last Laugh*. The rapidly moving camera, combined with the rapid overlapping dialogue of men and women purposefully, if somewhat frantically, at work, perfectly expresses the excitement of this world, the thrill of living life in the fast lane. An almost imperceptible dissolve[11] takes us to shot 2, a medium-close shot of women busily operating a switchboard. The camera pauses on them briefly and then follows a reporter on his way out of the newsroom who just catches an elevator on the way down. The adjoining elevator door opens, and out walks Hildy Johnson with Bruce (Ralph Bellamy), her fiancé. The camera then reverses direction to follow Hildy, who strides into the newsroom, leaving Bruce at the entrance gate, on which is posted a sign reading "NO ADMITTANCE." Because the camera immediately follows Hildy's movements, she becomes identified with the vital world of newspaper reporting, a world to which Bruce is pointedly denied entry.[12]

Hildy greets everyone by first name or nickname—"Hi ya Skinny, hello Ruth, hello Maisie"—her words reinforcing our sense of her comfortable familiarity with the world of the press. Her language, moreover, is rich in irony and verbal play, confirming her identity as a lover of words, a born writer. At the switchboard, she refers to Walter Burns as "the Lord of the Universe." One of the switchboard operators offers to announce her, but she answers, "Oh, no. I'll blow my own horn." At this point the camera follows Hildy back to where she left Bruce at the gate. Her speech to Bruce is plain and literal in contrast with her earlier verbal playfulness, and the change is a subtle indication of all she will have to give up if she marries Bruce. "He's in," she informs him. "Wait here. I'll be back in ten minutes."

The camera starts to follow Hildy as she hurries off in the direction of Walter's office, but Bruce calls after her, his words literally stopping the camera in its tracks. "Even ten minutes is a long time to be away from you," he says. Hildy stops, turns around and walks back to Bruce, the camera following her movement until she and Bruce are framed in a static medium two shot. "What did you say?" she asks. Bruce says, "Well . . ." and bashfully hangs his head. "Go on," Hildy urges. At this point there is a cut to a medium-close shot of Bruce from over Hildy's shoulder. "Uh . . ." Bruce mutters. "Go ahead," Hildy coaxes. "All right—Even ten minutes is a long time to be away from you," Bruce repeats.

The line, "Ten minutes is a long time to be away from you," is not in and of itself necessarily sappy. One can imagine that if someone like Humphrey Bogart delivered it with the right intonation, it would sound sexy. But when said (twice) by the soft-featured Bellamy in a slow, slightly hesitant manner (in contrast to the fast-talking Hildy—who never says "well," or "uh"), the words make Bruce seem babyishly dependent, like a child who can't tolerate being away too long from his mother. A dynamic woman like Hildy, we imagine, will not be charmed by such devotion for very long. In addition, the close-up on Bruce in which Hildy obliges Bruce to repeat his sentimental words seems to skewer him in his embarrassment. He hangs his head and casts down his eyes. It is something of a surprise and relief (if we at all identify with Bruce) that Hildy seems pleased by his words: "I can stand being spoiled a little," she replies, as the camera cuts to a reverse angle close-up of her, smiling. "The gentleman I'm going to see did very little spoiling."

Although her words, and the close-up that gives them emphasis, both suggest that she is charmed by Bruce's affection, and that she is happy to leave the newspaper world to settle down with him, an element of the film's mise-en-scène, the design of Hildy's outfit, gives us pause. The jaunty hat and stunning, matching zigzag design on her suit visually establish her as a dynamic, powerful person unsuited (pun intended) to a partner as bland as Bruce appears to be. (See figure 21.) And when Hildy reassures Bruce that "I'll come runnin', pardner" if she needs help with Walter, she delivers this line while running away from Bruce and toward Walter, a wonderful instance of dialogue in subtle counterpoint to the image. Once Hildy is back in the newspaper world, her verbal playful-

Figure 21. The jaunty hat with the matching zigzag design of her suit defines Hildy as a dynamic and powerful woman, and not a fit mate for the bland Bruce. (*His Girl Friday,* 1939, D3K Films.)

ness returns, in her rapid-fire responses to the greetings and comments of her ex-colleagues. The fundamental incompatibility of Bruce and Hildy so carefully set up aurally and visually in this scene is further reinforced in the next scene between Hildy and Walter. Here Hildy's voice rhythms, so different from those of the slow-speaking Bruce, mirror and match the fast-talking Walter's, suggesting once again that the two are meant for each other.

I have gone into these opening moments in detail in order to demonstrate how dialogue in conjunction with editing and dynamic camera movements work together to create a highly sophisticated and delightful melange of mixed messages. The combination of sound and image makes us feel viscerally that despite Hildy's words—her spoken commitment to Bruce—he is not the right man for her and Walter, her ex-husband, is. This, of course, sets up suspense in viewers' minds. Will Hildy ever come to realize her mistake? And if she does, how will she ever get out of her engagement to Bruce?

Not only do Hawks's characters (with the exception of Bruce) talk fast, their conversations often overlap, and in some instances up to three separate lines of conversations occur simultaneously in one scene. At one point in the film, when the reporters are phoning in the news that Earl Williams, a man who is supposed to be hanged the next day, has escaped from jail, Hawks combines rapid-fire editing with rapid-fire dialogue, all in the service of viscerally conveying the adrenaline rush a newspaper reporter experiences when breaking a big story. In Eisenstein's silent films, it was the fast editing that created the exciting sensation of events occurring at breakneck speed; in *His Girl Friday* it is the pace of the dialogue in conjunction with the editing. By overlapping dialogue, Hawks was able to eliminate all pauses between speakers, further speeding up the pace of the talk.[13] Later, when the same reporters phone in dramatic accounts of Earl Williams' recapture even as it is happening before their eyes, they embellish their accounts in ways that are in hilarious counterpoint to the image. Williams is very much awake, but a reporter phones in the news that he was completely unconscious when captured. Another reporter relates that "he put up a desperate struggle, but the police overpowered him," when in fact we see him surrender quietly. Another reports that Williams broke through a whole cordon of police, when in fact only one policeman is involved in the arrest. In the tradition of the best modern sound films, the respective contributions of cinematography, editing, and sound are truly equal and complementary.

HIS GIRL FRIDAY AS A CLASSICAL HOLLYWOOD FILM

While a large part of *His Girl Friday's* charm resides in its synthesis of witty, fast-paced dialogue with rapid editing and quick camera movements, another way of understanding why the film is so enjoyable and engaging is to see it as a quintessential example of a classical Hollywood film. According to André Bazin, "what makes Hollywood so much better than anything else in the world is not only the quality of certain directors, but also the vitality and, in a certain sense, the excellence of a tradition. . . . The American cinema is a classical art, but why not then admire in it what is most admirable, i.e., not only the talent of this or that filmmaker, but the genius of the system."[14]

Bazin's point is that Hollywood films had certain rules, formulas that had to be followed by directors working within the confines of the Hollywood studio system, and in compliance with the production practices of Hollywood companies between the 1920s and the 1950s. In order to create motion pictures on a mass scale, film production was highly systemized in a manner that resembled the division of labor in a factory. But the most gifted directors, Bazin argues, thrived under the studio system's restrictions and restraints. Rather than enslaving them or inhibiting their creativity, the limits of the system brought out their best. In their influential book *The Classical Hollywood Cinema,* David Bordwell, Janet Staiger, and Kristin Thompson note that Bazin's ideas were validated when the studio system was in decline and hitherto venerated filmmakers such as Anthony Mann, Nicholas Ray, and George Cukor began turning out mediocre works. They quote François Truffaut: "We said . . . that the American cinema pleases us, and its film makers are slaves; what if they were freed? And from the moment that they were freed, they made shitty films."[15]

His Girl Friday has all the features of the classical Hollywood narrative film, as set forth in *The Classical Hollywood Cinema.*[16] Bordwell and his cowriters justify their use of the term "classical" to define the Hollywood cinema as follows: "It seems proper to retain the term in English, since the principles which Hollywood claims as its own rely on notions of decorum, proportion, formal harmony, respect for tradition, mimesis, self-effacing craftsmanship, and cool control of the perceiver's responses—canons which critics in any medium usually call 'classical.'"[17] To construct a model of the classical Hollywood film, Bordwell and his colleagues randomly selected one hundred films made in Hollywood between 1915 and 1960 and studied them on a viewing machine, recording in detail stylistic features as well as summarizing each film's action scene by scene. Below is a brief and necessarily simplified summary (the book runs in excess of five hundred pages) of the results of their research.

The Hollywood cinema is first and foremost a psychological cinema. Its plots tend to focus on a central character, with clearly delineated psychological traits, whose desires motivate the action, setting off a chain of cause and effect. Bordwell calls this trait "character-centered causality." In most of the plots, the central character lacks something vital which he or she must overcome obstacles to obtain. Whatever it is the character is after, he or she has a limited amount of time in which to acquire it: this deadline enhances the Hollywood film's dramatic power. Two lines of action often intermingle in the Hollywood film, one involving the public world (success in a job, politics, art, etc.) and one involving love between a heterosexual couple, the "heterosexual imperative" of the Hollywood film. Usually the two lines of action are intricately intertwined, as when a man who wants to make a success in business falls in love with the boss's daughter. The ending of the Hollywood film, contrary to the impression most people have, is not necessarily happy. The plot does, however, end in closure, with all loose ends tied up, all questions the plot poses answered, and all mysteries solved. In the majority of Hollywood films, the ending seems inevitable, a definitive outcome of what we might expect, given the clearly delineated personality attributes of the protagonists.

Thus defined, classical Hollywood films share a basic plot synopsis: they share certain characteristics of content. The cinematic *style* of the classical Hollywood film is just as well defined. In addition to the familiar glossy images, three-point lighting,[18] and generally high production values, Hollywood style comes down to this: An illusion is carefully constructed to convey the impression that we are gazing into a three-dimensional world that seems utterly real and unconstructed. It is as if we were looking through an invisible plate-glass window into "life," that is, at events that would occur whether or not we were there to see them. (In Don Delillo's novel *White Noise*, the narrator remarks that the dead have great power because the living imagine the dead can see everything they do. As spectators at a Hollywood film, we are something like Delillo's dead.)[19] In most classical Hollywood films, the narrator is omniscient, an overseeing presence who knows everything, and who can pick and choose exactly what information to share with the spectator and in what order. The narrator's omniscience is expressed by omnipresence. That is, the camera is not restricted to the point of view of one character or set of characters, but is free to move around in space to reveal information to the spectator that is not shared by the characters in the film.

Yet, while we seem to be looking at life flowing by, at a story not "told" but just "happening," at the same time, and somewhat paradoxically, we find ourselves perfectly positioned to see everything important that happens in the plot from the best perspective. The action we see appears as an uninterrupted flow of life. In fact, it is constructed from multiple shots taken from many perspectives, whose order and selection are carefully chosen to enhance the dramatic and thematic effect of the film. The illusion is created primarily through the match cut (invisible editing) and other techniques Griffith pioneered, which were discussed in chapter 1. While Sergei Eisenstein strove to make his cuts noticeable by deliberately creating graphic or thematic conflicts in adjoining shots, Hollywood-style editing went more in the direction of the self-effacing realist style favored by André Bazin, and employed by Charles Chaplin, among others. Hence the seemingly artless artfulness of the Hollywood film.

His Girl Friday has all the traits of the classical Hollywood film set forth above, and illustrates how a brilliant director like Howard Hawks exploits the conventions for maximum effect. Two lines of action, one involving love and one involving work, are ingeniously intertwined. There is a heterosexual love plot (Will Walter and Hildy get back together?) and a plot concerned with public success (Will Walter and Hildy get a scoop, prevent Earl Williams from being hanged, and rid their city of the corrupt politicians who seek to hang an insane man in order to get themselves reelected?) The goals of the protagonists are clearly set forth at the beginning of the film: Hildy wants to break her ties to Walter and the newspaper by marrying Bruce, an insurance salesman, who will give her a conventional life as a wife and mother. Walter wants Hildy back, as a newspaper reporter and a wife. The personalities of the protagonists are clearly delineated. We know in the first ten minutes that Hildy only thinks she wants to leave the newspaper to marry Bruce and have babies. Her true desire resides with Walter and the newspaper. Walter will do anything in his considerable power (lie, cheat, shamelessly manipulate people) to win Hildy back.

There are not one but two deadlines in *His Girl Friday*, which puts the machine of the plot in high gear, lending it urgency: Hildy is getting married to Bruce the very next day, and Earl Williams is to be hanged at dawn. Both of these deadlines are shortened as the film progresses. Walter learns not only that Hildy is getting married the very next day, but that she is leaving on a train with Bruce (and his mother) in the next few hours. It is all the more remarkable that, after Walter receives this bad news, we hear him confidently tell his manager Duffy over the telephone that "Hildy is coming back." This information sets up a wonderful anticipation in the viewer's mind. How, we wonder, will Walter accomplish this task in so little time? In the second line of action, once Earl Williams breaks out of prison, the corrupt sheriff gives orders to shoot him on sight and announces a $500 reward to the person who does it. Earl's "deadline" could occur any minute.

The urgency of deadlines in *His Girl Friday* is made even more compelling because time passes in this film at a quicker rate than it does in real life. When Bruce and Hildy exit the elevator at the beginning of the film, the clock behind them reads 12:35. When Hildy returns to Bruce after her scene with Walter, a conversation that takes eleven-and-a-half minutes in real time with no time ellipses, the clock has jumped ahead to 12:57. Twenty-two minutes of story time have elapsed in just over eleven minutes of real or screen time. Time is rushing by at nearly twice the normal speed.[20]

Hawks uses the omniscient, unrestricted narrator deliciously to thicken the plot. For example, as Bruce sits alone in Walter's office, shortly after he has received a huge certified check from Walter (partial payment for a life insurance policy), there is a cut to Walter lifting up Louie, Walter's "heavy," to the window. This, we infer, is so Louie will be able to recognize Bruce, the better to pick his pocket later and return the check to Walter. Thus the spectator is given information that Bruce does not have. Interestingly, just before this scene, Hildy has called Bruce to advise him to keep the check not in his wallet but in his hatband. We realize in retrospect that Hildy has anticipated Walter's treachery. The battle of the sexes is launched. Walter will stoop to the lowest means to keep Hildy from leaving him and the newspaper, but Hildy, at this point, is one step ahead of him.

The editing technique of *His Girl Friday* conforms to classical conventions of "invisible editing." Most shots flow together so smoothly that most people are unaware of the cuts unless they are specifically pointed out. The first shot of the film, for example, a lateral tracking shot of the length of the newsroom, is joined to the second shot (of the women at the switchboard) by a dissolve, which smoothly blends one shot into the next. The smoothness of the cut is further enhanced because the camera tracks at the same speed in the two joined shots, thereby encouraging the spectator to concentrate on the uninterrupted flow of the camera movement and not on the cut. The cut between the second and third shots is hardly noticeable because Hildy's movement is carefully matched. Her action of walking away from the women at the switchboard in shot 2 is smoothly continued in the medium shot of Hildy in shot 3. Again, our eye tends to focus on Hildy's continuous movement rather than the cut. Other types of cuts that appear frequently in the film, such as point-of-view shots, shot/reverse shots,[21] and the cross cut, seem smooth mainly because they have become so conventional in Hollywood films that we are hardly aware of them. Even when the cuts are not technically smooth or seamlessly matched, they are strongly motivated by the plot or a line of dialogue, and hence invisible. After Walter announces to the befuddled Bruce that he will be taking Bruce and Hildy to lunch, for example, the next shot is of the threesome arriving at their table at a restaurant. So strongly is this shot motivated by Walter's words that the cut goes unnoticed. (A quick dissolve between the two shots also smoothes out the transition.)

As noted above, invisible editing techniques help create the illusion in the Hollywood film that we are watching "real life," not a movie. But occasionally, the Hollywood film does call attention to its status as fiction, making viewers aware that they are watching a movie, not "real life." These moments are rare, however, and tend to occur only at the beginning or end of classical films. Thus, *His Girl Friday* opens with a written title card which tell us that the story we are about to see "all happened in the 'dark ages' of the newspaper game." The title then calls attention to the fact that we are watching a "picture" (not real life) and even ends with those time-honored words that signify a story—"Once Upon a Time." But when the film proper begins, all such signs disappear and we are plunged into a hyperrealistic, three-dimensional, deep-focus view of what looks like a highly efficient newsroom.

Hollywood comedies, as opposed to serious dramas and melodramas, are given more license to call attention to themselves as movies, not life, and Howard Hawks makes wonderful use of this license in two moments in *His Girl Friday*. In the first, Walter is trying to give Louie's blond girlfriend a means of recognizing Hildy's fiancé Bruce. Unable to come up with a good description (because Bruce's features are so nondescript), he finally asks, "Do you know what Ralph Bellamy looks like?" When the blond nods her head, Walter says, "Well, this fellow looks just like him." The joke, of course, is that the actor who plays Bruce is Ralph Bellamy. In the second such moment, the mayor, who has caught Walter red-handed in a conspiracy to obstruct justice by hiding escaped murderer Earl Williams, says, "You're through." Walter retorts, "The last man who said that to me was Archie Leach, just a week before he cut his throat." This is an insiders' joke for those aware that Archie Leach was Cary Grant's real name before the studio changed it.

At the end of *His Girl Friday*, as at the ending of most Hollywood films, there is closure. Everything is resolved. Hildy becomes aware that her true vocation in life is being a reporter and she and Walter plan to remarry. Walter and Hildy expose the mayor and sheriff as corrupt (getting their scoop and hence succeeding in work as well as love). Earl Williams gets a reprieve from the governor. Bruce, who is characterized as a momma's boy throughout the film, is reunited in the end with his mother. We see them embracing as the door to the criminal courts newsroom closes on them, shutting them out of Hildy and Walter's world forever. Here the closure at the end of the film becomes literal. As in the majority of classical Hollywood films, the ending seems inevitable, fulfilling all we might expect given the way Walter and Hildy's personalities are defined at the start of the film.

The conventions of the classical Hollywood film became relatively fixed because they offer us so much pleasure. The device of the deadline makes the plot especially compelling, as do the two intertwined lines of action, involving the hope for success in love and in work, important goals in everyone's life. As spectators identified with an omniscient point of view, gazing at people to whom we are invisible and about whom we have superior knowledge, we experience the feeling of having a power, perspective, and knowledge that we lack in life. The closure at the end of a Hollywood film makes the world seem more just, predictable, logical, and often more hopeful than it is in fact. No wonder billions of people love Hollywood films.

At the same time, if Hollywood conventions are adhered to too rigorously—if the characters are too predictable, the closure at the end too pat—Hollywood movies can seem silly or empty, too obviously escapist. The best Hollywood directors were able to exploit the intrinsic appeal of established Hollywood conventions while injecting original or personal elements into their films, adding something of themselves to give their films an edge. The films we value most not only calm and reassure us, but unsettle and challenge us too, even (or especially) when they are comedies. Now that I have discussed how *His Girl Friday* follows the conventions of the classical Hollywood cinema, I'd like to conclude with a discussion of how these conventions are inflected with the personal imprint of its director, Howard Hawks.

HOWARD HAWKS: AN INDIVIDUAL TALENT IN A RICH TRADITION

Although Howard Hawks has directed films in almost every Hollywood genre, Peter Wollen has pointed out that one can divide his work into two basic kinds: action-dramas such as *Rio Bravo* (1959), *Only Angels Have Wings* (1939), *Dawn Patrol* (1930), *Red River* (1948), *Air Force* (1943), and crazy or "screwball" comedies such as *Twentieth Century* (1934), *Bringing Up Baby* (1938), *Ball of Fire* (1941), *I Was a Male War Bride* (1949), and *Gentlemen Prefer Blondes* (1953).[22] *His Girl Friday* is a fascinating synthesis of the ingredients of Hawks's action-dramas and crazy comedies, making it a darker, richer, more subversive and interesting film than the typical Hollywood comedy.

Hawks's action-dramas tend to center around self-sufficient, all-male groups whose members pride themselves on their professionalism. A man's worth, how "good" he is, is measured according to his proficiency in his job. These groups tend to be cut off from society in general and in particular they exclude women, who, unless they prove themselves worthy of entry by behaving just like a man, are shunned as threats to the value system (or, in another way of looking at it, to the defense mechanisms) of the all-male group. Women bring trouble and sometimes death to the tightly knit enclaves of Hawks's isolated all-male preserves.

The world Hawks creates in his screwball comedies is the inverse of his action-drama world.[23] While action-drama heroes are serious and professional, screwball characters seem to share a disdain for propriety combined with a penchant for madcap behavior. While in Hawks's action-dramas men are strong and powerful, the screwball comedies abound in sex role reversals and feature dominant women and dominated men. In the action-drama *Only Angels Have Wings,* for example, Cary Grant plays the tough-minded director of an airline specializing in deliveries to dangerous mountainous outposts. In the screwball comedy *Bringing up Baby,* he plays a befuddled scientist at the mercy of Katharine Hepburn, who runs rings around him. At one point, obliged to wear a frilly dressing gown, he announces to the old battle-ax who discovers him so attired, "I've suddenly gone gay!" In the comedy *I Was a Male War Bride,* Grant dresses in drag for a good part of the film.

A theme that is taken seriously in action-dramas like *Only Angels Have Wings,* that the presence of women will demoralize men and prevent them from pursuing their higher goals, is often treated with humor in the comedies. In *Gentlemen Prefer Blondes,* Jane Russell finds herself on board a ship with an all-male enclave—in this case, the entire United States Olympic team. In a huge production number, she desperately (but to no avail) tries to seduce the athletes away from their training regimen by seductively singing to anyone who will listen, "Is There Anyone Here for Love?" The team responds by throwing her into a swimming pool to cool her off. She fails to excite the interest of the Olympic team, but does attract a detective, hired to expose her friend Lorelei (Marilyn Monroe) as a gold digger. Interestingly, at one point in the film, after Jane and Marilyn have drugged him and stolen his pants, the detective ends up wearing a frilly robe like Grant's in *Bringing up Baby.* The crazy comedies, it would seem, give humorous expression to male fears about what a woman might do to them, as well as about themselves becoming too much like women, that motivate the need for all-male cliques in the action-dramas.

In *His Girl Friday* the all-male clique or enclave appears as the tight-knit group of cynical newspapermen who play cards and crack jokes in the newsroom of the criminal courts building. At one point in the film their all-male territory is invaded by Molly Malloy, a streetwalker with a kind heart, about whom they have written a trumped-up story calling her Earl Williams's sweetheart. In a truly unpleasant scene that seems oddly out of harmony with the film's zany atmosphere, the newspaper men taunt Molly savagely for having compassion for Earl Williams, who is to be hanged the next day. When the sound of the gallows being built ominously resonates through the newsroom, one of the reporters says cruelly, "They're fixing up a major pain in the neck for your boyfriend." This interchange is reminiscent of a scene in *Only Angels Have Wings*, in which the pilots taunt Jean Arthur for expressing her grief about a pilot just killed in a plane crash. Their answer to her expressions of sadness is to sing a jolly song and swig another glass of whisky. They can "take it" (where "it" is loss and sudden death); she can't. In both films, women threaten the men because they acknowledge feelings the men are frightened to feel. If they allowed themselves such feelings, they could not go on doing their jobs. As I noted above, in Hawks's action-dramas, doing a job well, being "good" on a job or even just "good enough," is the be-all and end-all of existence. Failure through loss of nerve is a fate worse than death.

In *His Girl Friday*, after Hildy escorts Molly out of the newsroom to spare her more humiliation, the reporters are subdued. Without Molly to jeer at, they have to face their own bad feelings about the unjust hanging they will have to write about. Molly Malloy returns to the criminal courts newsroom once more in the film. This time, she jumps out an upper-story window, presumably to her death, in order to divert the reporters' attention away from Earl Williams (who she knows is hiding in a desk). By sacrificing her life to save Earl from recapture, Molly becomes an object lesson on the dangers of feeling too much for others: You become everyone's victim, even your own.

Hildy Johnson, of course, is the cosmic opposite of Molly Malloy and a far better "man" (in the terms defined by Hawks's action-dramas) than her intended second husband. When Hildy describes Bruce's attributes to Walter, Walter quips: "That's the kind of man I should marry." Like so many of Hawks's crazy comedies, *His Girl Friday* abounds in sex-role reversal jokes, beginning when Walter tells Hildy that his chief writer Sweeny is "having a baby." At the heart of *His Girl Friday* lies the biggest sex-role reversal joke of all. In the play from which the film was adapted, *The Front Page* (by Ben Hecht and Charles MacArthur), Hildy was not a woman, but a man—one Hildebrand Johnson whose nickname was Hildy. In the play the male Hildy also wants to leave the newspaper world in order to get married and lead a more conventional life. Hawks, apparently, happened to have a woman read the part of Hildy when he was considering the script, and this made him realize the amusing possibilities of having a woman play the role. The substitution, of course, also allowed the film to conform to the Hollywood convention of the heterosexual imperative.

The character of Hildy, brilliantly played by Rosalind Russell, is an ideal Hawksian heroine. She has the outward beauty of a Hollywood movie star with the interior characteristics of a tough-minded male. For all her feminine beauty, Hildy does not have a maternal bone in her body. Near the beginning of the film, when Beatrice, the advice to the lovelorn columnist, announces to her proudly that "My cat just had kittens again," Hildy retorts, "It's her own fault." Although she claims that she wants to settle down and have children, she is clueless about the joys of motherhood. In her goodbye speech to her fellow reporters, she equates taking care of babies with giving them cod liver oil and watching their teeth grow. If she catches them even looking at a newspaper, she promises to "brain 'em." This speech hilariously reveals not only that she is protesting too much (her desire to leave newspaper life), but also that her prospects of becoming a good mother are only slightly better than, let us say, Lady Macbeth's.

Hildy agrees to write an interview that will help Earl Williams get a reprieve, but not because of compassionate feelings for the man. She essentially does the interview for money, in exchange for Walter's purchasing a huge life insurance policy from her insurance salesman fiancé. While I enthusiastically agree with many of the insights in Gerald Mast's chapter discussing *His Girl Friday* in his book *Howard Hawks: Storyteller,* and have drawn on his insights in formulating many of my ideas about this film, I strongly disagree with his reading of the scene between Hildy and Earl Williams. Mast writes that this scene demonstrates "Hildy's ability to be a woman, a newspaperman, and a sensitive human being at the same time."[24] But I find Hildy's interview with Williams cruel in the way she manipulates him to reveal his craziness while she pretends to be writing an account that will prove him sane. Her "good-bye, good luck" to Earl, once she has gotten what she wants from him, is chillingly perfunctory. Although the newspapermen who read her interview proving that Earl Williams is crazy (and hence not fit for execution) are impressed by its brilliance, she tears it up once she realizes that Walter has double-crossed her by contriving to get Bruce arrested. So much for any desire on her part to use her skills to save the life of an innocent man. All she cares about is one-upping Walter. When looked at objectively, Hildy is hardly more sensitive than Walter, and just as much of a stinker as he is.

Many film scholars and critics applaud Hawks for his portrayal of Hildy Johnson as a strong, powerful smart, gutsy woman, one who breaks the mold of the common Hollywood female stereotype. Not all women have a maternal instinct and many prefer career fulfillment to being a house-wife, though one rarely sees this in a Hollywood film made in the 1940s, especially when the woman is sympathetic and beautiful as well.[25] *His Girl Friday* has the audience rooting for the heroine not to settle down into a conventional life of marriage and motherhood but to fulfill herself as a talented writer in an unconventional marriage. In her pioneering work on the representation of women in film, *From Reverence to Rape*, Molly Haskell praises *His Girl Friday* for celebrating "difficult and anarchic love rather than security and the suburban dream."[26] In this regard, Howard Hawks has made a genuinely subversive film which challenged the prevailing gender ideology of the day. Hawks's personal preference for beautiful screen heroines who behave like men gives a conventional Hollywood formula film a radical edge. Yet this being Hollywood, Hawks could not stray too far from conventional presentations of women. A woman as talented and powerful as Hildy also had to be put in her place, where she most certainly is, not only at the end of *His Girl Friday* but throughout the film.

Despite Hildy's strength, assertiveness, beauty, grace, and wit, which endear her to men and women spectators alike, she is never given any real power in the film, or not for very long. It is clear from the start, to the viewer as it is to Walter, that Hildy is making a mistake in thinking she could be happy with a man like Bruce. All along, it turns out, Hildy was hoping Walter would rescue her from a disastrous marriage. This comes out explicitly at the end of the film when Walter pretends to be noble and advises her to marry Bruce. She breaks down in tears, crushed that Walter is "letting" her go and does not love her anymore. Walter, from the very start, has understood that it is his mission to prevent the marriage. After he invites himself to lunch with Bruce and Hildy, Hildy says, "It won't do you a bit of good," as if to say, "I'm getting married and nothing you do can stop me." Walter responds, "Glad to do it. Glad to do it," as if she had said—"Help, do something to get me out of this marriage." The omniscient, unrestricted narrator of *His Girl Friday*, as in the example cited above when we see Walter secretly giving Louie a look at Bruce, regularly reveals Walter's schemes to the spectator, which subtly works to put us on Walter's side. The joke, so to speak, is always on Hildy. Though in the above instance we know that Hildy has anticipated Walter's treachery, her brains and cleverness are working at cross-purposes to what she really wants.

All of the sexist and even racist connotations implicit in the wording of the film's title are made explicit at the end of the film as Hildy, having totally surrendered and still in tears, runs out after Walter carrying a suitcase. She is "his," not her own person; she is a "girl," not a woman; and just as the Carib Friday was to Robinson Crusoe, she is Walter's "natural" servant, not his equal. Walter achieves both of the goals he set forth at the beginning of the film—to get Hildy back as his reporter and as his wife. Hildy accomplishes none of hers—to leave the newspaper world and to marry Bruce. Hildy makes a total about-face, while Walter doesn't change one iota. Nor is there any indication that he will treat her any differently after all they have gone through. After winning her consent to remarry him, he blithely cancels the honeymoon he has just promised her when he learns of a strike in Albany. Stanley Cavel, in *Pursuits of Happiness*, a study of Hollywood comedies of remarriage, notes that in all of the films in that category "the goal of the woman's education [is] to demonstrate that change in or by the object of her love is unthinkable, and that this is after all acceptable to her."[27] Hawks has pulled off a brilliant coup in *His Girl Friday*. He has created a strong, smart, talented, beautiful, and powerful woman, thus subverting the usual gender stereotypes in classical Hollywood films, while leaving the structure of male power and privilege intact. In this kind of adeptness at having it both ways, of finding a means to please everyone, may well lie the real genius of the Hollywood system.

5

Expressive Realism
Orson Welles's *Citizen Kane*

ORSON WELLES'S EARLY CAREER

In August of 1939, at age twenty-four, Orson Welles signed a contract with RKO Radio Pictures, Inc. to make three films, one a year. His pay would be 25 percent of the gross profits of each film with an advance of $150,000. At his own choosing, he could be producer, director, writer, actor, or all of the above.[1] It was unprecedented in Hollywood for a director to have so much control over all aspects of his film. Welles entered Hollywood with such power because of his success as a theater director in the thirties. He first attracted attention at age twenty with a project sponsored by the New Deal's Works Progress Administration (WPA), a production for the Negro Theater Project in Harlem of *Macbeth* in a Haitian setting and with an all-black cast. He was later commissioned by the WPA to create, in partnership with John Houseman, his own company, for which he directed a Brechtian jazz opera, *The Cradle Will Rock,* with a score by Marc Blitzstein. The subject was the unionization of the steel industry, and the work opened despite a government ban. He then founded The Mercury Theater, which got off to a successful start with a modern-dress *Julius Caesar,* which Welles directed as a meditation on fascism.

The production that catapulted Orson Welles to national fame and garnered him his Hollywood contract was his 1938 Mercury Theater radio adaptation of H. G. Wells's *The War of the Worlds*. Welles's brilliant idea was to narrate the tale of the first landing on Earth of flying saucers from Mars through a series of fictional news bulletins. A program of ballroom dance music kept getting interrupted by increasingly hysterical reports, first about the landing of a flying saucer from outer space, and then about sightings of little green men near Princeton, New Jersey. Listeners who happened to tune in late took the bulletin for real. *The War of the Worlds* created a national panic, resulting in miscarriages, broken bones, and near suicides. The recent news of Hitler's annexation of Austria, which was also broadcast by radio bulletins, must have increased the readiness of the nation to believe a tale of insidious invasion.

The notoriety from Welles's broadcasting disaster brought him to the attention of the new president of RKO, George Schaefer, who needed someone to put new life into his stagnating studio. At the time, Welles was not particularly interested in cinema. He claimed he was going to Hollywood in order to get enough money to finance future theater projects. Not surprisingly, Welles was received in Hollywood with great bitterness because of his youth, his beard, and his contract. Nor did Welles improve his popularity when he exclaimed on his first tour of RKO: "This is the biggest electric train a boy ever had!"[2]

After a number of expensive false starts, including a plan to film Conrad's *Heart of Darkness* using an experimental, purely subjective camera that would literally equate Marlow's "I" with the eye of the camera, and with only three months left before his contract ran out, Welles settled on an idea, suggested by Herman Mankiewicz,[3] that resulted in *Citizen Kane*. The film centered on the life of a big American capitalist and was partially based on the life of the newspaper tycoon William Randolph Hearst. When Hearst got wind of the news that Welles was making an unauthorized biography of his life, he tried to destroy the picture. After failing to buy the picture himself and destroy all negatives, Hearst attacked it through his newspapers—by not advertising it, insinuating that Welles was a communist, and threatening to retaliate against theaters who showed it.

CRITICAL RECEPTION OF *CITIZEN KANE*

In spite of or perhaps because of Hearst's threat to destroy the picture, *Citizen Kane* opened to extraordinary critical acclaim. According to

Pauline Kael, "it was more highly praised by the American press than any other movie in history."[4] Bosley Crowther's review for the *New York Times* is representative. "*Citizen Kane*," he writes, "is far and away the most surprising and cinematically exciting motion picture to be seen here in many a moon . . . it comes close to being the most sensational film ever made in Hollywood."[5] Orson Welles was extravagantly praised for his acting but critics reserved special favor for his direction. He was seen as a kind of savior of the cinema, bringing a moribund medium back to life. Cecelia Ager wrote for *PM*, "Before *Citizen Kane*, it's as if the motion picture was a slumbering monster, a mighty force stupidly sleeping, lying there, sleek, torpid, complacent—awaiting a fierce young man to come kick it to life, to rouse it, shake it, awaken it to its potentialities, to show it what it's got. Seeing it, it's as if you never really saw a movie before."[6]

But Hearst's vendetta against *Citizen Kane* was successful in drastically reducing the film's box office revenues. While the film did manage to recoup its surprisingly modest production costs, that was not a sufficient return on investment in Hollywood to inspire confidence in a director. And Welles, who, in addition, had got the reputation of a man who did not much care about money, was doomed never to have total control over his work or funds sufficient to fully realize his ideas. *Citizen Kane*, for many critics, remains his one undisputed masterpiece.

The more one is sensitive to the aesthetic effects of the technical choices that go into constructing film narratives, the more one can appreciate the groundbreaking cinematic experiments in *Citizen Kane*. The film was highly praised by the realist theorist André Bazin for its use of long takes and deep-focus photography, which Bazin felt brought a heightened realism to the screen and constituted "a revolution in the language of the screen."[7] At the same time, Welles elaborated on the use of expressionist techniques associated with Soviet montage and German Expressionism. As many critics have observed, *Citizen Kane* marks a grand synthesis of realism and expressionism in film form. The richness of the imagery in *Citizen Kane* is further enhanced by the film's intricately structured sound track, which opened up fresh possibilities of combining sound and image. Finally, the way the story is told, in flashback through the eyes of six narrators, brought complexity and ambiguity to film narrative. Yet one never forgets that Welles was first and foremost a supreme showman and entertainer. The rich inventiveness of Welles's filmic and narrative techniques makes *Citizen Kane* both an astute, complexly told portrait of an American tycoon and a film that stays fresh and entertaining even after repeated viewings.

NARRATIVE INNOVATIONS IN *CITIZEN KANE*

Most Hollywood films of Welles's time, like *His Girl Friday*, were narrated primarily from an omniscient or unrestricted point of view by an invisible narrator. Because of our omniscient perspective, our ability to see and know more than the characters on the screen, and our illusion that we are looking with impunity into a world which is unaware of our gaze, Hollywood movies give us a feeling of power. *Citizen Kane* begins by luring us into the pleasure of being the all-knowing spectator. At the start of the film the camera effortlessly pans up and over a sign on a wire fence reading "No Trespassing," thereby foregrounding the privilege of the film spectator.[8] Through a series of slow dissolves we are transported beyond the "No Trespassing" sign to penetrate deeper and deeper into the inner sanctum of Xanadu, Charles Foster Kane's opulent, eccentric private castle. Finally, we find ourselves inside the room where Kane (played by Orson Welles) lies on his deathbed. With our eyes identified with the eye of the camera, we are the privileged, omniscient spectators of Kane's last moments before he dies. He is holding a glass ball that encloses a snow scene. His last word is "Rosebud."

At the moment of Kane's death, the glass ball drops from his hand and shatters into pieces. We see a distorted image of a nurse entering the room as the camera shoots through one of the fragments of the shattered glass. (See figure 22.) The distorted image of the nurse signals the end to our privileged omniscience. From this point on, with only a few exceptions, the film's narrative itself shatters, fragmenting our vision through six different perspectives on the life of Charles Foster Kane, each one distorted in its own way. The six narrators are: a "News on the March" newsreel obituary; Walter P. Thatcher (George Coulouris), the irritated, exasperated Wall Street banker to whom Kane's mother entrusted her son's upbringing and education after she was left a gold mine by a defaulting tenant; Mr. Bernstein (Everett Sloane), Kane's business manager and greatest admirer; Jed Leland (Joseph Cotten), Kane's bitter, disillusioned best friend; Susan Alexander (Dorothy Comingore), Kane's psychologically abused but still sympathetic second wife; and finally, Raymond (Paul Stewart), Kane's mercenary, tell-all butler.

Figure 22. The distorted image of the nurse through the fragment of broken glass signals the end of our privileged omniscience. (*Citizen Kane,* 1941, Turner Entertainment.)

The newsreel obituary is all-inclusive but superficial. It offers only a general overview of the significant events in Kane's public life. These include the source of his great wealth, his creation of a newspaper empire and his campaigns against monopolies and trusts, his marriage to the niece of the President of the United States, his campaign for governor, his defeat in this campaign when his opponent exposes his adulterous affair, his efforts to make his second wife a great opera singer, his contradictory politics as both a supporter and denouncer of Hitler, and his final retreat to Xanadu until his death.

Because all the major events in Kane's life are thus laid out, we are never in suspense about what is going to happen to him. Our attention is focused instead on why his life turned out the way it did. Rawlston (Philip Van Zandt), the director of the newsreel, thinks the story on Kane lacks "an angle," a personal dimension to the "man who could have been President, who was as loved and hated and as talked about as any man in our time . . ." In order to fill in this gap, to add more juice to Kane's story, he decides to hold up the release of the newsreel, and directs his reporter Thompson (William Alland) to interview key people in Kane's life, primarily in order to find out what Kane meant by his last word, "Rosebud." Rawlston hopes that the meaning of "Rosebud" will provide insight into who Kane was as a man, and what really made him tick. Thompson's quest for the meaning of "Rosebud" provides the pretext for the series of interviews, told as flashbacks, which recount the story of Kane's life.

Citizen Kane's narrative strategy, in which the whole story is told in flashback from slightly different points of view (the equivalent of the unreliable narrator in fiction), was unprecedented in a Hollywood film. The technique of telling the story of Kane from multiple points of view dispels the illusion that we are learning the "truth" about Charles Foster Kane. As numerous commentators have observed, the film is like a complicated jigsaw puzzle which the viewer must piece together, bit by bit, in order to see the whole picture. Only in the final moments of the film, when we despair of ever discovering the meaning of "Rosebud," does the film's narration return us to a privileged omniscient perspective, revealing the final missing piece.

The final scene in *Citizen Kane* takes place at Xanadu. Thompson admits to his fellow reporters that he has failed in his mission to find out the identity of Rosebud. A colleague remarks: "If you could have found out what Rosebud meant, I bet that would've explained everything." Thompson replies: "No, I don't think so. No. Mr. Kane was a man who got everything he wanted, and then lost it. Maybe Rosebud was something he couldn't get or something he lost. Anyway, it wouldn't have explained anything. I don't think any word can explain a man's life." As the reporters go off to catch a train, the camera shoots down from above at a massive collection of crates, statues, etc.—all the objects Kane has accumulated in his lifetime—finally pausing on belongings associated with Kane's childhood home in Colorado. A worker picks up a sled. Raymond, the butler, refers to the sled as "junk," and directs the man to throw it into the furnace. A slow dissolve into the mouth of the furnace shows us the sled going up in flames. With just enough time to decipher the words before the flames obliterate them forever, we read the name inscribed on the sled: Rosebud. The film's final shot is of the exterior of Kane's castle. Smoke pours out the chimney as if Xanadu were a giant crematorium. The last words we see, before "THE END," are the first words we saw at the beginning, the sign reading, "NO TRESPASSING."

Citizen Kane thus has two endings: one for the characters inside the film and one for us, the spectators outside the film. The characters never find out what Rosebud signifies. We are privy to the knowledge, but our sudden return to omniscience is qualified. We know what Rosebud refers to—the sled young Kane was playing with before Thatcher took him away from his home to be educated in New York—but what does it mean? Critics are still debating the significance of Rosebud. In general, there are two camps: those who believe that Rosebud does explain the solution to the mystery of why Kane, for all his advantages, failed in his political and personal life, and those who agree with Thompson, who declares at the end of the film that the life of any human being is too intricate and complex to be reduced to one explanation. The sled may explain some things, but not everything. Most critics share the latter view.[9] To them, that "No Trespassing" sign has protected Kane's privacy after all.

DEEP-FOCUS PHOTOGRAPHY

The cinematic style of *Citizen Kane,* especially its use of extreme deep-focus photography in many crucial scenes, was as innovative and groundbreaking as the film's narrative technique. Working in collaboration with his cinematographer Gregg Toland, Welles shot scenes in which we can see objects a few inches from the lens just as clearly and sharply as objects 200 feet away.[10] This practice was counter to the prevailing Hollywood style in 1941, which was characterized by diffuse lighting and images with a shallow depth of field, in which objects in the foreground are clear but the background appears blurry or out of focus. André Bazin was especially impressed with Welles's use of deep focus. "Depth of focus reintroduced ambiguity into the structure of the image," he writes. "Hence it is no exaggeration to say that *Citizen Kane* is unthinkable shot in any other way but in depth. The uncertainty in which we find ourselves as to the spiritual key or the interpretation we should put on the film is built into the very design of the image."[11]

It is clear that Welles's choice to shoot many of his scenes in deep focus and in long takes had their origin in his past as a stage director: he was trying to preserve the integrity of theatrical space on the screen. In numerous sequences in *Citizen Kane,* because of the use of deep-focus photography in conjunction with long takes, our eyes have the same freedom to wander around the screen image as we have in the theater. We can focus on the actor who is speaking or instead watch the actor who is listening. Our eyes can move around the frame, focusing on whatever we choose. The realist director may design the mise-en-scène artfully, thereby guiding our attention to significant actions, but he or she does not have autocratic control over what we see, as happens when the action is broken down into short shots by editing or photographed in soft focus so that we can see only images in the foreground.

Chaplin favored the use of "realist" techniques because they were best suited to capturing on film the intricacies and subtle timing effects of his comic choreography, but Welles's deep focus was much deeper than Chaplin's and his long takes much longer and more intricately structured, to create dramatic (as opposed to comic) effects. The following analysis of just one shot in *Citizen Kane* demonstrates the subtle dramatic effects Welles's innovative cinematographic style enabled him to achieve.

SEQUENCE ANALYSIS OF A LONG-TAKE DEEP-FOCUS SHOT

Early in the film Charles Kane's mother (Agnes Moorehead) signs the papers handing over her eight-year-old son (Buddy Swan) to Mr. Thatcher, a Wall Street banker. There is something chilling in Kane's mother's willingness to send her young child off into the world in the hands of a stranger, but evidence later in the film suggests that Kane's father is abusive and that the mother gives her son away, at great personal cost, in order to protect him. The mother's feelings about handing over her son, like almost everything in *Citizen Kane,* are left ambiguous, and the complex way this scene is photographed allows multiple interpretations of it, as well as adding dramatic resonance to this crucial moment in the film.

The shot lasts over two minutes. (As a point of comparison, the longest shot in *The Adventurer* was only 47 seconds.) It begins with young Charles Kane in long shot, playing with his sled in the snow. The camera then pulls back to reveal that it has been shooting through a window. This effect creates a visual metaphor. The boy playing in the snow is not as free as he at first seems. Just as his image is suddenly confined by a window frame, so his life will be circumscribed by a decision that is being made for him inside the house. Kane's mother appears at the window calling out to her son to "Be careful," and "Put your muffler around your neck, Charles." As the camera tracks backwards from the window into the space of the house, it reveals Mr. Thatcher standing at the right of the window. He says, "We'll have to tell him now." Ignoring this comment, the mother replies, "I'll sign those papers now, Mr. Thatcher." From frame left Kane's father appears, saying, "You people seem to forget that I'm the boy's father." The camera tracks backwards as Mrs. Kane walks over to a desk in the foreground of the image and sits down to sign the papers, with Thatcher seated next to her. An argument ensues in which the father, who appears in the middle ground of the image, strongly protests the mother's decision to hand his son over to a bank and threatens to take the case to court. The mother is icily adamant in honoring the agreement she has made with Thatcher. In exchange for the bank's full assumption of the management of the gold mine (the Colorado Lode), the bank which Thatcher represents will assume full responsibility for all matters concerning the boy's education and place of residence. Mr. and Mrs. Kane will receive fifty thousand dollars a year as long as they both live. This last bit of information, which Thatcher reads aloud, silences the father, who mutters, "Well, let's hope it's all for the best."

Throughout the scene, while all this activity takes place, we can see the boy Charles playing with his sled far in the back of the image, in extreme long shot, framed by the window pane, and totally oblivious to the momentous decision his mother has made about his life. Because of the length of the shot and the careful blocking of the action, our eye is free to focus on whichever player we choose, or our attention can wander from one player to another, as if we were spectators in the theater.

At the same time, the camera places us sufficiently close to the actors in the foreground of the image that we can read their expressions with much greater clarity than would be possible in the theater. We can look for clues in the frozen but somehow anguished expression of Mrs. Kane for why she is so determined to separate herself from her son. We can wonder in observing the slightly exasperated and nervous expression on Thatcher's face what kind of guardian he will make for a young boy. Or we can observe the father's angry, worried expression and wonder why he backs down. The father's position further back in the screen space makes him seem smaller than his wife and Mr. Thatcher, his diminished size somehow appropriate to his lack of power to influence his son's fate. The crowning brilliance of the scene is the tiny image of Charles Kane far in the depth of the screen space. Although the film is about him and in later scenes he will loom large indeed, here he is a tiny speck. On first viewing the film, some may not even notice him. But his understated presence playing outside the window, shouting "Union forever" as his mother is about to send him off into the world without her, is one of the most poignant moments in film. (See figure 23.)

Figure 23. The understated presence of the young Charles Kane playing outside the window shouting "Union forever!" as his mother is about to send him off into the world without her is one of the most poignant moments in film. (*Citizen Kane,* 1941, Turner Entertainment.)

Welles used similar deep-focus long-take techniques in numerous other scenes in the film, such as Thompson's first meeting with Kane's second wife Susan at the bar where she works as a singer, the scene in which Kane fires Jed Leland in the newspaper office, the scene in which Thatcher takes control of Kane's newspapers when Kane goes bust during the depression, and the scenes of Kane and Susan sitting in empty splendor in the halls of Xanadu. In a way unique to each of these scenes, their dramatic power is enhanced by the deep-focus techniques.

DEVIATIONS FROM STYLISTIC REALISM

Welles does not confine himself to a realist style in *Citizen Kane.* In one notable instance, he adds dramatic power to a scene by using a standard Hollywood shot/reverse shot technique. In the scene in which Susan Alexander and Charles Kane first meet, Welles alternates between long takes of Kane and Susan talking together in a medium two shot

Figure 24. Close-up of Susan Alexander, the night she meets Kane. (*Citizen Kane,* 1941, Turner Entertainment.)

and a series of alternating, soft-focus, reverse-angle close-ups. (See figures 24 and 25.) Because Welles avoids such shots throughout most of the film, when he does use them, they are all the more effective. While the couple clearly seems to be falling in love, their being so emphatically framed in separate shots as they speak to each other (not sharing the screen space as they would if they were photographed together in the frame in a long take), suggests that each is off in a separate fantasy world, cut off from the other person mentally. Here Welles, by using a standard Hollywood technique sparingly, revitalizes its psychological expressiveness.

Not only did Welles occasionally employ conventional Hollywood-style editing, he also borrowed from the Soviet montage style of Sergei Eisenstein. Eisenstein, as discussed in chapter 2, tried to keep his viewers alert, their attention cemented to the screen, by the frequent use of shock cuts created by sudden graphic or associative contrasts. Welles uses these effects sparingly, but effectively. At the beginning of the film, after Kane dies, Welles cut from the somber darkness of Kane's deathbed scene

Figure 25. Reverse shot of Kane. (*Citizen Kane,* 1941, Turner Entertainment.)

to the bright image of the flags that begins the "News on the March" newsreel. The loud voice of the announcer and high volume of the music that accompanies it compound the shock effect produced by the contrasting tones. Moreover, the juxtaposition of a dead man with jaunty images of flags and upbeat music creates the impression that no one much cares that Kane has died. Welles uses another shock cut at the beginning of the sequence in which Raymond recollects Kane's tantrum in response to Susan Alexander's leaving him. A somberly lit medium shot of Raymond is followed by a close-up of a shrieking white cockatoo flying away. The image associatively recalls Susan, whose voice has become shrill and harsh, before she too flies the coop, abandoning Kane.

The editing of *Citizen Kane* is innovative in another respect as well— the imaginative way in which Welles constructs transitions to signal temporal and spatial gaps in the narrative. Because of its complicated narrative structure, the plot of *Citizen Kane* continually leaps forward and backward in time. Welles used standard, traditional transitional devices to signal these leaps, but embellished them to add psychological and thematic implications. A good example of the subtle psychological sugges-

Figure 26. The lengthy lap dissolve of the young Kane's face on the snow-covered sled suggests that although he is on his way to a new life, something of himself will forever remain behind. (*Citizen Kane,* 1941, Turner Entertainment.)

tiveness of Welles's transition shots occurs at the end of the sequence in which Kane's mother sends her son away with Thatcher. As he is playing outside his home with his sled, the boy is abruptly given the news that he is to leave home with Mr. Thatcher that very day. He does not take the news well. In the final image of this sequence we see a big close-up of young Kane's face framed by the body of his mother. He is glaring offscreen in the direction of Thatcher, whom he has just attacked with his sled. Through a long-held lap dissolve,[12] the image of Kane's face is superimposed onto the image of the sled, which is now covered with snow. (See figure 26.)

Dissolves are a conventional way for a director to signal the passage of time. In this case, the amount of snow that has accumulated on the sled and the sound of a distant train whistle suggest that a good deal of time has elapsed and that Thatcher and Kane are on the train to New York. But the lengthy lap dissolve superimposing the young Kane's face onto the snow-covered sled has symbolic significance as well. It suggests that although the boy is on a train on the way to a new life, something of himself is being left behind. Another dissolve reveals the sled more deeply blanketed in snow, as if part of the boy will remain forever frozen and undeveloped as well. The abandoned sled stands in symbolically for the abandoned child.

At this point, dissolved onto the image of the sled is an image of white wrapping paper. Because the whiteness of the paper matches the whiteness of the snow, the transition is very smooth. We don't realize we have been transported to a new time and place until the wrapping paper is whisked away (accompanied by a tearing noise on the sound track), to reveal the sullen face of Charles Kane glumly contemplating a shiny new sled, a Christmas present from Thatcher. The camera tilts up the body of Thatcher who is standing by a huge Christmas tree. He wishes Kane a "Merry Christmas." There is a cut back to Kane, whom we see from the high angle of Thatcher's perspective. Kane sarcastically replies "Merry Christmas." The new, shiny sled is clearly no compensation for all that he has lost.

The next shot is a medium close-up reverse-angle shot of Thatcher saying "And a Happy New Year." In this shot Thatcher is now an old man with gray hair. In a split second of screen time more than fifteen years of story time have elapsed. Charles, we learn, has reached his twenty-fifth birthday. So innovative was Welles in executing rapid time transitions that a new term was coined for his technique—the "lightning mix." In a lightning mix, images separated from one another by vast gaps in time and space are seamlessly melded together by continuity on the sound track, usually by using the dialogue. (In this instance, Thatcher's phrase "Merry Christmas . . ." is not completed until the next shot fifteen years later, when he adds ". . . and a Happy New Year.") Welles's use of a lightning mix to catapult young Kane into adulthood perfectly conveys the idea of a child who had to grow up too fast. Welles also uses a series of lightning mixes in the famous "breakfast montage" to present in a few minutes the ten-year deterioration of Kane's first marriage. Here the lightning mixes dramatize how rapidly young love can turn into mutual hatred and contempt.

EXPRESSIONISM IN *CITIZEN KANE*

André Bazin puts Welles in his pantheon of realist directors, along with Renoir, Rossellini, De Sica, Stroheim, Flaherty, and even Murnau (whom he praises for choosing the moving camera over editing in the construction of many of his filmic scenes). Yet *Citizen Kane* is also a film in the tradition of German Expressionism. Like Murnau, Welles externalized the subjectivity of his characters (and especially of Kane) by means of psychologically charged settings, acute camera angles, distorting lenses, and disconcerting camera movements.

The demented architecture of Xanadu in the mist-enshrouded shots at the beginning of the film recalls Edgar Allan Poe's "The Haunted Palace," in which an unhinged house metaphorically stands for an unhinged mind.[13] Near the end of the film both Susan and Kane are dwarfed by the oversized ornaments and statuary that furnish Xanadu, and serve as external projections of Kane's inner deadness and mindless materialism. The gargantuan rooms through which their voices echo—they nearly have to shout at each other to be heard—reflect the distance that has grown between them. When Kane steps into an enormous blazing fireplace and informs Susan that "Our home is here," he metaphorically becomes the host of hell. After Susan leaves him, Kane, now utterly alone, wanders past a structure of double reflecting mirrors which reflect his image into infinity. As far as he looks, all he can see are images of himself, a perfect physical representation for a man trapped within his own narcissism.

Like Murnau, Welles also used extreme camera angles and strange camera movements in conjunction with his expressive mise-en-scène. When Thompson makes his first visit to Susan Alexander at the nightclub where she works, he comes in the midst of thunder, lightning, and torrential rain, weather suggestive of the emotional storm inside Susan after she gets the news of Kane's death. Unlike most directors, Welles does not show Thompson entering the nightclub through the door. Instead, an "unchained" camera travels up the side of the building that houses the nightclub, passes by a huge poster of Susan Alexander, and then moves past a lurid neon sign identifying the club as the El Rancho. From the rooftop, the camera looks down through a skylight to capture, from an extreme high angle, the watery image of Susan collapsed over a drink. The camera penetrates the glass, descending to a close shot of Susan. The initial high-angle shot of Susan through the glass skylight suggests Susan's despair (the high angle makes her seem tiny and extremely vulnerable). Moreover, as Laura Mulvey has noted, by shooting down at Susan Alexander through glass, Welles creates a subtle associative link between her and the snow dome Kane is holding the night he dies and utters the word "Rosebud," thus linking Susan to this mysterious word.[14] The camera's movement through the glass roof, finally, suggests the in-

Figure 27. The extreme low angle of this shot emphasizes Kane's demented, unbalanced grandiosity. (*Citizen Kane*, 1941, Turner Entertainment.)

trusive voyeurism of the media, hungry for details of Susan's private life with Kane.

Equally expressionistic is Welles's use of low angles to project extreme psychological states. While shooting from a low-angle perspective can make a character seem dominant and confident, Welles's camera plays an interesting variation on this technique by shooting Kane from a low angle when he is most defeated. When Gettys (Ray Collins), Kane's opponent in his campaign for governor, exposes Kane's adulterous affair to Kane's wife and threatens to expose him to the media as well, an action equivalent to political checkmate, Kane shouts at Gettys, "Don't worry about me. I'm Charles Foster Kane. I'm no cheap, crooked politician. . . . I'm going to send you to Sing Sing." As he says this he is photographed from an extreme low angle (see figure 27). Because his threats are so clearly empty, the low angle makes him seem demented and grandiose, rather than powerful and dominant. The use of a wide-angle lens[15] in this shot in combination with the low angle and slight tilt of the camera makes the planes in the image above Kane seem jagged and off-kilter, again exteriorizing Kane's mental state. In an even more extreme example, after Kane has lost the election and along with it the friendship of Leland, Kane is photographed from such a low camera angle that in order to get the shot, the cameraman had to shoot from below the floor level of the set. The effect of the shot, once more, is to emphasize Kane's demented, unbalanced grandiosity.

Citizen Kane also contains amusing feats of trick photography, such as when photographic images of *The Chronicle* staff come to life as employees of Kane's newspaper, *The Inquirer*. In an example of the opposite effect, an image of the exterior of the apartment building in which Kane "keeps" Susan Alexander imperceptibly dissolves into a photographic image plastered on the front page of *The Chronicle*, publicizing the scandal that will end Kane's career as a politician.

One could write an entire book, and many people have, about all the visual inventiveness that went into the making of *Citizen Kane*.[16] As the above examples testify, Orson Welles brought a new richness to the expressiveness of cinema through his tweaking of conventional film techniques for startling new visual effects. The scenes discussed here are just the tip of the iceberg.

INNOVATIONS IN SOUND EDITING

The visual inventiveness of *Kane* was by no means the only reason for its success. It is just as groundbreaking in its use of sound. Welles's experience in radio made him understand that there is much more to film dialogue than the meanings the words convey. The loudness of a voice, its pitch, timber, or accent, all convey worlds of information about the speaker. The voices of the actors in Welles's film, his own included, are thus richly textured for added emotional expressiveness. Just a few examples will suffice. The shrill pitch of Kane's mother's voice when she calls to him from the window expresses the tension she feels as she is about to send away her son. Susan Alexander's voice starts out as soft, warm, and modulated when Kane first meets her, but as her marriage draws to an end, her every sentence is a scream. The increasingly high pitch of Susan's voice becomes a vocal barometer of the rage and frustration she experiences as Kane's wife. Almost every character except for Kane has a marked accent that lends subtle dimensions to their characterizations. Susan has a lower-class Midwestern accent, which is in marked contrast to the upper-class accent of Kane's high-born first wife. Jed Leland has a rich Southern gentleman's drawl, Mr. Bernstein (who is never given a first name) has a Brooklyn accent that marks him as Jewish. Kane has no discernible accent, but his rich baritone voice exudes confidence and authority at the height of his power yet seems pompous and hollow as he grows older in defeat. Welles also understood from his radio experience that the sound quality of the dialogue can give psychological dimension to a story, and he applied this knowledge to the screen. The vast rooms of Xanadu are made to seem even more alienating because of the reverberating echoes whenever Kane and Susan shout at each other from across the room. A similar high reverberation of voice tones is used to suggest the sterile hollowness of Thatcher's library. Kane's voice mightily reverberates through the hall during his political rally speech when he is at the height of his power. In contrast, his words ring totally flat when he threatens to send Gettys to Sing Sing.

Just as Welles has been praised for bringing a heightened realism to the film image, he is also praised for bringing heightened realism to the soundtrack of *Citizen Kane*. Numerous commentators have remarked on the way the deep focus of the images is accompanied by a corresponding deep focus in the sound. Welles carefully regulated his sound levels so that voices in the depth of the image sound farther away than voices in the foreground of the image. The best example occurs in the "signing the papers" sequence in the Colorado cabin. The voice of the boy playing in the background is faint in comparison to the voices of his parents and Mr. Thatcher in the foreground. As the father turns away and heads toward the background, his voice becomes muffled and fainter as well. While Rick Altman convincingly demonstrates that Welles is not consistent throughout the film in maintaining this kind of spatial sound realism,[17] Welles's experiments with sound perspective in *Citizen Kane* influenced other filmmakers (and Orson Welles himself) to continue experimenting with deep-focus sound.

For the film's score, Welles hired Bernard Herrmann, who later became famous for his scores for Hitchcock films such as *Psycho* (1960) and *North by Northwest* (1959). *Citizen Kane* was the first film Herrmann had ever worked on (just as *Kane* was Welles's first feature film). According to Bernard Herrmann's personal account of his association with Orson Welles in "Score for a Film," Welles recognized Herrmann as an extremely talented novice, like himself. Just as RKO gave Welles unprecedented freedom and control over his film, Welles gave Herrmann unprecedented freedom and control over the musical component of the sound track. Herrmann was permitted to do his own orchestration for his music, to conduct the music, and to consult on the sound levels and dynamics of the score. Moreover, Hermann writes, "Most musical scores in Hollywood are written after the film is entirely finished, and the composer must adapt his music to the scenes on screen. In many scenes in *Citizen Kane* an entirely different method was used, many of the sequences being tailored to match the music."[18]

There is an old saying about background music in Hollywood films: If the viewer becomes aware of it, it isn't functioning properly. The music should work subliminally and unobtrusively to create a mood or comment on the action. Bernard Herrmann's score for *Citizen Kane* casts doubt on the validity of this statement. The music adds such energy to the images that it becomes a very overt presence in the film. The more we are aware of it, the greater is our pleasure in watching the film. For the many montage sequences throughout the film, rather than creating vague background music, Herrmann composed complete, self-contained musical pieces that pointedly reflected the content of the scenes. For the "breakfast montage" sequence in which Kane's first marriage dissolves, for example, Herrmann composed a theme and variation on a waltz. The waltz, with all of its romantic connotations, plays at the beginning of the sequence, when Charles and Emily (Ruth Warrick) are very much in love. But as the marriage becomes discordant, so does the music. At the end of the sequence the waltz theme can still be faintly heard, but it has become sad and bleak, played in the high registers of the violins. Discordant chords accompany Kane's increasingly harsh words to his wife.[19]

Herrmann carried over to the screen the technique familiar in radio of blending sound effects with musical instruments in order to add further dimensions to the meaning of the image. In the shot in which Kane's sled becomes increasingly covered with snow, for example, the combination of the train whistle with mournful musical chords adds poignancy to the image. Overlapping fragments of Susan Alexander's singing voice are combined with driving, discordant musical rhythms to create the effect of Susan's rising hysteria and mental disintegration as she is forced by Kane to pursue a disastrous singing career. A final example of the way Herrmann's music provides more than neutral background atmosphere, instead adding intensity to the image, is when his musical score simulates the ticking of a clock as Susan and Charles Kane are languishing in boredom in the empty halls of Xanadu.

Herrmann composed two main *leitmotifs*, or recurring musical themes, for the film. These give the score unity and underline two sides of Kane's personality. One leitmotif emphasizes Kane's power. Herrmann describes it as "a simple four-note figure in the brass." These notes are first heard at the beginning of the film as the camera explores the grounds of Xanadu. Herrmann writes that this motif is transformed in the course of the film, "becoming a vigorous piece of ragtime, a hornpipe polka, and at the end of the picture, a final commentary on Kane's life."[20] The second motif is that of Rosebud. According to Herrmann, it is first played as a solo on the vibraphone at Kane's deathbed scene, but it is heard again and again throughout the film, providing a musical clue, for those who catch on, to the identity of Rosebud.

Not all the leitmotifs in the film are musical. The sound of clapping hands is brilliantly organized in a series of important sequences of the film to add psychological depth to the action. The sequence in which Kane meets Susan Alexander ends with Kane clapping as Susan sings for him in their private love nest. The sound of Kane's hands clapping segues into a shot of a small group of people on the street clapping as Leland delivers a speech in support of Kane's campaign to become governor. In another lightning mix transition, a sentence begun by Leland is completed by Kane some time later, as Kane is now seen speaking in a huge hall, not to a few claps, but to thunderous applause. This sequence is followed by the scene in which Kane's affair with Susan Alexander is exposed by Gettys. Kane is defeated at the polls, after which Kane launches Susan Alexander on her ill-fated career as an opera singer. At the end of one of Susan's disastrous performances, Kane is the only one left applauding. The film has come full circle. By using applause as the link that binds these scenes together, Welles suggests that Kane's desire for political power comes less from his progressive ideals than from his excessive need for approval and love, a desire satisfied by applause. The sound of applause is a leitmotif that symbolically links Susan's singing career to Kane's political career, exposing the raw (unacknowledged) need that makes both of these projects, as well as his marriage, fail.

Just as with the visual effects, the sound effects in *Citizen Kane* are so rich and subtle that one could almost endlessly go on pointing out interesting examples. With every repeated screening of the film, one can discover more. It is a mark of Welles's achievement that these effects are never merely clever gimmicks. They invariably work both to amuse by their wit and to deepen the film's psychological and thematic meanings. These meanings are never directly spelled out, but implied through a visual and aural symbolism that encourages a level of audience participation in creating meaning that was (and remains) rare in a Hollywood film. Welles's groundbreaking synthesis of realism and expressionism in the images and sounds of *Citizen Kane* more than justifies the critical acclaim with which it was first received and the high praise it receives to this day.

6

Italian Neorealism
Vittorio De Sica's *The Bicycle Thief*

DEFINING ITALIAN NEOREALISM

In my history of film courses I have at various times taught three films defined in film histories as quintessential examples of Italian neorealism: *Open City* (Roberto Rossellini, 1945), *The Bicycle Thief* (Vittorio De Sica, 1948), and *Umberto D* (Vittorio De Sica, 1952). *Open City* is famous for launching the movement, *The Bicycle Thief* for reaffirming the neorealist aesthetic, and *Umberto D* for being the last "real" or genuine neorealist film. Before showing the film, I try to define Italian neorealism by listing the stylistic and thematic features of the movement that the film will exemplify. The problem is that for each film I have to create a different list.

While neorealism cannot be pinned down or defined according to one style or even in terms of the themes or kinds of stories told, scholars agree on its origins and some of its basic traits.[1] Neorealism emerged in Italy in the aftermath of World War II, the product of filmmakers who were trained in Mussolini's state-subsidized film school (the Centro Sperimentale) and who learned to make films in the lavishly well-equipped studios that Mussolini fostered (in a complex called the Cinecittà), but many of whom were politically on the left and in revolt against the kind of cinema produced under Mussolini's fascist regime. So, in some respects, neorealism is best defined by what it is not. Mussolini's cinema was a cinema of distraction, one whose primary goal was to entertain, and indeed the films had enormous popular appeal, rivaling Hollywood on the world market. Although scholars are continually pointing to exceptions, discovering films made under Mussolini's regime that anticipated neorealism, the fascist cinema's most characteristic genre was scornfully described by Giuseppe De Santis, a neorealist film director and critic, as *calligraphism*, which he defined as decoratively photographed adaptations of late-nineteenth- and early-twentieth-century fiction. Since calligraphism drew on materials from the past, it was seen as an escapist retreat from the social and economic problems of contemporary Italy. Mussolini's cinema was for the most part studio-bound, representing the world through elaborately constructed sets. The plots were also elaborate constructs, following formulas and conventions similar to those of the classical Hollywood film.

When Fascism fell, not only was Italy liberated from the Nazis, but its most talented filmmakers—such as Roberto Rossellini, Vittorio De Sica, Luchino Visconti, and Giuseppe De Santis—were freed from making what they saw as artificial, contrived, escapist films. Rather than projecting a falsely optimistic picture of Italian society, as they felt the films under Fascism tended to do, by focusing on the wealthy classes and the images of Italy that tourists see, neorealist filmmakers sought to expose the poverty and social malaise of a postwar Italy in shambles. Vittorio De Sica wrote: "We strove to look ourselves in the eyes and tell ourselves the truth, to discover who we really were and to seek salvation."[2]

Neorealist films tell stories that take place in the present day, not in the distant past. They also focus on the lives of the lower rather than the upper classes: on workers, not professionals; on the poor, not the rich; on the ordinary man, not the superhero. The problems and conflicts of neorealist protagonists derive less from inner psychological turmoil than from external social conditions. Most of the filmmakers associated with Italian neorealism were political leftists whose goal was to bring about social change through the creation of a new, socially engaged, national cinema, one that would replace the sanitized, retouched Italy of the films made under fascism with films that reflected the reality of contemporary life in Italy.

In our postmodern era, of course, we look with skepticism upon the claim that any film or group of films can reflect reality. All film images are representations, different ways of signifying the world. Even in a medium based on the seeming objectivity of the photograph, there is no such thing as a direct, objective recording of reality on film. As the Czechoslovakian filmmaker Alexander Hammid observes:

> the camera records only in the manner in which the man (or woman) behind it chooses to direct it . . . even if we put the camera in front of a section of real life, upon which we do not intrude so much as to even blow off a speck of dust, we still arrange: by selecting the angle, which may emphasize one thing and conceal another, or distort an otherwise familiar perspective by selecting a lens which will concentrate our attention on a single face or one which will reveal the entire landscape and other people; by the selection of a filter and an exposure . . . which will determine whether the tone will be brilliant or gloomy, harsh or soft. . . . This is why, in films, it becomes possible to put one and the same reality to the service of democratic, socialist or totalitarian ideologies, and in each case make it seem realistic.[3]

Although we can agree that no film movement has a pipeline to the "real," neorealist films broke with the conventions and practices of Mussolini's cinema of distraction in a number of ways that made their films *seem* more real, especially in comparison to the films that came before them. The most obvious way neorealist films differed from their predecessors was that rather than being made in the well-equipped studios of Cinecittà, neorealist films were shot on location. At first this was out of necessity. At the end of World War II, Cinecittà had been heavily damaged and was mainly utilized to house refugees. Thus, Rossellini and his crew took to the streets to photograph *Open City,* a tense drama of partisan resistance to the Nazi occupation. After the huge international success of *Open City,* it soon became evident that shooting in the streets of Italy was an aesthetic plus, lending an aura of authenticity to the filmed fictions.

A second way neorealist films differed from their predecessors was in their use of post-production sound. Because of the difficulty and expense of filming on location, Italian neorealist directors, beginning with Rossellini in *Open City,* shot their films silent, dubbing in the dialogue and sound effects later. Unburdened by cumbersome sound equipment, the camera had greater freedom of movement, creating the effect of capturing events fortuitously, on the run, the way images of life appear in documentaries and newsreels. *Open City,* moreover, was shot on a very low budget at a time when film stock was scarce, mostly of poor quality, and had to be bought on the black market in bits and pieces. These circumstances, in combination with Rossellini's lack of reliable power units, gave the film a grainy, grayish, uneven, rough-hewn look which also contributed to its documentarylike aura. And some of the footage of *Open City* does not just resemble documentary footage, but is actual docu-

Figure 28. Expressionist lighting in *Open City* during the scene in which the priest, Don Pietro, witnesses Manfreddi's torture. (*Open City,* 1947, Film Preservation Associates.)

mentary footage secretly taken of German troops in the final days of their occupation. So powerfully did the documentary appearance of *Open City* heighten the dramatic effect of the film's story that future filmmakers imitated its location shooting, post-production sound, and low-budget look, even when they could afford better. These stylistic traits became hallmarks of Italian neorealism.

I also should point out, however—and now come the sputtering and contradictions—that many neorealist films, including *Open City* itself, do not adhere to a spartan documentarylike aesthetic. Not all of *Open City* was shot on location. The interiors were shot on constructed sets created in an abandoned warehouse. For most of these interior shots, Rossellini used standard three-point lighting, a style associated with mainstream commercial Hollywood filmmaking. Occasionally, Rossellini even employed artificial, expressionistic lighting techniques to heighten the drama in *Open City,* as, for example, in the powerful scene in which the priest, Don Pietro, witnesses Manfreddi's torture. (See figure 28.) *Paisan* (1946), Rossellini's second influential neorealist film, which also dramatized the final days of Nazi occupation and Italy's heroic and often tragic resistance efforts, likewise has many conventionally lit sequences obviously shot in a studio. *Umberto D* had no scenes at all shot on location. But despite the inevitable exceptions, Italian neorealist films have, nevertheless, become strongly associated with location shooting, poor-quality black-and-white film stock, post-synchronized sound, and the use of a mobile camera, all of which contribute to producing films that look more like newsreels than fiction films, and hence seem starkly realistic.

Aside from their look, Italian neorealist films also seem more real than Hollywood films or the films made under Mussolini's regime because of the kinds of stories they tell. Rather than recounting extraordinary exploits of the high and the mighty, neorealist scenarios focus on common, even banal events in the lives of humble working-class people. For some reason, the depiction of lives of workers or the poor strikes us as more real than the depiction of the more insulated lives of the rich. Neorealist stories also tend to end abruptly, without closure, with loose ends dangling and problems unresolved, also making them more like life and less like fictions. The actors who play the leading roles in neorealist films, moreover, are often nonprofessional actors or stage actors who are cast because they look like ordinary people. Hence they give the appearance of being authentic, not glamorous stars "playing" at representing real people.

The above description of Italian neorealistic storytelling may well make us pause to consider an important question: Why was Italian neorealism as a film movement such an international success? What exactly is the appeal of films about poor or common people to whom nothing extraordinary happens and whose fates are left unresolved at the end? Why would anyone want to watch such films? In order to answer this question, I would like to focus on Vittorio De Sica's *The Bicycle Thief,* a film that epitomizes the peculiarly intense pleasure and pain of the Italian neorealist aesthetic.

NEOREALIST AESTHETIC: *THE BICYCLE THIEF*

The Bicycle Thief,[4] made in 1948, appeared at a time when the Italian economy was improving and the neorealist movement was on the wane, but, even so, to quote André Bazin, "it reaffirm[ed] anew the entire aesthetic of neorealism."[5] More than any other film of the period, *The Bicycle Thief* exemplifies traits associated with Italian neorealism. Set right after the end of World War II, it depicts an Italy of poverty and desperation. Unemployment is soaring and the paltry amount of the welfare checks allotted by the government can barely sustain life. The film focuses on the life and misfortunes of Antonio Ricci, a common worker. Photographed in grainy black and white, the entire film—interiors and exteriors alike—was shot on location. Most of the film takes place against the background of overcrowded city streets, or tenement housing for the poor. Not one professional actor played in the film. The man who plays Ricci was an actual worker in a steel factory.[6] According to André Bazin, De Sica was offered millions of *lire* to film the script with Cary Grant playing the lead, but he refused.[7] Ricci's wife is played by a woman who in real life was a journalist and the boy cast as Bruno, Ricci's son, was discovered by De Sica playing in the street. De Sica chose him because he was charmed by the way the boy's short trotting gait contrasted with the long strides of the man who plays Bruno's father.

The story the film tells, given its painful, inconclusive ending, is also characteristically neorealist. The film begins on what seems to be Ricci's lucky day: after two years of unemployment, he is finally offered a good government job putting up posters around the city. In order to accept the job, however, he must have a bicycle, and he has recently had to pawn his bicycle in order to feed his family of four. When his wife learns of his dilemma, she pawns the family's linens (which are her dowry, and the last objects of value in the stripped down household) to get Ricci's bicycle out of hock. Then, tragically, on Ricci's first day of work, a thief makes off with his bicycle. The rest of the film follows Ricci and his son Bruno as they desperately search for the stolen bicycle. At the end of a long day searching, in terrible frustration at his failed efforts to retrieve his bicycle, and desperate to hold on to his job, Ricci makes a botched attempt to steal a bicycle himself. The owner catches him in the act, calls for help, and Ricci is soon apprehended by an angry crowd. Although there is some relief when the owner does not press charges, Ricci is left at the end of the film without a bicycle and hence is once again without a job.

Despite the bleakness of its story, people who love movies are passionate about *The Bicycle Thief*. Many claim it as their all-time favorite film. Whenever the film is revived, it fills theaters. For André Bazin, much of the power of *The Bicycle Thief* lies in the way De Sica brings alive the political point that social institutions have become so ineffective that the poor are obliged to prey on the poor.[8] The boy who steals Ricci's bicycle, it turns out, not only suffers from epilepsy, but is even more impoverished and disadvantaged than Ricci. When Ricci and a policeman search the apartment in which the thief lives with his mother, the evidence of poverty is appalling. Bazin calls *The Bicycle Thief* the first communist film, and demonstrates convincingly that every seemingly coincidental episode in the film is in fact carefully chosen to add subtle ammunition to its political point.

PSYCHOLOGICAL THEMES

While *The Bicycle Thief* is clearly a film with a powerful political sub-text, one that needs to be understood in the context of the very real difficulty of survival in postwar Italy, it also has a fascinating psychological dimension. Ricci's troubles are shown to be internal as well as external. From the film's very first shot, Ricci is isolated from the men around him. While his fellow unemployed crowd the steps leading up to the unemployment bureau hoping their names will be called for a job, Ricci sits across the street, as if he has given up hope of ever being employed. As a result, he is so remote from the action that he does not even hear when his name is called. Someone has to seek him out to inform him of his good fortune.

When he is offered the coveted job, but cannot provide the requisite bicycle, he responds with despair. "Damn the day I was born. I feel like jumping in the river." Ricci's passive, fatalistic response to his dilemma is emphasized by the contrasting way his wife responds. She leaps into action, ripping off the sheets from the family's beds so they can pawn them in exchange for the bike. Ricci's passivity is again highlighted by the contrast of his behavior with his son's. Bruno, while scrupulously cleaning the recently retrieved bicycle, notices a new dent and angrily insists that Ricci should have informed the pawn shop about the damage. In numerous ways throughout the film Bruno is shown to be more competent than his father. He knows the bicycle's serial number by heart, he has mathematical abilities his father lacks, and several times in the film he saves the day by summoning a policeman, and bailing out his father when Ricci has gotten himself in trouble with a crowd. Finally, despite his young age, Bruno holds down a job at a gas station, making him the only member of the family who is employed.

While Ricci appears to be the victim of bad luck when his bicycle is stolen (a ring of bicycle thieves spots his unattended bicycle as he is concentrating on putting up a poster), De Sica suggests in an earlier scene that Ricci is not sufficiently protective of this most precious commodity. When he accompanies his wife to see a psychic, he casually leaves the bicycle by the door, asking (but not paying) a young boy to watch it for him. Most first-time viewers of the film get very nervous at this point, assuming that his nonchalance will result in the bicycle's loss. Moreover, Ricci is presented as incompetent once he is on the job. The man who trains Ricci instructs him to be sure to flatten out the lumps in a poster because if the inspector sees any lumps he will fine him. Soon after, we see Ricci doing a blatantly messy job of smoothing out the lumps in the poster (ironically, one of Rita Hayworth bursting out of a low-cut dress). Worse, he rips the second half of the poster as he imperfectly aligns it with the top half.

On the surface it might seem that De Sica's characterization of Ricci as a loser vitiates the film's political message. We could well conclude that it is his fault he is unemployed, and not that of the economic inequities of his society. But we can also read Ricci's character flaws as a response to his circumstances. After two years of unemployment it is not surprising that he would have given up hope, become depressed, and lost the drive to succeed and excel. We might also speculate that part of Ricci's almost childlike passivity results from his having come of age in a fascist, paternalistic state that infantilized its citizens. Bruno, who is growing up in a liberated Italy, would naturally have more confidence and drive. Beginning with *Open City,* which ends with a group of children whistling a song of liberation after a partisan priest is executed by the Nazis, many neorealist films place hope for a better future in the hands of Italy's youth. In any case, Ricci's very human vulnerability makes his plight all the more affecting. The weak are always the most seriously affected by a disintegrating social order.

CLASSICAL HOLLYWOOD ELEMENTS

Despite its flawed hero and depressing plot, *The Bicycle Thief,* from start to finish, is a dramatically powerful, highly entertaining, and utterly compelling film. This is owing, in large part, to De Sica's synthesis of neorealist style and content with the style and content of the classical Hollywood film. *The Bicycle Thief* most strikingly resembles Hollywood films in the device used to set the plot in motion: the main character's lack. As I pointed out in chapter 4, in most classical film plots the central character lacks something vital which he or she must overcome obstacles to obtain. According to Alfred Hitchcock, this object of desire (which he refers to as the MacGuffin)[9] could be anything, as long as it provides a goal that sets off an intense quest, a pretext for the action of the plot. The spectator derives pleasure, Hitchcock believes, not from the importance of what is sought, but from watching the quest.

In *The Bicycle Thief*, De Sica gives us the classical Hollywood pleasure of identifying with a character in a quest to recover something he
has lost, but in this film the lost object in and of itself is supremely important, and not just a device to set the plot in motion. Although the policeman in charge of Ricci's case dismisses his loss as "just a bicycle,"
the comment is heavily ironic in the context the film establishes: Ricci
needs the bicycle to be able to work and feed his family. De Sica suggests
that even more is at stake than unemployment and hunger by giving the
lost bicycle the brand name "Fides," which in Italian means "faith." Unemployment threatens Ricci not only with physical hunger but with a
terrible spiritual despair. This despair is hinted at, as we noted above, in
Ricci's suicidal remarks to his wife when he fears he will not be able to
take the job. Once his bicycle is redeemed, so is Ricci. He becomes happy
and hopeful, sexually playful with his wife, and at last a proud model
for his son. Thus the loss of the bicycle means much more than the loss
of material security. It also means the loss of Ricci's pride and hope for
a better life, the loss of his manhood, and ultimately the loss of a reason
to live. The film demonstrates how material well-being is a prerequisite
for spiritual well-being. The loss of "Fides" thus means both literally and
figuratively the loss of Ricci's "faith"—in himself and in his future. By
raising the stakes of finding the bicycle so high, De Sica heightens the
viewer's involvement in and anxiety about the outcome of Ricci's quest,
making the experience of watching *The Bicycle Thief* far more compelling
(and, yes, entertaining) than most conventional Hollywood films.

Our emotional involvement in the action is further intensified by the
use of another feature common to classical films: the deadline. Whatever
the task the protagonist needs to accomplish, it must be accomplished
soon—or else. Thus, Ricci's friend at the political party headquarters tells
him he must find the bicycle immediately because stolen bikes are quickly
disassembled and sold in parts. Late in the film, when Ricci's desperation is so great that he stoops to seeking help from a psychic, the psychic intones: "You will find it now or not at all." In other words, he has
a deadline.

Although the story of a weak, passive common man who loses something he desperately needs might seem unremittingly grim, this is not the
case. The film remains compelling to watch because of the way the script
of *The Bicycle Thief* balances moments of hope that the bike will be easily retrieved with moments of despair that the search is futile. When the
bicycle is first taken, there is a moment of hope when a man appears saying "I saw him. He went this way." Ricci jumps into a car whose driver

obligingly pursues the man indicated. After an exciting chase, when the car catches up with the man, he turns out not to be the thief. Ricci's despair is increased because he has lost valuable time on a wild-goose chase. (In subsequent viewings of the film, it becomes clear that a ring of thieves is involved in stealing Ricci's bike. The supposedly helpful man, one of them, has deliberately led Ricci astray.)

At the marketplace Ricci visits the next day to seek his lost bicycle, the camera tracks past row after row of bicycles and bicycle parts, giving Ricci's search a needle-in-a-haystack feeling of futility, vividly conveying his despair that he will never find it. But suddenly he comes upon a man painting the frame of a "Fides." The hope that the bicycle is Ricci's is drawn out when the man refuses to reveal the bicycle's serial number, as if he has something to hide. When a policeman finally forces him to reveal the serial number, despair returns because the number does not match the one on Ricci's bike. Despair continues when a downpour prevents Ricci from looking for his bike at another market, but hope returns when, in an extraordinary stroke of good luck, Ricci recognizes the thief (whom he had seen stealing his bike) talking to an old man. The thief rides away on the stolen bicycle (despair), but Ricci and Bruno follow the old man into a church, intending to persuade him to lead them to the thief (hope). The man manages to elude them (despair), but Ricci, through another coincidence, later encounters the thief again and follows him to his neighborhood (hope). A policeman is summoned to search the boy's home (hope), but the policeman finds nothing (despair). Ricci is threatened by the boy's mother for accusing her son and he is also mocked and physically threatened by the thief's neighbors (despair). The carefully modulated alternation between hope and despair keeps the film forever fresh and fascinating to watch. Even though I have seen the film countless times, with each viewing I keep hoping—in the irrational way we do at the movies—that this time Ricci will apprehend the thief right away, that this time the painted Fides will have the right serial number, or that this time the policeman will find the bicycle in the thief's room. Something will go right for a change and Ricci will get his bicycle back.

The Bicycle Thief departs from conventional mainstream cinema in its use of grainy black-and-white film stock, location shooting, and use of nonprofessional actors—all the conventions that give the film the patina of documentary realism. However, these very reality effects actually work to increase another major pleasure we get from classical films, the illusion that we are not at the movies but looking into a real world,

Figure 29. The camera moves back to reveal that we have been viewing this intimate morning scene literally through an open window. (*The Bicycle Thief,* 1948, Richard Feiner & Company.)

as if through an open window. So seemingly real is *The Bicycle Thief* that after seeing it, most studio-made films seem phony or fake in comparison. De Sica playfully comments on the window-on-the-world illusion he creates in his film in a sequence in which Ricci and Bruno prepare to set off to work on the first day of Ricci's new job. Right before they leave the house, Bruno walks toward the camera to close the shutters on the window. As he moves forward, the camera pulls back and out the window to reveal that we have indeed been viewing this intimate morning scene literally through an open window. (See figure 29.)

The Bicycle Thief also adheres to the Hollywood conventions of filmmaking in its use of invisible editing. The shots in *The Bicycle Thief* are for the most part edited together smoothly by match cuts and conventional editing devices such as point-of-view shots, shot/reverse shots, and crosscutting. As a result, the narrative flows so smoothly that the events in the film do not seem to be narrated. They seem just to happen. A close examination of the final sequence of *The Bicycle Thief,* however, illustrates the complex moral and psychological effects De Sica achieves through the artful synthesis of realist images with a classical editing style.

SEQUENCE ANALYSIS: RICCI BECOMES A BICYCLE THIEF

The sequence begins immediately after Ricci has lost his last best hope of finding his stolen bicycle. He has found and confronted the thief, but it is too late. The thief has already disposed of the bicycle and Ricci cannot prove that he has taken it. Not only can we infer that Ricci has lost all hope of being able to keep his job and hence his faith and hope for a better future, we can also intuit his pain at being mocked and humiliated in front of his young son, who, he must fear, has lost faith in his father's ability to get justice from the world. It is truly a bitter moment in the film, which De Sica forces us to contemplate at length as he cuts to several long takes of Ricci and Bruno walking through the city streets in defeat.

In shot 1 of the sequence, Ricci and Bruno arrive at a part of town near a soccer stadium with a game in progress. People are lined up on a curve listening for the results of the game. Bruno, who has been trailing behind Ricci in the long trek across town, immediately sits down on a curb to rest. Crowd noise from the stadium swells up on the sound track, motivating shot 2, a medium-close shot of Ricci reacting to the crowd noise. Shot 3, from Ricci's point of view, is the huge soccer stadium where the game is being played. This shot signifies more than the source of the crowd noise. The stadium is designed in the monumental style of fascist architecture. Rimming its walls are gigantic statues of heroic, idealized athletes, a cruel reminder to Ricci of all he does not represent to his son. (See figure 30.) Shot 4 returns to a medium-close shot of Ricci. His gaze turns in the direction of Bruno. Shot 5 is a full shot of Bruno sitting on the curb, seen from Ricci's point of view. Bruno is holding his head in his hands, as if he is suffering the deepest anguish. Shot 6 is a reaction shot of Ricci taking in the immensity of his son's distress. He turns away, but then his gaze settles on something equally distressing. Shot 7 reveals the object of his gaze, multitudes of parked bicycles. (See figure 31.) Although there is no dialogue, the sight of these bicycles from Ricci's point of view allows us to "hear" a nonverbal interior monologue. "Look at all these bicycles. If I could just have one of them. . . ." But any larcenous thoughts Ricci may have at this moment are dispelled by his sight of a policeman patrolling nearby. Shot 8 is a reaction shot of Ricci. He turns his back on temptation. Shot 9, a position and movement match, reveals Ricci walking toward the camera, but suddenly something else

Figure 30. The gigantic statues of heroic, idealized athletes on the stadium walls are a cruel reminder to Ricci of all he is not to his son. (*The Bicycle Thief*, 1948, Richard Feiner & Company.)

Figure 31. The image suggests a nonverbal interior monologue: "Look at all these bicycles. If I could just have one of them." (*The Bicycle Thief*, 1948, Richard Feiner & Company.)

Figure 32. From Ricci's point of view, a lone, unattended bicycle on a deserted street. (*The Bicycle Thief,* 1948, Richard Feiner & Company.)

captures his attention. In shot 10, from Ricci's point of view, we see a lone, seemingly unattended bicycle parked by a door on a deserted street. (See figure 32.)

With this shot, De Sica tells us in a flash exactly what is running through Ricci's mind. "No one is watching this one. I could easily take it and solve all my problems." In shot 11, a reaction shot, Ricci abruptly turns away, his back to the camera, as if rejecting the idea. (See figure 33.) But in shot 12, Ricci is suddenly facing the camera again and staring intently offscreen, as he was in shot 6. (See figure 34.) The temporal and spatial dislocation caused by the jump cut subtly reflects Ricci's moral disloca- tion, the internal "about-face" he has to make in order to seriously con- template the idea of becoming a thief. Shot 13 is another shot, from Ricci's point of view, of the bicycles we have seen in shot 7. Their mocking mul- titude seems to confirm Ricci in his decision to become a bicycle thief. In shot 14 he begins walking back in the direction of the unattended bi- cycle. In shot 15, a movement and direction match on Ricci, the camera follows Ricci as he continues to walk in the direction of the spot where he first saw the lone bicycle. In this shot we can see it tiny in the depth

Figure 33. Ricci abruptly turns away from temptation. (*The Bicycle Thief,* 1948, Richard Feiner & Company.)

Figure 34. Ricci's about-face. (*The Bicycle Thief,* 1948, Richard Feiner & Company.)

of the frame, parked by a doorway, still unattended. Ricci again turns away, as if changing his mind, but he cannot resist just one more look back. The camera then tracks with him as he turns back and joins Bruno.

The relatively long take in shot 15 brilliantly illustrates the point André Bazin makes in his influential essay "The Virtues and Limitations of Montage." Here Bazin argues (and I have already touched on this in chapter 3) that certain filmic situations are aesthetically more powerful if captured in one long take as opposed to being fragmented into a number of short shots through editing. Editing creates abstract or approximate spatial relationships between objects. When, for example, a person is shown looking intently at something in one shot and then we are shown the object of his or her gaze in the next, we get the impression that the space in the second shot is nearby, but we never know for sure how much space actually separates the two images. In the sequence under analysis, for example, there are several point-of-view shots of the stadium seemingly taken from where Ricci is standing. But because we never see the stadium and Ricci in the same frame, or within the confines of one shot, we have no idea of the true spatial relations between them or, indeed, if a stadium really exists in the vicinity. Its existence could be purely an illusion created by offscreen sound effects and editing. While Bazin does not argue that one should never create fake spatial relationships through the use of editing, he does believe that certain dramatic situations demand the long take in order to preserve for the viewer the real time and space in which the action occurs.

Up until shot 15, De Sica has fragmented the space of the action, breaking it up into little pieces—point-of-view shots, reaction shots, shots held together through movement matches, and so forth, with each shot lasting from three to four seconds. But in shot 15, which is held for eighteen seconds, De Sica preserves the temporal and spatial unity of Ricci's actions by following him with the camera. We witness his movement first toward the bicycle (his temptation), then toward Bruno (his conscience) in real time and space, as we would if we were seeing the action in the real world, or in the theater. By capturing Ricci, the bicycle, and Bruno within the confines of the same shot, De Sica gives us a more vivid experience of Ricci's internal conflict.

Bazin, as discussed in chapter 5, preferred long takes with deep-focus images because they allow the viewer's eyes to wander around the image and construct meaning for themselves. Nothing is forced on the viewer's attention. Earlier in the sequence, when we first saw the unattended bicycle from Ricci's point of view, our eyes were directed to it through the use of a close shot. In shot 15, however, the bicycle is tiny in the background of the frame. As in the example from *Citizen Kane*, when young Charles Kane appears tiny in the image while his mother signs papers that will change his life, the most important image is the tiniest object in the frame. In both cases the use of the long take and deep-focus shot creates an effect that is roughly equivalent to understatement in literature.

At the end of shot 15, Ricci sits down on the curb next to Bruno and looks up. Shot 16 is his view of the soccer stadium. The game is still in progress. This shot imbues the action with a certain amount of time pressure—another deadline. Probably Ricci would have more success in stealing the bicycle before the game lets out and too many people are around. Shot 17 is a reaction shot, taking us back to the same set-up as at the end of shot 15, of Ricci sitting on the curb next to Bruno. Ricci puts his hands to his face very much as Bruno had done earlier, but this shot speaks Ricci's temptation and conflict. Should he act? Should he try to steal that bicycle? Bruno is watching him intently and warily, almost as if he can read his mind.

Shot 18 is an abrupt cut to a blurry close shot of bicyclists whizzing by from screen right to screen left. The camera pans left with their movement until it reveals Bruno and Ricci still sitting on the curb. At this point, the camera slowly moves closer to Ricci and Bruno, zeroing in on their reaction. The contrast between the static, forlorn pair and the dynamic motion of the bicyclists increases our sense of all Ricci and Bruno have lost. They follow the movement of the bikers with their eyes until Ricci can stand it no longer. He rises from the curb. His action is completed in shot 19 (through a smooth movement match). He looks off in the direction of the stadium. Shot 20 is a high-angle shot of the stadium. People are pouring out of it now. In shot 21, the camera follows Ricci as he goes back to the place where he first observed the unattended bicycle. It is still parked by the door. He turns back in the direction of Bruno.

In the previous series of shots (shots 1–21) as well as the ones that follow (shots 22–28), De Sica builds suspense through the technique of retardation—delaying the outcome of an action so that when it comes it will be all the more explosive. Here the delaying tactics are dramatically motivated because they also serve to heighten audience identification with Ricci by allowing us to observe every nuance of his mixed feelings. The silent discourse of images tell us that he would like to steal the bicycle, but he cannot do so in front of his son. At the same time, the multitudes of people retrieving their parked bicycles and riding away make

Ricci's desire to have one himself almost unbearable. His action of taking off his hat and pulling his hair speaks volumes about the pain of his conflict. Shot 27, in which Ricci looks offscreen in the direction of the unattended bicycle and puts his hat back on, signals that he has made a decision. In shot 28, Bruno looks at his father almost accusingly, again as if he intuits what Ricci is thinking.

In shot 29, another long take lasting twenty-two seconds, Ricci pulls Bruno up from the curb, hands him money and speaks the first line of dialogue in over thirty shots: "Here. Take the streetcar—wait at Monte Sacro." Thinking he has rid himself of his inhibiting son, Ricci turns around and heads toward the object that tempts him. But Bruno, like a sticky conscience, disobeys his father, following closely in his footsteps. Ricci, exasperated, yells, "You heard me. Go on." This time Bruno, looking troubled and bewildered, exits from the frame as his father glares after him. The camera follows Ricci's movements as he turns the corner and heads in the direction of the unattended bicycle.

At this point comes what is for me the most powerful moment in the film. Shot 30 is a cross-cut to Bruno running for the streetcar, but he just misses it. Now the audience knows something that Ricci does not. He has not gotten rid of Bruno after all. This shot is so powerful because it adds a new layer of suspense to an already almost unbearably suspenseful situation. The first layer of suspense involves the questions: Will Ricci give in to the temptation to steal a bicycle and, if he does, will he get caught? Bruno's missing the streetcar complicates that suspense by adding another dimension to the suspense, a moral and psychological dimension. Now we are made to wonder what will happen if Bruno witnesses his father's thievery. How will he react?

I cannot speak for every spectator of this film, but in trying to figure out why this moment in the film has such power for me, I arrive at this formulation: I have come to share Ricci's alienation and desperation and hence I want him to succeed in stealing the bicycle. I want his life to get better no matter what the moral cost. This is not so unusual. Many movies encourage transgressive identifications, and thus seduce us into rooting for someone to get away with a crime. But Bruno's presence at the scene of Ricci's temptation is a complicating factor. Knowing that Bruno may witness his father's thievery puts me in conflict. Because I am so identified with Ricci at this point, Bruno functions as my conscience as well as his. But—and here is the real sticking point—as much as I cringe at the possibility that Bruno may see his father succeed at becoming a thief, at the same time, more than ever, I do not want him to get caught and hence fail once again in front of his son.

Because of the above context, shot 31, a cross-cut back to Ricci now lurking in closer proximity to the bicycle, creates mixed feelings of excitement, suspense, and dread that remind me of the best moments in Alfred Hitchcock's films. Ricci casually walks past the door adjacent to where the bicycle is parked, and looks in to see if anyone is watching. Then he turns around, mounts the bicycle and begins to ride away. A split second later a man comes out of the door crying at the top of his lungs, "Thief. Help. He's got my bicycle. Thief. Stop him." In shot 32 a group of men nearby hear the man's cry and come running. Shot 33 is a long shot of Ricci trying to escape on the bicycle, a group of men in close pursuit. Ricci emerges from screen right in shot 34, having gained no distance from his pursuers. We know he is doomed.

Shot 35 is a cross-cut to a medium close-up of Bruno. His anxious stare suggests he is witnessing his father's futile attempt to escape. Shots 37 and 38 are particularly emotionally intense because they are from Bruno's point of view: The spectator is placed, as it were, in the shoes of the son as he sees a group of angry men close in on his father and bring him down. Shot 39 is a medium close-up of Bruno's stunned reaction. The camera holds on his stricken face until he runs out of the frame in the direction of his father.

In the subsequent shots, once again Bruno witnesses his father being mocked and reviled, his face slapped. In an extraordinarily touching shot, as a group of men lead Ricci away, Bruno finds his father's hat and dutifully brushes it off, as if preserving the little dignity that his father has left. Not only does Bruno try to save his father's dignity, he effectively saves Ricci from criminal prosecution. The man whose bicycle was stolen is so moved by the sight of Bruno's anguish that he refuses to press charges against Ricci. "The man has enough trouble," he explains. In the final sequence of the film, as Ricci and Bruno head for home after their devastating day, Bruno saves his father once more—through the gesture of taking his hand. (See figure 35.)

Bruno's gesture has been interpreted in numerous ways. Viewers will dismiss it as sentimental or feel it as profoundly moving depending on what experiences they bring to the film. I tend to agree with André Bazin's reading of Bruno's gesture as a sign that "the son returns to a father who has fallen from grace. He will love him henceforth as a human being, shame and all. The hand that slips into his is neither a symbol of for-

Figure 35. Bruno saves his father once more—through the gesture of taking his hand.
(*The Bicycle Thief*, 1948, Richard Feiner & Company.)

giveness nor of a childish act of consolation. It is rather the most solemn
gesture that could ever mark the relations between a father and his son:
one that makes them equals."[10]

This moving solidarity between father and son is not, as some critics
claim, a concession to the feelings of the audience, but an integral part
of an important theme that plays throughout the film and is part of the
film's political message. Ricci realizes earlier in the film, when he fears
that Bruno may have drowned, that the loss of the bicycle is insignificant
in relation to the possible loss of his son. Yet the film makes clear that
the loss of the bicycle has threatened Ricci with the loss of Bruno throughout the film. So preoccupied is Ricci with finding his Fides that he dangerously ignores his son's needs and even his safety. When Ricci himself
becomes a bicycle thief, he is threatened not with the physical loss of his
son but with the loss of his son's admiration and respect.

While De Sica persuades us that people matter more than things, and
that Bruno's love for Ricci, despite everything that has happened, is a
kind of saving grace, he simultaneously makes it clear that neither people
nor love are safe in a world of economic scarcity. At the core of De Sica's

and his scriptwriter Caesare Zavattini's brand of neorealism was a strongly humanist and reformist impulse. They hoped that by honest portrayals of ordinary life in which human bonds are threatened by a disordered and unjust society, they could create a bond between the audience and the characters in the film so that those who saw their films would be sharply aware of how society needed to change if human life is to prosper.[11] The final shot of the film, a static shot of Ricci and Bruno disappearing into the crowd, becomes a bitter cry of protest. It leaves us with the feeling that theirs is only one sad story among countless tales of suffering in the dysfunctional social order of postwar Italy.

7

Auteur Theory and the French New Wave

François Truffaut's *The 400 Blows*

The 400 Blows is the autobiographical first feature film by François Truffaut, who was twenty-seven years old when he made it in 1959. Aside from its intrinsic value as a moving, psychologically acute portrait of the artist as a young man, *The 400 Blows* is historically important because its instant commercial and critical success helped launch a national film movement known as the French New Wave. The New Wave flourished for a relatively short period, between 1959 and 1963, when certain historical, technological, and economic factors combined to give considerable influence to a number of young French filmmakers who had started out as film critics, theorists, and historians. Aside from Truffaut, the most well known New Wave directors were Jean-Luc Godard, Claude Chabrol, Jacques Rivette, and Eric Rohmer, all of whom wrote polemical articles on the cinema in the 1950s for the film journal *Cahiers du Cinéma*, founded and edited by André Bazin. Although the style and content of the films they eventually would make varied considerably, New Wave directors resembled the Soviet filmmakers in the 1920s in that their cinematic innovations were strongly influenced by their theories about film and the nature of the film medium.[1]

NEW WAVE THEORY

A major inspiration for the New Wave critics-turned-filmmakers came from the writings of the French film critic Alexandre Astruc, who published an influential article in 1948 called "Camera Stylo" (Camera-Pen). Astruc argued that cinema was potentially a means of expression as subtle and complex as written language. He argued that cinema too was a language, "a form in which and by which an artist can express his thoughts, however abstract they may be, or translate his obsessions exactly as he does in a contemporary essay or novel."[2] Influenced by Astruc, New Wave directors embraced what was then a revolutionary new way of understanding and interpreting films. They promoted in their critical writings what Truffaut called *"les politiques des auteurs"* (the author policy), which the American film critic Andrew Sarris referred to as "auteur theory."[3]

An underlying assumption of auteur theory was Astruc's idea that, despite film's status as primarily a commercial entertainment medium, it could potentially be an art form as powerful in its means of expression as literature or poetry. In order to propose filmmaking as an art, however, there had to be an artist, a central consciousness whose vision is inscribed in the work. How was this possible in a medium that is basically collaborative, a combination of the efforts of producers, directors, scriptwriters, set designers, editors, cameramen, actors, and others? For the French New Wave theorists, the author of the film (the auteur) was the director.

Traditionally the "author" of the film was thought to be the screenwriter, the author of the script upon which the film was based. The French New Wave theorists disagreed. They believed that the written script of a film is only a blueprint, raw material that achieves meaning or significance only when the words are embodied in images on the screen. As they saw it, since the director is responsible for the images, he oversees the set designs, cinematography, editing, and performances of the actors, and also, in many cases, reworks the screenplay or script. Thus, according to the New Wave critics, it is the director and not the screenwriter whose artistic vision is inscribed onto the film.

Certain directors, to be sure, had long been understood as artists, but only in the noncommercial art cinema of Europe and Japan: filmmakers such as Bergman, Bresson, Ozu, and Murnau, who had a great deal of creative freedom in the making of their works. But the French New Wave theorists believed that even in that most commercial realm—the Hollywood film factory, where directors were under contract to the studios and thus assigned the works they were to direct—the works of certain filmmakers were always marked by the director's individual themes, psychological preoccupations, and stylistic practices. They singled out and praised such directors as Alfred Hitchcock, Howard Hawks, John Ford, and Orson Welles, calling them auteurs, film artists of the highest order.

Proponents of the French New Wave differentiated auteurs from *metteurs en scène*, directors who faithfully adapted the work of others and did not inscribe their individual personalities or styles onto their films. In Truffaut's most famous attack on classic French film, an article entitled "A Certain Tendency of the French Cinema," he especially criticizes the writing team of Jean Aurench and Pierre Bost for being merely literary men and thus disdainfully underestimating the unique power of cinematic language. He praised French directors like Jean Renoir, Robert Bresson, Jean Cocteau, Abel Gance, and Max Ophuls (who had emigrated from Germany to France), for making visually innovative films in their own distinct styles and for creating their films from their own stories.[4] These directors were true auteurs.

VIRTUES AND LIMITATIONS OF AUTEUR THEORY

The public and many academic critics embraced auteur theory for the simple reason that this approach to understanding and categorizing films was and still is so compelling. General audiences and film specialists alike have strong feelings about certain favorite directors and continue to think about what makes a particular director's work individual and distinct. This book is itself a testament to the ongoing popularity and influence of auteur theory in academia, because its chapters are organized to highlight the stylistic innovations of individual directors. Nevertheless, auteur criticism came under attack in the late 1960s and early 1970s by academic critics who pointed out its limitations. Auteur theorists, it was argued, had simply revived the nineteenth-century Romantic tradition of viewing the artist as a creative genius who stood apart from society and enriched the world with his unique, often liberating vision.[5]

This Romantic conception of the artist was criticized from a number of perspectives. The idea of the auteur as visionary genius assumes that the artist is a unified subject, who consciously inscribes a profound meaning upon his or her works. This view was seen as hopelessly naïve by psychoanalytic critics, who understand the artist not just as a conscious producer of messages but as someone prone to unconscious impulses as well. Although the artist may intend a certain message or theme, the psychoanalytic critic can read beneath the surface of the text to reveal other themes and preoccupations of which the artist may be entirely unaware. Interestingly, in this regard, until Alfred Hitchcock was confronted with his obsessive preoccupations with guilt and voyeurism in his films by the French auteur theorists, he was largely unaware of them.

The Romantic conception of the artist was also undercut by sociological critics. Claims for the artist as an individual genius, they argued, failed to take into account the effect of society on the artist's work. While few would deny that the will and talent of the artist play a role in the creation of a work of art, it is true as well that the artist's products are also determined by historical and social forces that act upon him or her. As André Bazin wrote as a corrective to the excesses of auteur theory, "The individual transcends society, but society is also and above all *within* him."[6] New theories were called for that locate directors within their historical and social contexts.

The strongest detractors of auteur theory were academic critics influenced by both Marx and Freud for whom this approach to film study was simply irrelevant. These critics were not interested in studying film as an art and in interpreting the artist's message. They were interested in understanding the process by which a culture's ideology, be it capitalist consumer values or patriarchal ideas about gender, were reproduced and maintained through mass media. Not surprisingly, these critics did not concern themselves with what makes a director individual and unique. They wanted to know how the operations of ideology spoke *through* a director's work in such a way as to maintain the status quo, and how the power structures of society were kept intact by works that reflected a world in which that power seemed natural and hence justified.[7] Feminist critics, for example, thought films helped maintain the power of patriarchy, the "natural" dominance of men over women. From the feminist perspective, it matters little who is directing the film. In every film the same stereotypes of women are regularly found—women appearing as either virgins or whores; the dumb blond; the smart, independent woman who ends up somehow punished by the film's plot—stereotypes which reinforce women's subordinate social place.[8]

Roland Barthes's influential essay "The Death of the Author" challenged auteur theory from yet another angle, by pronouncing the death of the author and the birth of the reader. Once the word is on the page (and by extension, once the image is up on the screen), Barthes argues, the author disappears behind the text. Meaning is determined not by the intent of the author, but by the mind of the reader or receiver of the text. For Barthes, then, it is the text which speaks, not the author. The author, from this perspective, is a fiction constructed out of traces in the text by the reader. Bathes was far more concerned with the fiction of the author than he was with the author of the fiction.[9]

Despite these critiques of auteur theory, it has nevertheless been highly influential in the establishment of film studies at the college and university level. Because it posited film as an art form and film directors as artists, the auteur approach established film as a serious object of study. College courses are regularly organized around the works of one film-maker. Moreover, auteur theory's emphasis on a director's individual style and his or her thematic preoccupations was instrumental in encouraging close formal analyses of films, as opposed to far less rigorous, impressionistic forms of criticism that were the norm before. In order to detect just exactly what was individual about a certain director's style, critics began to scrutinize films minutely, frame by frame, shot by shot, on editing tables, well before video technology made this kind of study even more practicable. A sequence of film got the same kind of minute attention as a line in a poem or a paragraph in a novel. Finally, auteur theory remains an important critical approach to film if only because its very limitations raise so many interesting and important critical questions, opening up new paths for film study.

NEW WAVE THEORY IN PRACTICE

The New Wave theorists eventually succeeded in becoming filmmakers for a number of reasons. First of all, as was not the case in America, where the film industry was almost totally dominated by Hollywood, in France there were encouraging precedents for independent film production. Renoir, for example, was successful enough to form his own production company in the late thirties. The turning point for the New Wave came when Roger Vadim's independent production *And God Created Woman* became a huge international success in 1957. Vadim's success gave hope that filmmaking outside the established studio system in France could be commercially viable. It was in this context that Truffaut's father-in-law, a well-known film distributor whose films Truffaut scathingly reviewed, finally made him a proposition, saying, in effect: "If you know so much, why don't you make a film?" He advanced him about 100,000 francs. With this money, along with government subsidies[10] and the financial backing of friends, Truffaut made *Les Quatre Cents Coups (The 400 Blows)*. In 1958, Truffaut was banned from the Cannes Film Festival for his violent denunciation of festivals and his uncompromising attitude toward most of the films shown there. The very next year *The 400 Blows* was the official French entry at Cannes and Truffaut won the prize for best director. *The 400 Blows*, which is as fresh and moving today as when it first came out in 1959, wonderfully illustrates what was new about the French New Wave.

In *The 400 Blows*, true to the spirit of Alexandre Astruc's conception of the *camera stylo*, Truffaut creates a film language to translate subtle nuances of feelings and ideas into film, thereby demonstrating that film can be as emotionally and intellectually evocative and complex as a work of literature. The film itself is not a literary adaptation. Truffaut himself wrote the story and adapted it for the screen, with the collaboration of Marcel Moussy, who helped in the creation of the dialogue. The story of the film was patently autobiographical, based on Truffaut's own childhood experiences. Not all New Wave films, nor all of Truffaut's films, were autobiographical. Many of them were even based on literary works. Most New Wave films were personal, however, in that the directors usually worked from their own screenplays, and the films reflected their own personal styles and thematic preoccupations.

The "400 blows" of the film's title comes from the French idiom "*faire les quatre cents coups*" which means "to raise hell." While *The 400 Blows* is certainly about a child who raises hell—rebelling against authority by playing hooky and stealing—the title has a double meaning. It not only refers to the exploits of a hell-raising adolescent rebel, but also alludes to the blows dealt the child by his insensitive, neglectful parents and the stifling, bullying school and state authorities—the kinds of blows to a young person's psyche that could well cause a child to become alienated and raise hell. This is a subject about which Truffaut knew a good deal.

A short biographical sketch reveals the extent to which *The 400 Blows* was based on Truffaut's life.[11] Truffaut was born out of wedlock in Paris in 1932 to a seventeen-year-old mother who had little interest in raising a child. First, she turned him over to a wet nurse and, subsequently, to her mother. He returned to live with his mother when he was eight, after his grandmother died. In the meantime, his mother had married Rolland Truffaut, an architect who was not Truffaut's biological father but who gave him his name. (Truffaut never met his real father, who was later revealed to be a Jewish dentist.) An unwanted child, neglected by his parents, Truffaut took refuge in reading and the cinema.

Antoine Doinel, the protagonist of *The 400 Blows* (played by Truffaut look-alike Jean-Pierre Léaud), has the same life history as Truffaut. He too is born out of wedlock and his parents find him a burden. Just as Truffaut did as a child, Antoine plays hooky from school with his best friend (called René in the film and played by Patrick Auffay), sneaking into the cinema and committing petty thefts. Fittingly, Robert Lachenay, the real René, worked with Truffaut as an assistant on *The 400 Blows*.

Truffaut ran away from home at age eleven after an outlandish excuse for playing hooky backfired. He claimed he was not in school because his (adoptive) father had been taken away by the Germans, something that had actually happened to his uncle the week before. He was exposed when his father came to school to pick him up that day. (In the film, Truffaut makes the lie even more outrageous by having Antoine claim that he was not in school because his mother died.) Although his father tracked him down and returned him to school, Truffaut was so oppressed by the school authorities, who seemed to watch his every move, that he ran away again, living on a series of odd jobs and minor thefts, including the theft of a typewriter. It was during this period of his life that Truffaut started a film cub and met André Bazin, who was running a rival film club. Although Antoine Doinel plays hooky from school in order to see movies, Truffaut's systematic and scholarly interest in film at that age is not reflected in *The 400 Blows*.

Truffaut's adoptive father eventually found him and turned him over to the police, which also happens in *The 400 Blows*. Truffaut shares with his filmmaker idol Alfred Hitchcock the childhood trauma of having his father instruct the authorities to lock him up in jail for his misbehavior. But whereas Hitchcock was locked up for five minutes, Truffaut spent two nights in jail before being sent to an Observation Center for Delinquent Minors. The most poignant moments in *The 400 Blows* are those in which Antoine is being turned over by his father to the police, booked for vagrancy and theft, locked up in a holding cell with prostitutes and thieves, and transported by paddy wagon to the central prison in Paris.

At the end of *The 400 Blows*, Antoine makes a wild dash for freedom from the Center for Delinquent Minors. During a soccer game, he escapes through a hole in a fence and runs to the sea. He has achieved his goal of finally getting to see the ocean, but at the same time he realizes he is trapped. As he wades into the water, he sees he has nowhere else to run. This is where we leave Antoine, on the edge of the ocean, at the conclusion of *The 400 Blows*. In real life, Truffaut was rescued from the authority of the state by André Bazin who, though only thirteen years older than Truffaut, became his substitute father, taking him under his wing and giving him his first paying job writing about film. Truffaut writes: "From that day in 1948 when he got me my first film job, working along-side him, I became his adopted son. . . . Thereafter, every pleasant thing that happened in my life I owed to him."[12] Truffaut dedicates *The 400 Blows* to the memory of André Bazin, who had died in 1958 at the age of forty.

In addition to its highly personal content, *The 400 Blows* exemplifies New Wave policy in its allegiance to the image. As I noted above, the New Wave theorists believed that cinema should not be a transparent form through which other arts, such as novels or plays, are transmitted, but a unique aesthetic system in its own right whose essence was visual. In the introduction to his extended interview with Alfred Hitchcock, Truffaut praises Hitchcock's "unique ability to film the thoughts of his characters and make them perceptible without resorting to dialogue."[13] *The 400 Blows*, which also resembles *The Bicycle Thief* in this regard, is filled with long passages in which images rather than words tell us everything we need to know.

For example, Antoine Doinel's unhappiness in his home, his feeling of being an unwanted outsider whom his parents would like to get rid of, is given poignant visual expression when he is shown fulfilling his nightly chore of taking out the garbage. Truffaut's camera follows Antoine carrying the garbage down four flights of stairs to the basement of the depressingly shabby apartment complex in which he lives. His inner feelings of bleakness are manifest when the light in the cellar goes off just as he is depositing the garbage and, at that moment we hear an infant crying. While the infant's cry is realistically motivated, because we can interpret the sound as coming from one of the apartments, the cry, in conjunction with Antoine's act of throwing out the garbage, also expresses Antoine's bleak feelings of being an unwanted child. He is aware, as we learn later during his interview with a psychiatrist, that his mother had wanted to throw him away (by having an abortion). The light going out in the cellar foreshadows the light that will soon go out of his life when his parents in essence throw him away by signing him over to the state authorities.

Truffaut is equally effective in giving visual expression to Antoine Doinel's feelings of elation when he and René escape the stifling regime of the classroom when they play hooky. Their elation is expressed not in words but through their movements and the style in which they are photographed. The boys, followed by the camera, run down endless tiers of

Figure 36. Antoine's face is enframed by a segment of the imprisoning grid pattern, creating the effect of a noose tightened around his neck. (*The 400 Blows*, 1959, A. DINO / MK2 SA.)

steps, their arms extended, almost as if they were flying. Antoine and René are again visually associated with birds when a flock of pigeons takes glorious flight as the boys approach it. Truffaut photographs Antoine and René in their all-too-few moments of freedom with a moving camera in wide-angle, deep-focus long shots. Wide-angle lenses tend to exaggerate the distance between foreground and background planes, making the world seem open and expansive, the perfect lens choice, when combined with a freely mobile camera, for conveying a feeling of unbounded freedom.

Once Antoine is caught and jailed, the space around him in the frame shrinks as Truffaut photographs him in tightly framed close shots. Our view of him, moreover, is increasingly obscured as he is photographed through the grillwork of the cagelike holding cell where he must wait before being transported to a more permanent prison. In one shot, his face is enframed by a segment of the imprisoning grid pattern, creating the effect of a noose tightened around his neck. (See figure 36.) In addition, the point-of-view shots (from Antoine's position) become increasingly obscured by the structures in which he is imprisoned. This occurs, for example, when he is in the paddy wagon on his way to prison. The gleaming streets of Paris whiz by obscured by the vehicle's steel bars.

Throughout *The 400 Blows*, Truffaut's *camera stylo* visually expresses the film's over-arching theme—that children's natural desire for spontaneity and freedom is continually stamped out by social forces that entrap and constrict them. The schoolroom scenes at the beginning of the

Figure 37. Truffaut documents that magical time in children's lives when they still have the freedom and innocence to express what they feel, before they learn to hide their spontaneity and aliveness. (*The 400 Blows*, 1959, A. DINO / MK2 SA.)

film convey the tension between regimentation and freedom as the students create little moments of spontaneous pleasure even as they are fixed in the formal rows of the traditional classroom. They secretly pass around a figure of a seminude woman and erupt in suggestive amorous poses behind the teacher's back while he writes a poem on the blackboard about the love life of a hare.

In one of the most delightful sequences in the film, which we witness from a high-angle overhead shot, a physical education instructor herds his students on an exercise run through the streets of Paris. As the run proceeds, small groups of children sneak away, little by little, until the class of nearly thirty students has dwindled down to two. Even by including this extended sight gag in *The 400 Blows,* Truffaut does his own kind of breaking away from the conventions of the tightly constructed plot-driven films of the conventional cinema. This sequence does nothing to further the film's plot. It functions thematically as a visual riff on the subject of childhood rebellion against adult regimentation.

While Antoine and René make plans to steal a typewriter, Truffaut interrupts the narrative flow of the film once again to linger on the rapt faces of young children watching a "Little Red Riding Hood" puppet show. Their feelings of terror, amusement, pleasure, triumph, and surprise are written on their faces for all to see. (See figure 37.) Here Truffaut documents that magical time in children's lives when they still have the freedom and innocence to express what they feel, before social constraints oblige them to hide their spontaneity and aliveness. In addition, this scene exemplifies another feature of New Wave cinema, the appearance of tributes or homages to the cinema of the past which played such a large part in inspiring the New Wave theorists to become directors. In this instance, Truffaut's study of the children echoes a scene in the pioneering Soviet filmmaker Dziga Vertov's *Man with a Movie Camera* (1928), in which the camera dwells with the same kind of fascination on the uninhibited expressive faces of children watching a magic show.

SEQUENCE ANALYSIS: BAZIN'S INFLUENCE ON TRUFFAUT

Since many of the New Wave directors (Truffaut, Godard, Chabrol, Rohmer, and Rivette) wrote for *Cahiers du Cinéma*, a journal founded and edited by André Bazin, the style of their films was influenced by Bazin's realist aesthetic, though each of the above-mentioned directors adapted the style in distinctly individual ways. Two sequences from near the end of *The 400 Blows* demonstrate Truffaut's adaptation of Bazin's realist aesthetic for his own artistic ends. The first is a forty-five-second-long take near the end of *The 400 Blows* depicting the scene in which Antoine escapes from the soccer game, and the second is the even longer take that follows, which lasts seventy-five seconds as Antoine makes his run for the sea.

In the first shot, Antoine is playing soccer with the other inmates of the center for delinquent boys. When a ball goes out of bounds, the camera follows Antoine who, after rushing to retrieve it and tossing it back into the game, suddenly goes out of bounds himself. The camera pans with him as he runs toward frame left and slips through a hole at the bottom of a wire fence. At this point the camera swish pans[14] right, taking us back to the playing field, revealing that a guard has seen Antoine's escape. The camera follows the guard as he too slips through the hole in the fence in pursuit of Antoine. At this point the camera swish pans again, this time to the left, until it captures the image of Antoine in extreme long shot running along the edge of a pond. The guard then enters the frame from the bottom corner of frame right and begins running after Antoine, rapidly gaining ground.

In a classically edited film, the action of this shot would be broken down into a number of shots and there would be cross-cuts between shots of the escaping Antoine and the pursuing guard. Truffaut, by shooting the action in one long take, precisely defines the exact spatial relation between Antoine and the guard, and thus makes the action more compelling. Because in this shot the temporal and spatial dimensions of the action remain intact, we realize that the guard has seen Antoine's escape as it was happening and that he pursues the runaway without missing a beat. By preserving the actual spatial relationship between pursuer and pursued, we receive a heightened awareness of Antoine's danger of being captured.

The seventy-five-second tracking shot in which we focus on Antoine as he runs through the country landscape toward the sea also demonstrates Bazin's idea that some actions need to be represented in real time in order to be dramatically effective. Because we are permitted to see an unedited shot of Antoine running for a relatively long time without showing the least indication of fatigue, we are better able to experience along with him the pure adrenaline-fueled exhilaration of his bid for freedom.

THE FAMOUS FREEZE-FRAME

Antoine's exuberant run from the repressive reformatory to the boundless realm of the sea culminates in the famous freeze-frame and zoom shot which bring the film (and Antoine's hope of escape) to an abrupt halt. This film-ending technique, which subsequently became something of a cinematic cliché, came as a shock to audiences in 1959 and maintains its power to unsettle audiences. The use of the freeze-frame and zoom shot here epitomizes another aspect of New Wave style that distinguishes it from classical cinema. In films made in the classical Hollywood style, filmmakers conceal the traces of the cinematic apparatus so as not to interfere with the spectator's immersion in the fiction. Here, the sudden freezing of the frame foregrounds the film medium, reminding us that films are made up of segments of still frames which present an illusion of animated life only when projected at 24 frames per second. Truffaut, it seems, was willing to take the risk of exposing the artifice of his medium because by doing so he was able to take the medium to new expressive heights. Just as Eisenstein's animated stone lion violated realism to achieve a poetic effect in the Odessa Steps sequence, the freeze-frame at the end of *The 400 Blows* abandons Bazinian realism to function as a powerful metaphor for Antoine's final and definitive entrapment in a system from which there is no escape. Even the word of the title (FIN) functions not just as a word but as an image. Superimposed over Antoine's frozen face the letters F-I-N resemble the bars that obscured our view of him in the prison scenes, signaling not just that the film has ended but that Antoine's hopes for escape and freedom are finished too. (See figure 38.)

Figure 38. The letters F-I-N, superimposed over Antoine's frozen face, resemble the bars that obscured our view of him during the prison scenes. (*The 400 Blows*, 1959, A. DINO / MK2 SA.)

NEW WAVE SELF-REFLEXIVITY

In fact, the unique visual language of cinema is foregrounded not only in this final shot but throughout *The 400 Blows* in the flamboyance of the tracking and panning shots, high-angle shots, swish pans, lap dissolves, jump cuts, and freeze-frames—all of which draw attention to the filmmaking process. The use of the swish pan in the shot where Antoine escapes is typically New Wave because even as it allows Truffaut to adhere to Bazin's realist aesthetic by maintaining spatial unity within the shot, it is simultaneously self-reflexive in that the blurry, jerky movement of the swish pan loudly calls attention to the medium. We become aware not just of a tale but of a "teller," the auteur behind the camera, whose style is every bit as important as the content.

The 400 Blows is not only self-reflexive in its foregrounding of technique; the institution of the cinema is an overt presence in the film, another common feature of New Wave films. Thus the film repeatedly incorporates the cinema into its plot. It is the place of guilty pleasure where Antoine and René go when they play hooky. The rare moment in which the Doinel family are shown having fun together as a family is when they are playfully discussing a film they have just seen together, Jacques Rivette's *Paris Belongs to Us*, another landmark of the New Wave cinema. In addition to these literal references to the cinema, there are indirect, insider references as well, reflecting Truffaut's fascination with film history. Antoine, for example, goes for a ride at an amusement park on the

"Rotor," a large cylindrical drum which is photographed to resemble a giant Zoetrope, the eighteenth-century animation toy which was the precursor of the cinema. Antoine's long ride on the paddy wagon recalls Thomas Edison's (and hence the cinema's) first movie studio, which was called "The Black Maria," a slang term for paddy wagon. I have already mentioned the scene of the children at the puppet show, an homage to Dziga Vertov's *The Man with the Movie Camera*, a brilliant early example of a self-reflexive film.

Truffaut's use in *The 400 Blows* of cinematic techniques, such as the zoom shot and swish pan, that call attention to the film medium also illustrates how much Truffaut was indebted to "direct cinema," or *cinema verité*, a documentary film movement that began in the late fifties. Direct-cinema filmmakers utilized lightweight mobile equipment, fast film stock, and the hand-held camera to record events spontaneously, as they were happening. They frequently employed zoom lenses to bring the spectator closer to spatially distant events or used swish pans to follow rapidly unfolding actions. Truffaut adopted direct cinema's style, techniques, and location shooting partly out of necessity—it was cheaper to make films that way—but the fact that such techniques are associated with documentary truth lends an aura of authenticity to Truffaut's poetic fictions, just as it does to the Italian neorealist films discussed in chapter 6.

Truffaut employs jump cuts, or deliberately jerky edits, during Antoine's interview with the psychiatrist to give the interview a documentary quality. Jump cuts during an interview are often used in documentary films to indicate that parts of the interview have been elided and that we are seeing only the significant parts. To add further to the documentary effect, Truffaut directed Jean-Pierre Léaud to improvise his answers to the psychiatrist's questions rather than having him speak from a script. Truffaut writes of Léaud's performance: "He instinctively found the right gestures, his corrections imparted to the dialogue the ring of truth and I encouraged him to use the words of his own vocabulary. . . . When he saw the final cut, Jean-Pierre, who had laughed his way through the shooting, burst into tears: behind this autobiographical chronicle of mine, he recognized the story of his own life."[15]

The scene with the psychiatrist has a particularly disturbing effect because of the way Truffaut uses sound. The psychiatrist questioning Antoine never appears on the screen. We only hear her questions. Her presence as an interrogating voice without a body perfectly captures the cool impersonality of the system in which Antoine has been abandoned. Interestingly, the choice of constructing the scene in this way was not deliberate but was due to serendipity. The actress Truffaut wanted to play the part of the psychiatrist (Jeanne Moreau) was not available at the time the scene was shot and Truffaut could not afford to wait. His solution was to record her questions after the interview scene was filmed and later dub Moreau's voice into the interview scene. This scene, made chillingly effective because of Truffaut's improvised sound technique, marks the beginning of Antoine's final defeat, which is given powerful visual expression in the final freeze-frame.

The ending of *The 400 Blows,* like the ending of *The Bicycle Thief,* is painful. The pain, however, is made bearable because of Truffaut's cinematic virtuosity. The skill with which the events are depicted helps to contain the sadness of the story. Or perhaps in the case of *The 400 Blows* the pain is also alleviated because we know subliminally that the boy whose tragic story of freedom lost is told, is a stand-in for the man directing the film, who opened up new channels for freedom in filmmaking. Far from being punished like Antoine for breaking the rules, Truffaut has become the celebrated auteur whose first film ushered in the cinematic fresh air of the French New Wave.

8

Hollywood Auteur
Alfred Hitchcock's *Notorious*

HITCHCOCK AS AUTEUR

As I discussed in chapter 7, the New Wave theorists distinguished between those directors they considered auteurs, whose unique style and vision marked their films, and those directors who were merely faithful adapters of their literary sources or of other writers' screenplays. The Hollywood directors the French critics praised as auteurs include Howard Hawks, John Ford, Anthony Mann, Nicholas Ray, George Cukor, Orson Welles, and above all, Alfred Hitchcock. The French auteur theorists and directors Claude Chabrol and Eric Rohmer point out in their pioneering book *Hitchcock* (1957) that Hitchcock's films are deeply infused with anxiety, guilt, and existential angst, which they trace to his Catholic upbringing and education. They conclude their book with the claim that "Hitchcock is one of the greatest *inventors of form* in the entire history of cinema. . . . Our effort will not have been in vain if we have been able to demonstrate how an entire moral universe has been elaborated on the basis of this form and by its very rigor."[1]

Although a number of critics wrote about Hitchcock as a serious artist, notably Robin Wood, Ian Cameron, and the American director Peter Bogdanovich, Hitchcock's reputation as an artist was elevated in America by the translation in 1966 of François Truffaut's *Hitchcock*. In this book, based on fifty hours of interviews, Hitchcock and Truffaut discuss in chronological order the technical underpinnings and thematic implications of every Hitchcock film then made. The revised edition, translated into English in 1984, includes commentary on the films made after 1966. In the introduction to the 1984 edition, Truffaut makes the claim that Hitchcock was an explorer of metaphysical anxieties on a par with Kafka, Dostoevsky, and Poe, and that his works became more complex and profound as his career progressed.[2] Hitchcock continues to be the subject of numerous scholarly books and articles. Entire courses in colleges and universities are devoted to the study of his work. In this chapter I consider why Alfred Hitchcock, who devoted most of his career in Hollywood to making films in the popular genre of the suspense thriller, is considered a serious film artist, a quintessential auteur.

THE CASE OF *EASY VIRTUE*

According to the French critics who defined the term, even when an auteur makes a work based on someone else's novel, drama, or screenplay, he somehow manages to inscribe upon it his own thematic concerns. I became a believer in this aspect of auteur theory when I first taught *Easy Virtue* (1927), an obscure silent Hitchcock film, in my history of the silent film course.[3] Hitchcock made *Easy Virtue* when he was under contract to Michael Balcon, at a time when the British film industry was at a low ebb and film producers were grasping at successful Broadway plays to entice audiences into movie theaters. The film was based on a Broadway hit by Noel Coward about a woman whose second marriage is destroyed by a narrow society, which expels her when they find out about her tragic and somewhat scandalous prior divorce. This seems an unlikely subject for a Hitchcock film, a far cry from the suspenseful, even terrifying thrillers for which he is well known.

Yet when one watches *Easy Virtue*, one experiences reverse déjà vu: *Easy Virtue* contains numerous characteristics of the films Hitchcock was yet to make. The beautiful heroine Larita Filton (Isabel Jeans) is, like so many future Hitchcock heroines, a cool elegant blond whose presence seems to fascinate Hitchcock's camera. Furthermore, Larita's beauty and notoriety make her the subject of fascination to cameras within the film as well. Crowds of nosy, intrusive newspaper reporters ambush her outside the courtroom in a way strikingly reminiscent of Alicia's persecution by cameras in Hitchcock's later film *Notorious*

(1946). At one point in the film, Larita retaliates by throwing a book at a camera. Her last words in the film, after her second divorce is finalized, are directed at camera-wielding newspaper reporters: "Shoot: There's nothing left to kill."

Although Hitchcock claimed to be ashamed of this line of dialogue,[4] confessing in his interview with Truffaut that it was one of the worst he has ever written,[5] the words are, in fact, quite moving in the context of the plot. Moreover, by having his heroine complain about cameras, Hitchcock foreshadows a theme that will become increasingly explicit in his mature work, the subject of the moral dubiousness of the camera's intrusive voyeurism. This theme was made explicit in *Rear Window* (1953), about an immobilized photographer, aided by his telephoto lens, who guiltily amuses himself by spying on the activities of his neighbors.

Significantly, for all the emphasis the line "Shoot: There's nothing left to kill" is given in *Easy Virtue* (it appears at the very end of the film and not at the beginning, as Hitchcock claims in his interview with Truffaut), the camera is not presented in the film as Larita's real enemy. Her life already has been ruined by her mother-in-law (Violet Farebrother) (figure 39), a forbidding, severe woman reminiscent of many future terrifying mother figures in Hitchcock's films, including Mrs. Danvers (Judith Anderson) in *Rebecca* (figure 40), Madame Sebastian (Leopoldine Konstantin) in *Notorious* (figure 41), "Mrs. Bates" in *Psycho* (figure 42), and Mitch's disturbed and disturbing mother in *The Birds* (Jessica Tandy) (figure 43).

The mother-in-law in *Easy Virtue* takes offense at Larita at first glance and poisons her son's affections toward his bride before any news of her scandalous divorce has come to light. Hitchcock's interesting, though perhaps unconscious conflation of an (emotionally) annihilating mother with a (metaphorically) murderous camera in *Easy Virtue* again surfaces in the famous shower sequence in *Psycho* (1960). Here the camera, closely identified with Norman Bates's point of view, does not shoot, but stabs to kill. It rhythmically moves in and out on the body of a beautiful blond woman (Janet Leigh) as she is being stabbed to death just after she has been the subject of Norman's (and hence the camera's) guilty voyeuristic peeping. Norman kills, of course, possessed and dressed as his mother. Thus even in an ostensibly uncharacteristic Hitchcock film like *Easy Virtue* we can find in embryonic form—minus the shivers and suspense—characteristic Hitchcockian psychological themes involving evil mother figures, ambivalence toward beautiful blond women, and a

Figure 39. Mrs. Whittaker (Violet Farebrother). (*Easy Virtue*, 1927, British International Pictures.)

Figure 40. Mrs. Danvers (Judith Anderson) in *Rebecca*. (*Rebecca*, 1940, American Broadcasting Companies Inc.)

self-conscious and self-critical awareness of the sadism and voyeurism of the camera.

CHARACTERISTIC THEMES IN HITCHCOCK'S THRILLERS

Once Hitchcock began creating suspenseful thrillers the obsessive themes for which he is most famous began to appear. These include the

Figure 41. Madame Sebastian (Leopoldine Konstantin) in *Notorious*. (*Notorious*, 1946, American Broadcasting Companies Inc.)

Figure 42. Mrs. Bates (Tony Perkins) in *Psycho*. (*Psycho*, 1960, Universal City Studios.)

Figure 43. Mrs. Brenner (Jessica Tandy) in *The Birds*. (*The Birds*, 1963, Universal City Studios.)

transference of guilt from a guilty to an innocent person; the police pursuit of the wrong (innocent) man; the double-chase motif in which an innocent man pursues the real culprit while he himself is being pursued by the police; the deceptiveness of appearances; and the sudden outburst of violence and absurdity in the midst of the most mundane everyday activities.

Above all, Hitchcock seems intrigued by the theme of the double, in which an ostensibly innocent person is linked through plot devices or visual innuendo to the guilty party. This theme visually and thematically structures *The Lodger* (1927), *Blackmail* (1929), *Shadow of a Doubt* (1943), *Strangers on a Train* (1951), *The Wrong Man* (1956), and *Frenzy* (1972). *The Wrong Man* offers an excellent example of how Hitchcock uses visual and aural devices to link an innocent man with a guilty man. Near the end of the film, the protagonist, a man unjustly accused of a series of holdups, prays for vindication before a picture of Jesus Christ, the archetypal wrong(ed) man. Hitchcock lap-dissolves the face of the praying man onto the face of another man (the real thief, for whom he has been mistaken) just as this man is about to rob a delicatessen. The superimposition of the two faces seems to merge the identities of the two men. When the thief is caught red-handed in the holdup, he cries out: "I haven't done anything. I have a wife and children waiting at home," the same words that the film's unfortunate hero had uttered when he was wrongly apprehended by the police.

By visually and then verbally connecting an innocent man with a guilty man, Hitchcock implies that there is not, after all, so much difference between them. Anyone terribly strapped for cash with a wife and children to support might just be tempted to hold up a store. Great enough need and a sudden impulse, Hitchcock suggests, can turn any law-abiding man into a criminal. The juxtaposition of an innocent man praying before a picture of Christ and the subsequent merger of the innocent man's features with the guilty man's just as he is about to hold up another store is a brilliant pictorial rendering of the phrase, "There but for the grace of God go I."[6]

Unlike most popular entertainment, Hitchcock's films refuse a clear demarcation between good and evil, innocence and guilt, or love and hate. Whenever Hitchcock's films are viewed closely, despite the happy endings the studios or occasionally Hitchcock's own wish for commercial success compelled him to impose, they often leave the viewer uncertain, filled with a gnawing fear that what we think of as a safe and ordered world around us may be a sham. *The Lodger* (1927), for example, which

Hitchcock refers to as "the first true Hitchcock movie"[7] seems to end happily, in marriage. But as the beautiful blond heroine and her husband, a former lodger at her parents' boarding house, meet in a final embrace, behind them in the depth of the image flashes a sign: TONIGHT GOLDEN CURLS, the very phrase that at the beginning of the film is associated with the "Avenger," a serial strangler who targets light-haired women. Throughout most of the film Hitchcock has made us suspect that the lodger is the Avenger and in this context the words on the sign take on a sinister meaning. Thus *The Lodger* exhibits in embryonic form Hitchcock's predilection, first pointed out by Truffaut, to play his love scenes like murders and his murders like love scenes. In Hitchcock films the most trusted people can turn out to be the most treacherous, and often the most treacherous state of all is the state of matrimony.

Despite Hitchcock's reliance on literary sources for many of his spy thrillers, especially those he made in England, Hitchcock made his own unique contribution to the genre. Whereas the spy novels on which his films were based had a lone male for their hero, usually a bachelor who had no use or time for love, Hitchcock substituted a heterosexual couple in the structural position of the hero.[8] By changing the focus from the exploits of a master spy to the interactions of a couple working together, Hitchcock went beyond the limits of a popular genre to incorporate serious themes: the tenuousness of connections between two people, the hope for and fear of love, and the perversity at the heart of romantic desire. What is really at stake in a Hitchcock spy thriller is personal, not national, security. Nowhere is this better demonstrated than in *Notorious* (1946). This film, which Truffaut claims is "the very quintessence of Hitchcock,"[9] illustrates the complex moral and psychological undercurrents that circulate beneath the surface of a Hitchcock spy thriller when the hero becomes a couple.

NOTORIOUS: PLOT SYNOPSIS AND THEMES

The film begins in Florida, shortly after World War II. Alicia (Ingrid Bergman) is the daughter of a Nazi agent who has just been imprisoned for his treasonous activities. Disillusioned by her father, Alicia has become notorious in her own right for her sexual promiscuity. She is recruited by Devlin (Cary Grant), a U.S. intelligence agent who knows that she strongly disapproved of her father's activities, to undertake a secret mission in Brazil to uncover the activities of a Nazi cell whose members are still plotting world domination. Devlin and Alicia (the spy couple) go to Rio together, and while waiting for Alicia to get her instructions, fall in love. Devlin, however, remains wary of the former playgirl.

Alicia's assignment in Rio is to be a kind of Mata Hari. She is to establish intimate contact with a past friend of her father, Sebastian (Claude Rains), who harbors a cell of prominent Nazi refugees in his mansion. Alicia, by means of her sexual allure, is to gain entry to the house and then report to Devlin on the Nazis' activities. Sebastian, too, falls in love with Alicia and, despite the opposition of his jealous mother, proposes marriage. Alicia hopes Devlin will object, but when he does not she accepts Sebastian's offer, in order to prove her determination to redeem herself by carrying out her mission. Ironically, her willingness to go through with the marriage strengthens Devlin's suspicion that she is nothing more than an adventuress.

As the new mistress of the Nazi household, Alicia has access to every room in the mansion except for one—the wine cellar. Only Sebastian has the key to this room. Suspecting that something vital is hidden there, Devlin instructs Alicia to steal the key from Sebastian, which she does at great personal risk. Under cover of a formal reception at the mansion, Devlin and Alicia search the cellar and discover uranium ore hidden in wine bottles, part of a Nazi plot to create a bomb which will enable them to dominate the world.

According to Hitchcock, the politics of *Notorious* didn't interest him at all: "I wanted to make this film about a man who forces a woman to go to bed with another man because it's his professional duty."[10] The uranium ore found in the wine bottles was simply a "MacGuffin," Hitchcock's term for the sought-after secret that sets the plot going but in itself means little and could be any of a number of things. "It [the uranium] didn't really matter," Hitchcock commented, "We were telling a love story."[11] Hitchcock's comment would imply that *Notorious* was about Devlin's dilemma, his painfully conflicted emotions about what he forces the woman he loves to do. But the film actually focuses primarily on Alicia's predicament, building sympathy with her at the start of the film when she, like Larita in *Easy Virtue,* is being hounded by aggressive newspaper reporters.[12] The film's title *Notorious* refers to Alicia's reputation, and the film mostly centers on her feelings and the two impossible double binds in which the film's plot places her. First, to redeem her promiscuity and her father's treachery, Alicia must become both promiscuous and treacherous; and second, to win Devlin's love and respect she must sleep with another man, thereby losing Devlin's love and respect.

Figure 44. Hitchcock visually suggests that Sebastian has become reabsorbed into his mother's sphere of influence by the merging of their shadows. (*Notorious*, 1946, American Broadcasting Companies Inc.)

The other center of sympathetic identification in *Notorious* is, surprisingly, the villain, Sebastian, who according to Hitchcock loves Alicia more genuinely than Devlin.[13] Sebastian's love for Alicia is presented as a positive developmental step in his life. At long last he has freed himself from the domination of his jealous mother, who has hitherto successfully prevented him from marrying. When Sebastian learns he has been betrayed, he becomes once more engulfed in his mother's dominating sphere of influence, forced to murder the woman he loves. Hitchcock gives haunting visual expression to this theme when, from Alicia's point of view, we see Sebastian's shadow merge with his mother's as the two join forces to murder her (figure 44), a precursor to the moment in *Psycho* when Norman Bates, psychically and physically merged with Mrs. Bates, kills Marion. What Hitchcock says began as a fantasy, a man "forcing" a woman to go to bed with another man out of "duty," is developed into a complexly structured, deeply felt meditation on the perverse connections among love, hate, and self-destruction. Sebastian's love for Alicia leads to his humiliation and betrayal and then his desire to kill her, while Alicia's love for Devlin leads her to degrade herself as a Mata Hari and nearly die from poison when she is found out. Hitchcock was less interested in working out the twists and turns of a spy plot than he was in exploring the moral and psychological predicaments of human beings who become spies and hence, by necessity, must engage in illicit activities such as theft, murder, and especially, sexual betrayal. Thus while his spy plots have the dangerous situations and mysteries that appeal to a mass audience, they also provide pretexts to place his characters in a moral and psychological pressure cooker. Hitchcock's characters are never one-dimensional but are instead complex human beings who suffer terrible emotional and sometimes physical consequences when they pervert their morality out of need—for the sake of love or for a supposedly higher good, or both.

HITCHCOCK'S STYLE: PURE CINEMA

I have emphasized the complex emotional undercurrents of *Notorious* because I want to illustrate why Hitchcock's films are regarded as serious moral and psychological explorations. I will now turn to a consideration of Hitchcock's style, of how he compels his audience to identify with his precariously situated characters through virtuoso passages of "pure cinema." *Pure cinema* is a term dating back to the theoretical and aesthetic debates of French critics in the 1920s, some of whom believed that cinema was a distinct art form because it encompassed all of the other arts—literature, music, dance, drama, painting, poetry, photography— while others, advocates of pure cinema, insisted that films draw only on characteristics unique and specific to the film medium. The idea of pure cinema taken to the extreme meant that only visually abstract films could be considered "pure," because films that told a story borrowed from other arts—literature and drama. Hitchcock used the term in a less extreme way, referring to how a director can express thoughts or create a dramatic mood without the need for words, purely through the choice of and arrangement of images. Hitchcock gives the following account of his method for achieving moments of pure cinema.

> [Y]ou gradually build up the psychological situation, piece by piece, using the camera to emphasize first one detail, then another. The point is to draw the audience right inside the situation instead of leaving them to watch it from outside, from a distance. And you can do this only by breaking the action up into details and cutting from one to the other, so that each de-

tail is forced in turn on the attention of the audience and reveals its psychological meaning. If you played the whole scene straight through, and simply made a photographic record of it with the camera always in one position, you would lose your power over the audience.[14]

SEQUENCE ANALYSIS: STEALING THE KEY

A close analysis of the sequence in which Alicia, under Devlin's orders, steals the key off Sebastian's key ring just before a reception to celebrate their recent marriage illustrates how Hitchcock's deft manipulation of film techniques induces the spectator to identify with Alicia as she undertakes her risky mission. Hitchcock could easily have captured the action of Alicia's stealing the key in one shot, but chooses instead to break up this action into twelve separate shots. Of the twelve shots in the sequence, four are long or medium shots that function to establish or reestablish the larger context of the action. The majority are close-ups of Alicia's face, hands, or the key. Five of the shots are subjective, from Alicia's point of view. Hitchcock's frequent use of point-of-view shots is his primary means of "drawing the spectator right inside the situation." Because we are made to see so much of the action through Alicia's eyes we are pulled into a strong identification with her. We understand her thought process because we are compelled to see exactly what she sees.

In the first shot of the sequence we have a rather distanced view of her. She appears in long shot, framed by the door leading from the bedroom to Sebastian's dressing room. The deep focus of this image conveys a feeling of open space, room to move around in, and a background in which to retreat. (See figure 45.) This feeling of freedom is quickly dispelled as Alicia, in the same shot, moves toward the camera into a much tighter medium-close shot, and the background behind her goes out of focus. At this point Alicia's eyes gaze intently off frame left. (See figure 46.) Shot 2 reveals, from her point of view, what she is watching so intently: the door to Sebastian's bathroom, slightly ajar, with his shadow moving fitfully across it. (See figure 47.) Sebastian's shadow flickering on the door serves the double purpose of making him a menacing figure (since shadows are often associated with danger) and indicating his very close proximity to Alicia, making her attempt to steal the key seem terrifyingly risky. The third shot of this sequence is a reaction shot of Alicia, who moves forward into an even more tightly framed close-up. The calm expression on her face, in striking counterpoint to the danger of

Figure 45. The deep focus of this shot of Alicia (Ingrid Bergman) conveys a feeling of open space, room to move around in. (*Notorious,* 1946, American Broadcasting Companies Inc.)

Figure 46. Alicia moves into a tight medium-close shot and the background goes out of focus, dispelling the feeling of freedom. (*Notorious,* 1946, American Broadcasting Companies Inc.)

Figure 47. The shadow on the door indicates Sebastian's menace as well as his close proximity to her as she is trying to steal his key. (*Notorious,* 1946, American Broadcasting Companies Inc.)

her situation, makes her seem extraordinarily courageous. Her eyes glance down in the direction of Sebastian's dressing table, which, as we saw in the previous shot, is situated just outside the door to his bathroom.

Shot 4, from Alicia's point of view, begins with the dressing table seen from where Alicia was standing in the previous shot. Then the camera slowly tracks up to the dressing table, gradually revealing the focus of Alicia's gaze: Sebastian's key ring with the key to the wine cellar. The tracking shot, moreover, is accompanied by mysterious music, which rises to an eerie crescendo as the camera moves closer and closer to its target. The camera's movement toward the keys visually expresses the intensity of Alicia's desire for the forbidden object. The rise of the music's volume suggests a corresponding rise in the intensity of Alicia's emotions as she contemplates the riskiness of what she is attempting to do. The close shot of the forbidden key ring with which the shot ends signifies the huge importance of the key attached to it, whetting our appetite to discover what is behind the locked door that only it can open. Through such cinematic devices Hitchcock makes the viewer as determined as Alicia to appre-

Figure 48. Because of Alicia's closer proximity to the door, Sebastian's shadow looms larger. (*Notorious,* 1946, American Broadcasting Companies Inc.)

hend the key. Like so many of Hitchcock's shots which go beyond the simple function of giving plot information, this shot is instilled with nuances of feeling that can only be projected through the manipulation of the cinematic apparatus. Hence, it qualifies as a moment of pure cinema.[15]

In shot 5, a long shot of Alicia, she is still across the room from Sebastian's dressing table and the keys. She walks toward the dressing table until, at the end of the shot, she is framed in a medium shot. As she is about to grasp the key ring, Sebastian's offscreen voice suddenly addresses her: "I'm surprised Mr. Devlin is coming tonight." These words flow over into shot 6: a subjective shot from Alicia's point of view of the bathroom door with Sebastian's shadow moving across it. Now, because of her increased proximity to the door, the shadow looms even larger, making it even more menacing and a perfect visual correlative of her increased danger (see figure 48). Shot 7 returns us to the same vantage point as at the end of shot 5 (a medium-close shot of Alicia). She is still on the verge of grasping the key ring even as Sebastian's voice continues, "I don't blame anyone for being in love with you, darling." The question generated by

Figure 49. A subjective shot of the key. Everyone can identify with the difficulty of getting a key off a key ring. (*Notorious*, 1946, American Broadcasting Companies Inc.)

the way this sequence is edited is: Will Alicia have the nerve to attempt to steal the key with Sebastian so palpably present immediately offscreen, as was first indicated by his shadow and now by his offscreen voice?

Shot 8, a big close-up of Alicia's intrepid, determined face glancing down at the key chain answers the question. Shot 9 is a subjective shot, a big close-up of Alicia's hands struggling to remove the wine cellar key from the ring, identifiable by the initials UNICA, which in Spanish means "the only one." (See figure 49.) Placing the forbidden key on a key ring was a brilliant touch, because everyone can identify with the difficulty of getting a key off of a key ring. By making this a subjective shot, Hitchcock once again compels the viewer to identify with Alicia's dangerous and compromising action. Sebastian's voice continues from shot 8. He is still alluding to his discomfort at having Devlin at the party: "I just hope that, uh, nothing will happen to give him any false impression. . . . Be with you in a minute." Shot 10 is another close-up of Alicia looking toward the bathroom door, followed by shot 11, another subjective shot, from Alicia's point of view, of Sebastian's looming shadow. These shots are a reminder of how close she has just come to being caught. The tension is finally broken momentarily in shot 12, a long, deep-focus shot of Alicia returning to her bedroom, presumably with key in hand. In the very next shot, without missing a beat, Sebastian strides out of the bathroom, making us fear that he might be aware of the theft.

In the sequence just analyzed, Alicia is presented as extraordinarily brave in undertaking such a risky endeavor. She steals the key, as it were, from under her husband's nose, and Hitchcock's technique intensifies our awareness of her danger by putting us in her place. But our reaction to her physical danger is complicated and heightened by the morally ambiguous nature of the theft. It is one thing to steal a key from a villain for a good cause, but in this case the villain is also Alicia's husband, a man who loves and trusts her. She is taking advantage of her intimate access to his personal possessions in order to rob him. On top of this, the man for whom she is stealing the key is not just an agent of the law, but the man she loves. Because of these emotional complications, Alicia's theft of her husband's key is not just an uncomplicated heroic action done for the good of her country. She is also cuckolding and symbolically castrating him. Through the combination of close-ups and subjective shots, Hitchcock situates the viewer inside the action, giving us first-hand knowledge of what it feels like to be someone who is so desperate to redeem herself, to win love and self-acceptance, that she is willing not just to put herself in grave danger, but also to become a traitor and a thief. The suspense generated is so great because so much is at stake if she is caught, not the least of which is having to face the man she has falsely loved and betrayed. Hitchcock's systematic use of point-of-view or subjective shots implicates the viewer not just in suspenseful situations where one's life is at risk, but in actions so dangerous and subversive that what is really at stake is one's soul. If we allow ourselves to become engaged, pulled in by Hitchcock's seductive techniques, we learn about dimensions of our psychic and moral life that surprise us and give us pause.

Hitchcock summed up his motivation for making films in his interview with Truffaut: "My main satisfaction is that the film had an effect on the audiences, and I consider that very important. I don't care about the subject matter; I don't care about the acting; but I do care about the pieces of film and the photography and the sound track and all of the technical ingredients that made the audience scream."[16] Elsewhere, Hitchcock has said, "I aim to provide the public with beneficial shocks. Civilization has become so protective that we're no longer able to get our goose bumps instinctively. The only way to remove the numbness and revive our moral equilibrium is to use artificial means to bring about a shock. The best way to achieve that, it seems to me, is through a movie."[17]

Whether or not we scream at a Hitchcock movie, the best ones put us through an experience that frightens us, shatters our complacency, and brings us knowledge of parts of ourselves of which we may have been unaware. Hitchcock's genius is to create films that exploit the resources of the film medium to make us react, make us feel fear, or make us experience not just the chaos that may erupt from without, but that which unfurls from within us. His movies fit Kafka's definition of a good book: "an ax for the frozen sea inside us."[18] Hitchcock managed to be a superb entertainer whose films nonetheless have a very sharp edge.

9

The European Art Film
Federico Fellini's *8 1/2*

MODERNIST ASPECTS OF FELLINI'S STYLE

Federico Fellini's *8 1/2* (1963) is a radical departure in style and content from mainstream cinema. Unlike the typical Hollywood film, which has its roots in the clearly defined characters and unified, coherent plots of nineteenth-century popular fiction, *8 1/2* is a European art film, inspired by the forms and techniques of twentieth-century literary modernism.[1] Modernist novelists such as Virginia Woolf, Gertrude Stein, William Faulkner, and James Joyce adopted complex and often difficult new forms of representation that foregrounded the subjectivity of the narrator, undercutting the pretensions of nineteenth-century fiction to render characters, actions, and events objectively. Literary modernists questioned the belief that art can ever be an accurate mirror of nature and society, claiming instead that art can only mirror the external world as filtered through the mind.

When I first saw *8 1/2* in 1964 I was totally baffled. This was the result of the film's strange, stylized mise-en-scène and my confusion about just exactly what was happening in the plot. No film up until then had prepared me for Fellini's adaptation of a quintessential modernist technique—stream-of-consciousness narration. The stream-of-consciousness narrator does not convey events in a clear-cut linear order. Rather the story is told as if the narrator were lying on a psychoanalyst's couch and asked to relate an event using free association, including not just the "facts" of the story but all the feelings and mental associations the story triggers in the teller's mind. Thus, in *8 1/2* there is no easy-to-follow, linear, rational causal string of events, as there is in the classical Hollywood film. At any moment in the film, Guido's circumstances might trigger not an action but an interior vision—a dream, a childhood memory, or a scene from the film Guido is in the process of conceiving. The preponderance of interior visions reminds us that we are not seeing a replication of the world as it is, but a world as it is remembered in a free-associative manner, filtered through the mind of the teller.

In modernist literature, the goal is often not to tell an exciting story but to delineate a character suffering an existential crisis. Thus the emphasis is not on external action but on internal insight. As narrative theorist Horst Ruthrof observes, the narrative is "organized towards pointed situations in which a presented persona . . . in a flash of insight becomes aware of meaningful as against meaningless existence."[2] In the process, the narration becomes an implied pronouncement on the conditions of modern life. These traits all apply to Fellini's *8 1/2*. The film is about the existential crisis of a filmmaker who has a breakdown in the midst of a project, losing inspiration for the film he is under contract to make. The film lays bare the cultural and psychological conditions that inhibit the mind of the artist and presents a breakthrough moment when a sense of meaning (and hence a knowledge of what his film is about) returns to the artist. In both modernist literature and the art film, the point of the work is never obvious and easy to grasp. One has to work mentally to put together the pieces in one's mind, to figure out what the author or auteur is trying to say. Just as with any difficult modernist literary work, one needs to experience *8 1/2* more than once in order to "get" it.

8 1/2 also presents itself as a modernist work because of its self-reflexivity. Like modernist novels which draw attention to their own conventions and the words out of which they are constructed, *8 1/2* blatantly calls attention to its filmic techniques. The flamboyant camera movements, audacious edits, and self-conscious score make us aware that we are watching not life, but a cinematic rendering of life, a life as it is mirrored *on film*. Indeed, everything we see in *8 1/2*, beginning with the dream that opens the film, is blatantly filtered through the cinematic sensibility of Fellini's fictional protagonist, the film director Guido Anselmi, whose cinematic sensibility mirrors Fellini's. Even the title of Fellini's film is self-reflexive: it is also the title of Anselmi's film. Moreover, it literally enumerates Fellini's past endeavors in cinema. Before *8 1/2*, Fellini had directed six films, codirected another, and directed episodes in two films. According to his arithmetic, this added up to seven-and-a-half films. Hence *8 1/2* was Fellini's eighth-and-a-half film.

8 1/2 marked a departure, in style and theme, both from Fellini's earlier films and from the classics of Italian neorealism, such as Rossellini's *Open City* (1945) and *Paisan* (1946), both of which Fellini had worked on as a scriptwriter at the beginning of his career. As discussed in chapter 6, the goal of many Italian neorealist directors was the truthful depiction of the impoverished condition of Italy in the aftermath of World War II. Though Fellini's goal was also to tell the truth on film, that truth encompassed not just the director's vision of social reality but also his spiritual, psychological, and metaphysical reality. The least realistic films, he felt, were the ones that pretended to be the most objective. Under the influence of the ideas of the Swiss psychoanalyst Carl Jung, Fellini wrote: "Sometimes a film, while avoiding any precise representation of historical or political reality, can incarnate in mythic figures, speaking in a quite elementary language, the opposition between contemporary feelings, and can become very much more realistic than another film in which social and political matters are referred to much more precisely."[3] *8 1/2* is a radical departure from neorealism because its images do not purport to mirror the world, or present a "true" reflection of society, but they do mirror the mind—the interior, subjective world of a great, successful Italian film director.

PLOT SYNOPSIS

8 1/2 tells the story of Guido Anselmi (Marcello Mastroianni), a renowned film director who, in the midst of making a film, suddenly loses his inspiration and fears he will never be able to complete the project, an intellectually pretentious science-fiction blockbuster about the end of the world. The production crew has been hired, the actors have been cast, the sets have been built (including a gigantic space tower by the sea which has cost the producer millions of *lire*), but the director cannot come up with a script or any other inspiration for the film. The crisis in his career, which occurs as he is about to enter middle age, makes him question his talent as a filmmaker and brings to the surface conflicts in his personal life. He has been advised to visit a fashionable spa to relax, and he hopes to overcome his malaise. But Guido's troubles—in the form of his producer, his cowriter, his production crew, his cast members, and predatory journalists—all follow him to the spa. In a perverse moment, Guido even invites his wife to join him, even though his mistress is already there. This precipitates a quarrel which threatens his marriage. His personal and professional life seem headed for disaster.

The linear development of the plot is constantly interrupted, often without signals or cues to the spectator, by a stream-of-consciousness narration of Guido's dreams, visions, fantasies, daydreams, and childhood memories, evoked by his present crisis. The film is a veritable encyclopedia of types of interior visions. Guido's dreams, actually nightmares, tell of his guilt and anxiety. His visions, always of a beautiful girl in white, hold out an illusory promise of salvation and release from his mental stagnation, reflecting the common male middle-age fantasy that "If I could just meet the right young, beautiful woman, my vitality would come back and my problems would be solved." Guido's childhood memories enable him to relive and revise youthful experiences which have laid the foundation for his present conflicts, and his daydreams explore resolutions to his deepest and most guilty desires. As an example of the latter, he imagines his wife and mistress amiably meeting, complimenting one another, and dancing off together in perfect harmony. This daydream becomes a full-blown fantasy production in which he imagines himself the head of a harem comprising all the women he has ever desired—living happily and communally together, dedicated in their service to him, and with every woman over age twenty-six banished upstairs.[4]

But no amount of fantasizing can stave off a disastrous resolution to his real-life problems. His producer arranges a press conference to force him to say something definite about the film. Guido, unable to answer the hostile questions of the press and threatened with ruin by his producer if he doesn't, crawls under the table and shoots himself. But this dire action turns out to be only another fantasy, and Fellini at once provides us with another ending. Guido drives away from the news conference, apparently having announced that he is not making the film. His collaborator, Daumier, a harshly critical man who externalizes the director's self-hatred and lack of confidence in the expressions of his most genuine and authentic self, is overjoyed. He was certain the film would have been an aesthetic and intellectual disaster. But suddenly Guido sees his magician friend Mario waving a wand, and then he sees the beautiful girl in white. Now, all dressed in white, the people from his past and present who inhabit his dreams and fantasies appear: Carla, his mistress; the aunts who took care of him as a child; Saraghina, the prostitute who initiated him into the mysteries of sex; an ancient cardinal of the church;

his mother and father. Jacqueline Bon Bon, a striptease artiste whom we recognize from Guido's harem, walks alongside a tall graceful woman, a guest at the spa, who has fascinated Guido because she resembles a statue of the Virgin Mary he remembers from childhood. The director feels suddenly strengthened and renewed by these images, and able to love and accept them all. As a result, he is no longer frightened by the confusions and contradictions of his life. He asks his wife, to whom he has been unfaithful for years, to accept him as he is, and she promises to try. (This is, after all, still Guido's, and Fellini's, fantasy.)

His creative crisis magically resolved, Guido picks up a megaphone and begins to direct the long delayed film. He gives a signal to the image of himself as a child (the source of his poetic inspiration as an adult) to open a white curtain at the bottom of a spaceship tower, the last remnant of the science-fiction disaster film he was originally under contract to direct. At last this grandiose structure has a place in his film, not as a launching pad for an escape from his internal conflicts through fantasy, but as a means to confront and transcend his emotional problems. Down the tower steps marches a procession of all the inhabitants in his internal and external world. For a joyous grand finale (which is also a beginning), Guido directs everyone to join hands in a long line and dance around a circus ring. Soon, only Guido as a child and a small band of clowns are parading in the ring. As they march off, the scene fades into darkness and the title *8 1/2* appears. It suddenly occurs to us that we have not only just seen a film about a director struggling to make a film, we have in fact just watched the very film the director was struggling to make, complete with a happy ending. The name of that film is the name of the very film we are watching: *8 1/2*.

THE "DOUBLE MIRROR CONSTRUCTION" OF *8 1/2*

Although Guido Anselmi is by no means an exact copy of Federico Fellini, there is little doubt that through the creation of Guido, Fellini examines many of the internal conflicts that block his own creativity. It is well known that Fellini suffered a creative block similar to Guido's when he was in the midst of working on the film that later became *8 1/2*. As he relates the story, actors had been cast and sets had been constructed, but he no longer wanted to make the film. As he was in the midst of writing a letter to the producer to call it off, the chief machinist invited him to drink a glass of champagne with the film crew to celebrate the beginning of production. As Fellini recalls:

The glasses were emptied, everybody applauded, and I felt overwhelmed by shame. I felt myself the least of men, the captain who abandons his crew. . . . I told myself I was in a no exit situation. I was a director who wanted to make a film he no longer remembers. And lo and behold, at that very moment everything fell into place. I got straight to the heart of the film. I would narrate everything that had been happening to me. I would make a film telling the story of a director who no longer knows what film he wanted to make.[5]

As the critic Christian Metz observes, *8 1/2* has a double mirror construction: "*8 1/2* is not only a film about the cinema, it is a film about a film that is presumably itself about the cinema; it is not only a film about a director, but a film about a director who is reflecting himself onto his film."[6] Thus Fellini is reflected in Guido Anselmi, who, like Fellini, blocked in his efforts to make a film, liberates himself by turning the film into one about the social and psychological forces that have created the blockage. This, of course, explains the otherwise puzzling scenes in *8 1/2* in which we see Guido auditioning actresses not for roles in a science fiction fantasy but to play the parts of people significant in the director's life—his father, his bitter wife, his sensuous mistress, the prostitute Saraghina. The interior visions in the film—the dreams, visions, and memories—do not attempt to mimic interior reality as it is literally "seen" by Guido, but instead portray how an imaginative filmmaker would employ his medium to represent interior visions in such a way as to help him work through his complexes. Ultimately *8 1/2* does not mirror the inner or outer life of Guido Anselmi, but instead represents Guido's filmic expression of his inner and outer life. The film, that is, imitates neither lived reality nor a director's inner fantasies, but visually renders both reality and fantasy as a brilliant director would represent them on celluloid.

A close look at Fellini's rendering of Guido's childhood memory of his romp with the prostitute Saraghina and his subsequent punishment for his transgression by the priests at his Catholic boarding school (which I refer to throughout this discussion as the Saraghina sequence) demonstrates how Fellini avoids depicting this childhood memory as a conventional film flashback in which viewers have the impression they are seeing what "really" happened to him as a boy. Rather, the memory is presented in a distanced, highly stylized manner, embellished with symbolic overtones, satirical thrusts, and the unconventional use of music, photography, and editing. All of these unconventional filmic devices call attention to the fact that we are seeing Guido Anselmi's re-creation *on film* of his traumatic childhood experience: the sequence is his subjective, if not his literal, memory of the negative effects of his Catholic school upbringing.

SEQUENCE ANALYSIS OF THE SARAGHINA SEQUENCE

CONTEXT AND PLOT SYNOPSIS

The Saraghina sequence is triggered by Guido's consultation (on the insistence of his producer) with a cardinal of the Catholic Church about the Catholic themes of his film. During the interview, the cardinal questions Guido not about his film but about his personal life, questions that make the director clearly uncomfortable. Is Guido married? (he answers yes); does he have children? (he answers yes and then no); what is his age? (forty-three). The cardinal then directs Guido to listen to the cry of a bird and Guido obediently complies, but not for long. His attention is captivated by the sight of a heavy-set peasant woman carrying a basket, her skirt raised above her knees. It is this sensual sight that triggers, even in the presence of a church dignitary, Guido's sexually charged memory of Saraghina.

The cry of the bird segues into the sound of a harsh whistle blown by a priest who is umpiring a soccer game in a schoolyard. Guido, aged about eight, escapes from the schoolyard to join his friends on an expedition to see Saraghina, a wild-looking prostitute who lives in an old blockhouse on the beach. In exchange for money, the woman begins a suggestive dance, a cross between a rumba and a striptease. Guido, shoved forward by his friends, begins to dance with her. But just as she lifts him up into the air, two stern priests from the school appear in search of the runaway. Guido is captured and dragged back to school to face his punishment. In the office of the Father Superior he is told that his transgression is a mortal sin. His mother, overwhelmed with shame for what her son has done, rejects him. Guido's schoolmates holler and jeer when he appears in class wearing a dunce cap and a sign on his back saying SHAME. While the others are having supper and listening to a priest read aloud from the life of the pious Luigi, a saint known for his abhorrence of women, Guido is made to kneel painfully on kernels of corn.

Next we see Guido in meditation over the mummified remains of a decaying female saint. In confession he is asked if he is aware that Saraghina is the devil. His ordeal over at last, he kneels before a statue of the Virgin Mary, perhaps asking forgiveness. But despite the strong measures the church has taken to curb Guido's sexuality, Guido is drawn back to the scene of the crime. He is greeted warmly by Saraghina, whom he discovers sitting by the sea, singing. The scene switches back to the present. Guido and Daumier, his collaborator, are at a restaurant discussing the episode which we have just seen, the Saraghina sequence, which Guido intends to include in his film. At a nearby table sit the cardinal and his retinue. Daumier complains that the Saraghina sequence we have just seen is merely a childhood memory, bathed in nostalgia, with no true critical awareness of the Catholic experience in Italy.[7]

But Fellini's powerful filmic evocation of this event in Guido's life belies the critic's harsh words. As Fellini has related in an interview, this sequence is partially based on the negative effects of his Catholic education. The Catholic boarding school is modeled on a school he attended in his youth. This school, he claims, had "a tremendous influence in determining the way my mind works. . . ." Fellini remembers that "the discipline . . . was medieval. . . . For such small boys (I was only eight or nine) the way they disciplined us was very harsh indeed. For example, one of the most frequent punishments was to make the culprit kneel down on grains of Indian corn for half an hour . . . and was often very painful." Detailing other cruel ways in which the boys were disciplined, Fellini speculates that the severe treatment of such young children is "the sort of thing that might cause serious mental problems, serious complexes." He adds: "the feeling of guilt I drag around with me, which I can't really place, probably derives from the fact that I spent four or five years in that school."[8]

In *8 1/2*, Fellini condenses "four or five years in that school" into one traumatic episode. Although Saraghina is a genuine figure from Fellini's past, he was never really punished by the priests for his association with her. But the fictional linking of Saraghina with the school contains an important emotional truth: an overly strict Catholic upbringing, Fellini implies, can teach children to associate their natural impulses for freedom and sexual pleasure with guilt and punishment, and cause problems in their adult creative and sexual lives.

EXPRESSIVE (SUBJECTIVE) REALISM OF THE MISE-EN-SCÈNE AND CINEMATOGRAPHY

To visually emphasize how Guido's Catholic upbringing has shackled his spirit, Fellini, in a stylized and exaggerated way, opposes the constricted realm of the church with the open, anarchic realm of Saraghina. When we first see Guido as a child, he is enclosed by the high walls of the schoolyard (figure 50) and encircled by the arm of a looming statue of a church dignitary (figure 51). Saraghina's home, in contrast, is the wide open space of the seaside. Everything about her is exposed to the elements—her hair blows wildly, her feet are bare, she bursts out of her dress, and her movements are fluid and uninhibited. (See figure 52.) In contrast, the priests who come after Guido are living symbols of confinement: their long black robes appear particularly incongruous against the natural landscape of the beach. (See figure 53.) Fellini presents their capture of Guido in the sped-up motion of silent slapstick comedies. The acceleration exaggerates, to the point of caricature, the stiff mechanical movements of the priests. But at the same time that he makes them silly, he invests the priests with surprising power. As Guido flees from the priest who chases him from the left, it appears at first that he may escape his pursuer, but unexpectedly he collides with the second priest, who quite impossibly materializes from frame right to block his passage. Even in the unbounded realm of the seashore, the church manages to block and confine.

Once Guido is back at school, the open space of the sea is replaced by a narrow, windowless corridor. Flanked by priests, Guido has literally become a prisoner. While Saraghina is associated with the lively art of dance, the church is associated with portraits and statues, static forms in which images of life are permanently frozen and fixed. As Guido is being led by the ear to his trial, he passes a row of portraits, stern men of the church who accusingly fix him with their eyes. At the end of the row, Guido's prosecutor is photographed to appear like one of the portraits uncannily come to life. At the same time, the juxtaposition makes the man seem hardly more alive than the pictures on the wall.

Even the camera seems to lose its freedom of movement once it is back at the school. As Saraghina dances on the beach, the camera swings around freely to follow her movements, pausing only occasionally on the most awesome parts of her anatomy in imitation of the eyes of the boys, who observe her with the slightly fearful fascination of precocious lust. Back at the school, the action is taken mostly from static camera positions. When the camera moves it does not swing around as it does on the beach, but moves solemnly forward in straight lines to reveal painful and unpleasant static objects—the accusing portraits on the wall, the self-conscious sorrow of Guido's mother, the decayed face of the female saint who is intended as an object lesson in disgust for the female flesh. The camera movements in this portion of the Saraghina sequence are also characterized by rapid pans from the face of one priest to another, and

Figure 50. Guido enclosed by the high walls of the schoolyard. (*8 1/2*, 1963, Corinth Films.)

Figure 51. Guido encircled by the arm of a looming statue of a church dignitary. (*8 1/2*, 1963, Corinth Films.)

quick zooms into the faces of Guido's accusers, movements which add stinging emphasis to their cruel words.

One of the most striking features of the Saraghina sequence is Fellini's deliberate stylization of the mise-en-scène. At Guido's trial, for example, his mother is seated near a large portrait of a little boy wearing a halo, the kind of child she would obviously prefer to Guido. (See figure 54.) While

Figure 52. Everything about Saraghina is exposed to the elements—her hair blows wildly; her feet are bare; she bursts out of her dress; her movements are fluid and uninhibited. (*8 1/2*, 1963, Corinth Films.)

Figure 53. The long black robes of the priests are incongruous against the natural landscape of the beach. (*8 1/2*, 1963, Corinth Films.)

the literal presence of such a portrait in the courtroom is highly unlikely, its symbolic implication is clear: such little boys can only be found hanging on walls, forever imprisoned in idealized painted images. There are several other features of this scene that are not realistically motivated but are there to make a symbolic point. According to Fellini, a number of the

Figure 54. Guido's mother sits by the portrait of a little boy wearing a halo, the kind of child she wishes him to be. (*8 1/2*, 1963, Corinth Films.)

priests at the trial are played by women with shaved heads, their male voices dubbed in. As Suzanne Budgen noted, this symbolic touch makes Guido's accusers "far less wholesome than the company they have snatched him from."[9] Interestingly, Guido's mother is portrayed by an elderly woman with gray hair, even though the "flashback" supposedly refers to something that happened over thirty years ago, when his mother would have still been young. Fellini's projection into the past of Guido's mother as she is in the present conveys Guido's feeling that she is just as ashamed of him now as she was back then. The negative effect of this maternal condemnation (which Guido has internalized) is shown near the end of the film, in the scene in which Guido shoots himself because he is unable to answer questions about his film at a press conference. Immediately preceding this action is an image of his mother saying, "Where are you running to, you wretched boy?"

The Saraghina sequence is anything but, to paraphrase Daumier's words, a mere childhood memory bathed in nostalgia with no true critical awareness of the Catholic experience in Italy. The church's harsh punishment of Guido's erotic impulses and its valorization of a virgin as the ideal woman, Fellini implies, have had a devastatingly negative effect on Guido's adult life. The church has made him unable to combine his feelings of tenderness and love for a woman with his erotic desires. Guido's wife is a Madonna. His respect for her has made her a taboo object, not to be contaminated by his sexual desire (which the church designates as

Figure 55. The statue of the virgin merges with the image of Saraghina's blockhouse. (*8 1/2*, 1963, Corinth Films.)

sinful). Not surprisingly, when she visits him at the spa, he is "too tired" to make love to her. Sex is only permissible (and hence pleasurable) with "bad" or "degraded" women, women who have gone to the devil. Guido's mistress, the plump, voluptuous Carla, is a tamed and refined—but not too refined—version of Saraghina. In an earlier episode of *8 1/2* when Carla begins to sound too much like a wife, Guido makes her up to look like a whore and tells her to pretend that she has wandered into his room by mistake.

A subtle and moving bit of symbolism occurs when Guido kneels before the statue of the Virgin Mary after his confessor has told him that Saraghina is the devil. As the camera pauses on the face of the Virgin, there is a slow lap dissolve that momentarily merges the statue of the Virgin with an image of Saraghina's blockhouse. (See figure 55.) Next, Guido sees Saraghina sitting on a chair facing the ocean singing a sweet lullaby. She is wearing a diaphanous white scarf (an image associated with the purity of the young woman Guido sees in his visions) which blows in the breeze. She appears far more angelic than devilish, but perhaps a little bit of both. (See figure 56.) By superimposing the image of the virgin onto the blockhouse of the whore, and then presenting Saraghina as both a seductress and a maternal figure, singing a lullaby and smiling tenderly at Guido, Fellini contradicts the church's construction of the prostitute as purely evil, creating in Guido's filmed reminiscence a positive resolution

Figure 56. Saraghina now appears more angelic than devilish, but perhaps a little bit of both. (*8 1/2*, 1963, Corinth Films.)

to his childhood trauma. In his film, it is implied, Guido has healed a life-long church-induced split in his psyche, a split which Freud referred to as "the most prevalent form of degradation in erotic life," or as it is sometimes called, the Madonna-whore complex.[10]

FELLINI'S SUBVERSION OF CONVENTIONAL EDITING TECHNIQUES

As I discussed in chapters 1 and 4, certain rules of editing were established so that the spectators of the mainstream fiction film were not distracted by the editing and maintained their orientation in the screen space. By seamlessly conjoining shots through match cutting (also referred to as continuity cutting), film viewers were encouraged to become involved in the illusion that they were watching, not a film made up of multiple bits and pieces of celluloid, but an unmediated reality. In a modernist, self-reflexive art film, of course, this is no longer the goal. By partially adhering to the rules of continuity cutting, but at the same time slyly subverting them, Fellini deliberately calls attention to his own artifice in the editing of his film. The Saraghina sequence contains a number of striking examples of Fellini's playful subversion of conventional editing techniques.

At the beginning of the Saraghina sequence, to portray Guido's escape from the schoolyard, Fellini tweaks the convention of the movement-and-direction match. As I discussed in chapter 1, when the movement and direction of an actor are matched in conjoined shots, the usual effect is to create in the viewer's mind the illusion of temporal and spatial continuity between the shots. Fellini matches the movement and direction of Guido running in two shots, but not to create an illusion of temporal and spatial continuity. In the first shot we see Guido running out of the enclosing arm of the statue toward frame right, and in the next shot we see him continuing to run, also in the direction of frame right. But in the second shot he is suddenly on the other side of the wall running with his friends. The perfect match on the movement and direction of Guido running makes the action seem one continuous sprint, but because the location has radically changed in the second shot, Guido seems to have magically leapt over or run through the wall. As in a dream, an impulse for freedom is suddenly transformed into an instantaneous fait accompli. Here Fellini's editing mirrors not the logic of reality but the processes of the wishful, dreaming mind.

Fellini is just as adept at the use of unconventional editing to create the logic of nightmare. Guido's return to the school from the beach happens just as smoothly and quickly as his escape from it. After Saraghina lifts Guido into the air, suggesting the peak of his pleasure, Fellini cuts to two priests approaching, followed by a cut to Guido running away. Fellini does not dilute the impact of these actions by conveying this action realistically, showing us Guido's first sight of the priests, his disengagement from Saraghina, and the dispersion of his friends. Rather, the action is condensed to emphasize the psychological logic of guilty pleasures instantly followed by the specter of punishment, which is followed by flight. After Guido is captured in the comic collision with the priest, the camera moves up to show him being forcibly escorted by a priest on his right. In the next shot, a movement-and-position match, Guido is still being escorted by a priest on his right, but the location has changed—he is no longer on the beach but now back at school. Once again, Fellini's editing seamlessly merges disparate spaces and condenses time, here to emphasize the swiftness of the church's retribution in the memory of the young sinner.

Another example in which Fellini breaks the established rules of continuity cutting occurs when Guido is brought before his classmates as an object lesson in shame. As Guido's classmates jeer at him, Fellini abruptly cuts to a big close-up of a plate of corn kernels being emptied into the hands of a priest. Suddenly the camera pulls back to reveal that the scene has totally changed from the classroom to the school dining room where Guido is forced to kneel on the corn kernels. The conventional way of presenting this action would be to cut to a long shot of the dining room to establish the new location and then cut in the detail of the corn being poured. Instead, Fellini leaves out the shots which would help orient us in screen space for the purpose of giving greater emphasis to the cruelty of Guido's punishment. The unexpected, dislocating change in time and space and the confusion caused by the weirdness of the image of the corn evoke the feelings of the traumatized child, who experienced his punishment as a rapid, brutal chain of events.

Finally, Fellini subverts conventional practices in film editing by deliberately ignoring a fundamental rule for achieving smooth film continuity, the matching of the background and positions of the characters from shot to shot. In *The Technique of Film Editing*, Karel Reisz writes:

> The most elementary requirement of a smooth continuity is that the actions of two consecutive shots of a single scene should match . . . if a scene is shot from more than one angle, the background and positions of the players remain the same in each take. Clearly, if a long shot of a room showed a fire burning in a hearth, and the following mid-shot revealed the grate empty, then a cut from the one to the other would create a false impression.[11]

The fact that a film is constructed of pieces of celluloid spliced together becomes particularly noticeable when objects in the background of the shot are inconsistent from shot to shot, disrupting the viewer's illusion of the "reality" of the fiction. Fellini violates these elementary requirements in several scenes in the Saraghina sequence.

The scene in which Guido appears before a tribunal of priests begins with a subjective shot from Guido's point of view. The camera frames four priests seated in a row. (See figure 57.) In the same shot, the camera pans right to the Father Superior seated at a large desk. A cut then returns us to a medium-close shot of the first priest, who says, "It is a mortal sin." A pan to the right reveals the second priest who says, "I can't believe it." We naturally expect to see the third priest seated next to the second, but when the camera pans right again, the third and fourth priests are located in a far corner of the room. One is sitting and one is standing. (See figure 58.) In the last shot of this sequence, a long shot of the entire room, the four priests are once more positioned as they were originally, all in a row. (See figure 59.) A final example of mismatching of conjoined shots occurs in the scene of Guido's confession. The background of the point-of-view shot in which Guido approaches the confessional booth does not match the background when he leaves it. Although the confessional booth remains the same, the spatial configuration of the room and the furniture in it is totally changed.

Figure 57. At the beginning of Guido's trial, the camera frames four priests sitting in a row. (*8 1/2*, 1963, Corinth Films.)

Figure 58. When the camera pans back to the priests they are in a new location, the far corner of the room. (*8 1/2*, 1963, Corinth Films.)

Although most people may not notice that the backgrounds or players fail to match from one shot to the next unless it is explicitly pointed out to them, such shots, nevertheless, have a subliminally disorienting effect. Through them Fellini captures the distorting process of memory, which makes the placement of people and objects of the past shifting and

Figure 59. In the final shot of the sequence, the priests are once more positioned as they originally appeared. (*8 1/2*, 1963, Corinth Films.)

uncertain. The mismatching shots have one other important function: those who are aware of them are made very conscious that we are watching not life but a film. Since *8 1/2* is a film of a film, Fellini's foregrounding of the editing process through his mismatches is entirely appropriate.

CREATIVE USES OF SOUND

Following the practice in Italy, Fellini post-synchronized the sound track of *8 1/2*, adding sound effects, music, and dialogue only after the entire film was shot. Post-synchronization gives a director's creativity enormous play, freeing him from the constraint of recording sound realistically or naturalistically and allowing him to experiment with new combinations of sound and image for striking poetic or psychological effects. We discussed above the disturbing effect of Fellini's dubbing in of male voices over the priests who were played by women with shaved heads. Fellini also took advantage of post-synchronization to create an in-joke in the Saraghina sequence. The voice of the priest who reads aloud about the life of the pious Luigi, a man who abhorred women, while Guido is kneeling on the grains of corn, is clearly recognizable to his friends as the voice of Federico Fellini.[12]

The sound track in the Saraghina sequence makes a significant contribution to the mood, atmosphere, and meaning of the episode. Earlier I discussed how Fellini's mise-en-scène and camera movements created a stark contrast between Saraghina's realm and that of Guido's boarding school. Fellini's manipulation of the sound track also contributes to the opposition between the two places. Saraghina's realm is accompanied by the sound of the rhythmic pounding of the sea along with Nino Rota's melodic and freewheeling musical compositions, which accompany Saraghina's dance. The combination of the sea sounds and music contributes to Saraghina's symbolic status as a positive elemental life force. The school scenes, in contrast, are accompanied by harsh or unpleasant sounds. The flashback to Guido's school, for example, is introduced by a shrill bird cry which segues into the harsh piercing blast of the schoolmaster's whistle. When Guido is being escorted to his trial, he is surrounded by a deadly silence broken only by the faint but persistent ringing of a bell, as if life at school were a perpetual summons. The clamorous roar of Guido's classmates when he appears before them wearing a dunce cap is unnaturally loud, amplified by Guido's shame and humiliation.

Just as Fellini creates unexpected and disorienting effects from his subversion of conventional editing techniques, he also subverts long-established conventions of combining sounds with images. In order to demonstrate precisely how he does this, it is necessary to make a distinction between different ways sounds (speech, sound effects, and music) are linked to images in the conventional fiction film. The sound in the conventional fiction film can be divided into diegetic or nondiegetic sound. Diegetic sound is either sound whose source is visible on the screen or sound arising from the fictional world the film creates. We never see the source of the bells that are ringing as Guido is being led to the room with the priests, for example, but since the setting is established as a church school, it is plausible that bells would be ringing. Hence the sound of the bells is diegetic, as are most of the sound effects discussed above—the sound of the sea, the harsh whistle blown by the priest, and, of course, all the dialogue. Nondiegetic sound, in contrast, does not have a source in the fictional world of the film. It is added by the director to create mood or otherwise to enhance the dramatic meaning of the action. Most nondiegetic sound takes the form of music. When a couple kisses, for example, and the music swells, we do not expect to see an orchestra playing in the background, just as we do not expect to see the musicians who play the music as Saraghina dances on the beach. We accept nondiegetic music as a convention.

In conventional films, the distinction between diegetic and nondiegetic sound is clear-cut. Nino Rota's music in *8 1/2* is unusual because it calls attention to itself in a way that blurs the boundaries between diegetic and nondiegetic sound. Thus, even though the music on the beach is supposedly nondiegetic, with no source in the fictional world, the movements of the boys as they clap and stomp in reaction to Saraghina's dance are syncopated to the musical beat in a manner common in film musicals (where the music *is* diegetic). Saraghina too seems to dance in rhythm to the nondiegetic music, as if an orchestra were playing just offscreen on the beach.

Fellini's editing rhythms are also self-consciously coordinated to the musical rhythms, the beat of the music often corresponding to the "beat" of a cut, as happens more often in cartoons than in live-action films. For example, as Fellini cuts from the shot of Saraghina lifting Guido up into the air to the shot of the priests in pursuit of the sinner, there is a corresponding change on the sound track from the main Saraghina theme to the musical bridge. Previously, this bridge has been associated with Saraghina's most provocative movements and seductive wiggles. When the same music accompanies the stiff, awkward movements of the priests, the counterpoint between sound and image makes the men of the church seem all the more repressed and ridiculous.

When Guido returns to visit Saraghina after he has been punished, he sees Saraghina sitting by the sea singing the very same melody as the song that earlier accompanied her dance. Echoing the previous nondiegetic music with the diegetic song has a strange and uncanny effect, the result of blurred boundaries between diegetic and nondiegetic sound. Another instance in which these categories are blurred occurs at the end of the sequence, when Daumier, Guido's collaborator on the script, mercilessly criticizes the Saraghina sequence (which we have just witnessed). As his voice drones on, we hear a piano playing a theme we have come to associate with Guido's childhood innocence and creativity, the "Ricordo d'infanzia" music, which is fully orchestrated during the grand finale of the film. The music here could be purely nondiegetic: its sweetness a gentle counter to Daumier's harsh intellectual words, informing the viewer that Guido does not completely accept Daumier's unkind and uncomprehending criticism of his re-created childhood memory. But since the music is played by a piano, and Guido and Daumier are in a restaurant in which a piano could conceivably be playing nearby, the music could also be diegetic or actual. Daumier does walk by a piano at the end of the sequence. By blurring the distinction between diegetic and nondiegetic music, not just in this sequence but throughout the film, Fellini draws our attention to the way musical conventions work in film. The film's unconventional sound track, like the editing, photography, stylized mise-en-scène, and blatant use of symbolism, is self-reflexive, reminding us that *8 1/2* is a film of a film.

The critics who claim that the film's happy ending is unlikely and implausible fail to appreciate that the subject of *8 1/2* is not the triumph of do-it-yourself analysis but the triumph of art. The subject of the film is not life as it is but the creative resourcefulness of the imagination which can forge a great success out of the conflicts and failures of life. The ending finale is pure movie magic, concocted out of sweet music and powerful images of innocence and reconciliation, celebrating in a frankly symbolic way the triumph of the imagination. When the director joins hands in loving acceptance with all the people in his life who have potentially driven him crazy because of the conflicting demands they have made on his psyche—his parents, his aunts, the priests from his school, his producer, the cardinal, his wife, and his mistress—Fellini affirms the relation between conflict and creativity. Although Guido's conflicts may well be impossible to resolve in life, they can be addressed, confronted, and even joyfully resolved in the charmed circle of film art. The happy ending of the film would seem implausible had it accorded with the conventions of Hollywood classical realism. It works superbly, however, as the conclusion of a self-reflexive modernist art-film fairy tale.

10

Film and Postmodernism
Woody Allen's *Annie Hall*

DEFINING POSTMODERNISM

Postmodernism is such a notoriously slippery term that the word has become almost meaningless. This is ironically appropriate, because meaninglessness is a core concern of postmodernism. On the Internet, I came across the following quotation, which nicely sums up the indeterminacy of the term: "To some it's an excuse to pile together oodles of wild and crazy décor, to others it's another example of the weakness of standards and values, to others a transgressive resistance to the sureness of categories, to others a handy way to describe a particular house, dress, car, artist, dessert or pet and to others, it's simply already over."[1] I am not going to attempt a blanket definition of postmodernism in all of its many manifestations in art, architecture, literature, music, and film, but instead I will try to define what I mean by a postmodern cinematic sensibility by looking closely at Woody Allen's films, and *Annie Hall* (1977) in particular.

Some of the funniest moments in many Woody Allen movies revolve around the main character's depression, based on a horrified recognition of the meaninglessness of life. In *Annie Hall*, Alvy Singer's mother takes him to see the family doctor because "He's been depressed. All of a sudden, he can't do anything." Alvy explains that he has read that the universe is expanding and "Someday it will break apart and that would be the end of everything." As a result he has stopped doing his homework because "What's the point?" In *Deconstructing Harry* (1997), the theme comes up again, when the black prostitute Cookie asks Harry Block why he is so depressed and why he has to take so many pills. Harry, alluding to antimatter, which will cause the universe to implode in upon itself, asks her if she knows about "the black hole," to which Cookie answers, "That's how I make my living."

Like many of Woody Allen's one-liners, this one has more than one source of humor. On the one hand, we laugh because of the immense comic incongruity between two very different kinds of black holes, taking pleasure in Cookie's carnal deflation of Harry's cosmic angst. On the other hand, we recognize a certain plausibility in the connection. An addictive need for sex, the kind which could drive a man to seek a prostitute, could very well have its origin in feelings of vulnerability, fragmentation, and identity diffusion, projected onto a cosmos conceived as flying apart or collapsing into itself. In that sense, the black hole really is the means by which Cookie makes a living.[2]

It is also the means by which Woody Allen makes a living. From as far back as his days as a stand-up comic, Woody Allen has been trading on his ability to make jokes about human anxiety in a postsacred age in which the ontological rug has been pulled out from under us. With the loss of faith in God, an ultimate being from whom truth and moral values derive, human beings have only themselves to rely on in their quest to find meaning in life. Yet our belief in a coherent, unified self as a potential center of meaning has also come under attack by the teachings of postmodern psychoanalysis and philosophy, both of which suggest that the concept of a centered, unified authentic self is as illusory a hope as is that of an all-knowing God.

Sigmund Freud teaches that we continually struggle with conflicting internal impulses, some of them unconscious or repressed. Hopelessly split in our desires, and no longer certain of our motives, we literally do not know who we are or what we really want. Picking up where Freud left off, the French psychoanalyst and philosopher Jacques Lacan theorized that our sense that our selves and lives form a coherent, and thus meaningful, whole is based on an illusory, language-based fiction we create in order to hold our selves, which are actually not whole but fragmented, together. Drawing upon Lacan's observations, the French philosopher Jacques Derrida argues that all concepts of truth (or meaning) depend upon language, but words refer to nothing concrete in the world, only to other words. Through the technique of deconstruction,

Derrida demonstrates that all our certainties are based on assumptions that are themselves based upon assumptions in an infinite regression. Woody Allen jokingly expressed the tenuous sense of self promulgated by postmodern philosophy in an early stand-up comic routine when he complains that his first wife, a philosophy major, was always demonstrating to him that he didn't exist.

POSTMODERN THEMES IN WOODY ALLEN'S FILMS

The first film in which Woody Allen overtly reflected on the predicament of human beings in a postsacred world is *Love and Death* (1975). Here, the main character (and by implication the audience) is given hope that there is a God and hence a meaningful, coherent moral world order, only to have the illusion rudely exploded. The night before Boris (Woody Allen) is to be executed for the attempted assassination of Napoleon, an angel of God appears in his cell to reassure him that at the very last minute Napoleon will pardon him. Now that he has proof of God's existence, Boris immediately begins spouting fractured biblical nonsense in the reverent voice of a true believer. At dawn he goes to his execution with a display of great bravery and coolness, only to be executed anyway. The angel of God's information was not reliable.

Even less reliable than God, or God's agents, in Woody Allen's films are other people. His characters are often betrayed by individuals who seem to have bought the idea that since God is dead, everything is permitted. In *Crimes and Misdemeanors* (1989), Allen's most completely worked-out rendering of this theme, Judah literally gets away with the murder of his mistress. Not only do the police not suspect his part in the crime (he has arranged it), but also, after a short period of fretting, he no longer feels any guilt at all for the murder and leads a perfectly happy, prosperous, and contented life. Only in fiction, Allen suggests, are wrongdoers necessarily punished either by their own feelings of guilt or by external forces. Thus, whereas Raskolnikov's guilt in Dostoevsky's *Crime and Punishment* (to which the title of Allen's film alludes) leads him to collude in his apprehension by the police, the conclusion of *Crimes and Misdemeanors* suggests that in today's world, lacking belief in a God who punishes the unjust, the unjust as often as not go without punishment. Even the worst crimes are misdemeanors.

In *The Purple Rose of Cairo* (1985), Allen foregrounds the theme that the only world in which morality, honesty, commitment, and love prevail is the world created in fictions, which are vitally important, nevertheless, because without fictions life would be unbearable. In this film, Tom Baxter, a fictional character from a 1930s escapist film comedy, *The Purple Rose of Cairo*, emerges from the screen to court Celia (Mia Farrow), an abused Depression-era housewife with whom he has fallen in love because of her devotion to him. She has come back five times to see the film in which he plays a dashing Egyptologist and world-class adventurer. Gil Shepherd, the real-life actor who plays the part of Tom Baxter (both characters are played by Jeff Daniels) also courts Celia. She ends up choosing the "real" man over the fictional character, only to learn that the love of the fictional man was true (the ability for true love was written into his character), and the love of the real man was only a fiction. Gil Shepherd, it turns out, was only acting: pretending to love her in order to persuade his fictional character, whose escape from the screen could potentially ruin his career, to go back into the screen. Once his mission is accomplished, he abandons Celia with very little, if any, remorse. Celia finds relief from her crushing disappointment by going back to the movies.

Woody Allen's postmodern sensibility goes deeper than the depiction of a disturbingly centerless, morally vacuous world, which is also a late nineteenth-century problem and not postmodern per se. What is more characteristically postmodern about Allen's work is the highly self-reflexive, parodic way he uses the film medium. Most Woody Allen films mirror or imitate, not life, but only life as it is presented in other films. Unlike the classical Hollywood film, which, as I discussed in chapter 4, strives to create an illusion that the world we are watching is real, Woody Allen's films blatantly call attention to their fictiveness or artificiality. We discussed how the modernist filmmaker Fellini does this as well, by using complicated and flamboyant film techniques which call attention to the medium and make us aware of the artist behind the artifice. Woody Allen undercuts the realistic illusion of film in a very different manner— through parody and pastiche. That is, he uses traditional forms but in an ironic way, to undercut their realist pretensions.[3]

As Nancy Pogel pointed out in her book *Woody Allen*,[4] nearly every segment in *Everything You Always Wanted to Know About Sex* (1972) self-consciously imitates, parodies, or otherwise plays off of a particular film or television genre familiar to his film audience. In "What is Sodomy?" Gene Wilder plays a doctor who falls in love with a fickle sheep. Here Allen parodies the "dark naturalism" of films like *Sister Carrie* (William Wyler, 1952), based on Dreiser's novel of the same title, and *A Place in the Sun* (George Stevens, 1951), in which an upper-class male disastrously falls in love with a beautiful woman from a lower class. (Wilder ends up in the gutter drinking from a bottle of Woolite.) "Why Do Some Women Have Trouble Reaching Orgasm?" is photographed in the style of Italian art-film director Michelangelo Antonioni, complete with English subtitles. "What Are Sex Perverts?" parodies TV game shows such as "I've Got a Secret" and "What's My Line?" In "What Happens during Orgasm?" Woody Allen plays a soon-to-be ejaculated sperm with the odds of survival crushingly against him. This segment parodies both war films and science-fiction fantasies such as *Fantastic Voyage* (1966).[5] Other segments of *Everything You Always Wanted to Know About Sex* parody the horror film, the television sitcom, and the medieval historical romance.

Sleeper (1973) is another parody of the science-fiction film, while *Love and Death* spoofs the novels of Tolstoy and Dostoevsky, films that have been made of these novels, and the montage style of Soviet filmmakers Sergei Eisenstein and V. I. Pudovkin. *Stardust Memories* (1980) is an extended riff on Fellini's *8 1/2*, in both style and content: it is a wide-screen, black-and-white film about a world-famous movie director suffering from a creative block. *Everyone Says I Love You* (1996) sends up the aggressive nonrealism of the musical. The film within a film of *The Purple Rose of Cairo* imitates the look of the thirties screwball comedy, while the frame story, which takes place during the Depression, imitates the somber look of social-realist films.

Just as Derrida shows that language is infinitely referential, deriving its meaning only from other words, Woody Allen's films, through their self-reflexive borrowing or eclecting[6] of past film styles and genres, make us aware that the reality that seems so transparently mirrored in the film medium refers not to some foundational reality outside the film but only to other films. His films thus make us aware that the meanings they construct are as insubstantial as the material of their construction, the bits of celluloid which are only reflections of reflections.

Allen's intimation that there is no such thing as the truth and that film's pretense of showing us reality "as it is" is just that, a pretense, is especially evident in his parodies of the documentary film, the film form devoted to dramatizing real life as opposed to fiction. His first film, *Take the Money and Run* (1969), was a pseudodocumentary on the life of an unsuccessful crook. Here, Allen takes particular delight in comically deflating the all-knowing "voice of God" narrator whose bombastic pronouncements are continually undercut by the film's sight gags and absurd, surreal plot turns.

Allen also spoofs the pretensions of the documentary form to reveal the "truth" in *Zelig* (1983). This film imitates the form of a compilation documentary, made up from fragments of other films—newsreels, documentary footage, even feature films. The subject of this pseudodocumentary is a human chameleon (played by Woody Allen) who can miraculously change his shape to become a replica of any man (the process doesn't work with women) with whom he is in close proximity. When he is with African Americans, he becomes black, with Greeks he becomes Greek, with fat men he becomes fat. So great is his notoriety for this strange talent (a symptom of his pathological need to be accepted, to fit in) that he becomes world-famous, appearing in newspapers and newsreels alongside numerous historical figures such as Babe Ruth, Calvin Coolidge, and Adolf Hitler. In these impossible scenes, Allen foregrounds the ease with which photographic images can be manipulated through editing and special effects to make blatantly impossible actions seem real. Allen decisively undercuts the film medium's pretensions to represent the truth by juxtaposing footage from a Hollywood movie made of Zelig's life with "real" incidents of his life supposedly captured on newsreels. By putting Hollywood "reality" next to documentary "reality" Allen demonstrates that both modes rely on conventions. The "real" or documentary footage is just as contrived as the Hollywood footage.

Husbands and Wives (1992) is shot in a cinema verité style, imitating the style used to capture the dissolution of a couple's marriage in the Public Broadcasting Corporation's *An American Family* television series (1973).[7] Cinema verité, which also informed the style of *The 400 Blows* and other New Wave films, but for different aesthetic goals, refers to a way of filming real-life scenes without elaborate camera equipment, the goal being to interfere as little as possible with the events being photographed. In *An American Family* (a precursor to "reality television"), a camera crew moved into the suburban home of a Southern California family and photographed the everyday life of the family members, with the intention of bringing real life as it is spontaneously being lived to the screen. But although Allen shoots *Husbands and Wives* in a cinema verité style resembling that of *An American Family*, he undercuts any pretense of documentary authenticity by using widely recognized professional actors (Mia Farrow, Judy Davis, and himself) in the main roles. By using a style which proclaims "the truth" in order to tell an obvious fiction, Allen foregrounds the fictional underpinning of all supposedly realistic films.

In *Deconstructing Harry* Allen foregrounds the film medium in still another way. The film is composed of scenes that alternate depictions of

Harry's life with flashbacks and scenes from his novels and short stories. The enactments of Harry's fictions are shot in the seamless style of the classical Hollywood film, a technique which hides the constructedness of the film world by smoothing over evidence of cuts and thus preserves the viewer's orientation in screen space. In contrast, scenes from Harry's "life" are shot in a highly mannered ultra–cinema verité style, complete with glitches in the sound track and numerous disorienting, jittery jump cuts. Here Allen visually dramatizes the fact that Harry can feel "real"— that is, coherent, or "together"—only in his fictions, not in his life.

In *Husbands and Wives*, *Deconstructing Harry*, and most of Woody Allen's other films, the foregrounding of the film medium serves to make us hyperaware that when we are watching a film, that most mimetic of all media, nothing we are seeing is really real. Everything is a construct— a product of the director's brain—even, or especially, when the main character in the film strongly resembles the auteur of the film we are watching—Woody Allen himself. Allen uses his appearance as the star in his own films paradoxically, to foreground another important premise of postmodern thinking—the death of the author, or in this case, the auteur. In his fiction, plays, and films, Allen continually undercuts the pretensions of an author to be the one who knows some ultimate truth about life and who thus is in complete creative charge of his creations. *Annie Hall*, which I would now like to analyze in some detail, seems on the surface to be the intimate tell-all confession of a writer, with teasing intimations that that writer is really Woody Allen himself. At the same time, Allen in *Annie Hall* deconstructs the very possibility of an author's ability to know and to be able to present some foundational truth about his own or his characters' lives. Just as Allen undercuts the pretensions of documentary truth in his parodies of documentaries, in *Annie Hall* Allen undercuts his own pretensions to provide us with filmed autobiography. Autobiographical truth, like documentary truth, he demonstrates, is just another fiction.

THE DEATH OF THE AUTHOR IN *ANNIE HALL*

At the beginning of *Annie Hall*, after the credits fade out, we are stunned to see an image of Woody Allen himself in a medium close-up, speaking directly to the camera and by implication to us, the spectators sitting in the film audience. He is wearing clothing familiar to audiences who have seen him in his stand-up comedy routines or on late night talk shows—a tweedy sports jacket, a shirt but no tie, and his trademark horn-rimmed

Figure 60. Woody Allen seems to be speaking as himself directly to the film audience. (*Annie Hall*, 1977, Metro-Goldwyn-Mayer Studios.)

glasses. (See figure 60.) He tells a joke about two elderly women at a Catskills resort. "Boy, the food at this place is really terrible," one remarks, to which the other replies, "Yeah, I know, and such small portions." Woody Allen then comments, "Well, that's essentially how I feel about life. Full of loneliness and misery and suffering and unhappiness, and it's all over much too quickly." He then goes on to tell a second joke the essence of which is "I would never want to belong to any club that would have someone like me for a member." This joke, he claims, which he got from Groucho Marx, is the "key joke of my adult life in terms of my relationship with women." Next he comments on how he has just turned forty and he guesses he is going through a mid-life crisis. This leads to some defensive claims that he doesn't mind growing old ("I think I'm gonna get better as I get older"), a sentiment undercut by his vision of himself as "one of those guys with saliva dripping out of his mouth who wanders into a cafeteria with a shopping bag screaming about socialism."

The extraordinary and surprising aspect of this opening monologue (captured in one long, uninterrupted take) is that the audience is confronted in such an intimate way with the author of the film—its writer,

director, and star. When he employs the first-person singular in his monologue, we all assume he is referring to his real self—the real Woody Allen,
who in 1975 had indeed just turned forty. But Allen punctures our deliberately created illusion that we have been having an intimate chat with
the *auteur* with the following line: "Annie and I broke up and I—I still
can't get my mind around that." Subtly, the frame of reference has shifted.
Before our eyes Woody Allen has become Alvy Singer, the character he
plays in the film *Annie Hall*. As he begins to muse on the past in order
to try to make sense of what went wrong, why he and Annie broke up,
his speech takes on the kind of stuttering, pseudointimate tone that we
recognize from episodes in his stand-up routines when he is musing about
his life's difficulties. But now, we are listening not to Woody Allen but
to Alvy Singer, whose occupation in the film turns out to be that of a
stand-up comedian. In retrospect, *Annie Hall*'s opening address from the
very beginning can be read as one of Alvy Singer's (not Woody Allen's)
comedy monologue routines. The screenplay of *Annie Hall* preserves the
opening scene's deliberate conflation of Woody Allen and Alvy Singer.
After the credits, the screenplay states, "Sound and Woody Allen monologue begin," but then indicates an "Abrupt medium close-up of Alvy
Singer doing a comedy monologue."[8]

By seeming to speak directly to the audience in his own person at the
beginning of *Annie Hall,* and then seamlessly sliding into his film persona, Woody Allen makes us hyperconscious of the relation between himself as a director or writer and the character he creates. At the same time,
even though *Annie Hall* is nominally about a character Allen has written and created—Alvy Singer—we are made to wonder if this might not
really be a film about Woody Allen. Allen gives us a number of reasons
to think so.

First of all, the fact that Allen plays the title role dressed as himself,
or at least, as the self that he has constructed for his stand-up comedy
routines, plays into the illusion that we are seeing a first-person autobiographical film. In his biography of Woody Allen, Eric Lax points out
that the clothing of Allen's stand-up and film persona is identical to the
clothing Allen himself typically wears.[9] The connection between Allen
and his screen persona is further reinforced by Allen's giving Alvy a name
similar to his own—Alvy is close to Allen, with the "y" taken from the
"y" in Woody—as well as his own past profession of stand-up comic. The
boundaries between life and fiction are further muddied when we see a
clip of "Alvy" appearing on the *Dick Cavett Show*. I put Alvy in quotes
because the clip we see is actual documentary footage of Woody Allen

appearing on the show in 1975. In the reverse of what happens in the opening monologue, Allen turns his fictional persona back into his real self.

As if further to encourage the audience to connect his screen persona with himself, Allen gives Alvy some recognizable features of his own past relationships with women. Like Allen at the time he made *Annie Hall,* Alvy has been divorced twice. It was also well-known to audiences at the time that Allen had had an affair with Diane Keaton, the woman who plays the part of Annie Hall, and whose loss Alvy is trying to get over. In a further conflation of life and fiction, Diane Keaton's real name was Diane Hall. If you subtract the "di" from Diane, you get "An-e" Hall. Through these teasing references Allen creates the impression that Alvy Singer is a thinly disguised version of Woody Allen, who is using film as an instrument of self-analysis to figure out why he cannot have an enduring love relationship, and how he ever could have let someone as wonderful as Diane Keaton get away.

But most of *Annie Hall* is fiction. Allen's first working title for the film, according to John Baxter's biography of Woody Allen, was entitled "Anhedonia," a clinical term describing the inability to enjoy life.[10] This version *was* based on aspects of Woody Allen's own life (and unused parts of it reappear in both *Stardust Memories* and *Deconstructing Harry*), but he dropped much of the personal material in order to focus the film around Alvy's relationship with Annie, most of which is indeed fictional, made up by Woody Allen and his cowriter on the script, Marshall Brickman. Alvy Singer's wives, as they appear in flashbacks in *Annie Hall,* bear little resemblance to Woody Allen's actual past wives, Harlene Rosen and Louise Lasser, and the character Annie Hall, despite the life and vitality given to her by Diane Keaton, has only a superficial resemblance to Diane Keaton the person. Nevertheless, when Woody Allen complained in interviews that people got it into their heads that *Annie Hall* was autobiographical and he couldn't convince them that it was not, he is being disingenuous. In *Annie Hall* Allen deliberately sets up the illusion that the film is a personal recounting of his life, feeding the hungry voyeurism of the film audience, while mostly presenting them with fiction.

Woody Allen, it would seem, knows something about voyeuristic desires. Throughout his career, beginning with his stand-up comic days, he has joked about his own fascination with voyeurism, the desire to look into the secret recesses of someone else's life. In *Annie Hall* he repeats a joke from an early stand-up comic routine about being thrown out of New York University during his freshman year for cheating on a metaphysics final exam, because he looked within the soul of the student sitting next to him. In numerous other films, from *Take the Money and Run* to *Deconstructing Harry,* including *Zelig, Another Woman, Alice,* and *Everyone Says I Love You,* Woody Allen invites the film audience to peep into that most private of private realms in which people bare their souls—the psychotherapy session.

Within the fiction of *Annie Hall,* that Woody Allen is confessing all, is the fiction that Alvy Singer is baring his soul, confessing everything, as if to his analyst (for whom the movie audience stands in), in order to get to the bottom of what's wrong with him, why he can't accept himself, and why his relationship with a woman he still loves broke up. In this sense *Annie Hall* can be viewed as the film equivalent of Philip Roth's *Portnoy's Complaint,* which also features a Jewish man with relationship problems who tells all in a series of flashbacks to his analyst. Philip Roth, of course, explodes Portnoy's belief that his confession is the truth about his life in the famous line, spoken by Portnoy's analyst, that concludes the novel, "Now vee may perhaps to begin. Yes?" Allen also calls into question the authenticity or adequacy of Alvy's confession, not only by having Alvy's self-analysis end inconclusively, but also by foregrounding the fictional, reconstructed quality of Alvy's memories of his past. Some of Alvy's flashbacks in *Annie Hall* are photographed in a realistic mode, heightening the impression that we are seeing literal images of Alvy's past—the scene in which Alvy and Annie battle with the lobsters comes to mind, as well as the scenes in which Alvy recalls incidents from his first two marriages. Yet the delightful originality of *Annie Hall* derives from primarily patently fictional metaphorical images, not from Allen's realistic presentations of moments in Alvy's past.

Like all good therapy patients, Alvy begins his search for the sources of his adult neurotic hang-ups in his childhood. "I swear I was brought up underneath the roller coaster in the Coney Island section of Brooklyn," he tells us. Then we see the literal image of a house with a roller coaster built over it (figure 61) and then a shot of Alvy as a child eating soup and reading a comic book as the house convulsively shakes, presumably because a roller coaster is passing overhead. Because of the bizarre nature of the image, we do not take Alvy's image as literal but as a surreal representation of a figure of speech. This is analogous to the process of the dream work as Freud describes it, in which abstract ideas (the latent dream thoughts) are transformed into the concrete visual form of the manifest dream.[11] Interestingly, this strange construction was not a figment of Woody Allen's imagination, but a "found object." Woody

Figure 61. The house where Alvy grew up. (*Annie Hall,* 1977, Metro-Goldwyn-Mayer Studios.)

Allen had planned to base Alvy's childhood more literally on his own childhood until his set designer, Mel Bourne, drove him to see the Cyclone roller coaster at Coney Island, which actually had an apartment built into it. "This is where Alvy grew up," Allen supposedly said. "We're going to use this."[12] Woody Allen seems to have immediately understood that the image of a house built into a roller coaster was an apt image for the experience of a child who grew up surrounded by so much emotional turmoil that it felt like he lived underneath a roller coaster. Later in the film, Alvy, accompanied by Annie and his best friend Rob, go back into the past and witness one of Alvy's parents' crazy fights, which apparently were so unsettling to little Alvy that they shook the foundations of his security in childhood. (The memory of the fighting parents is one way in which *Annie Hall* could be considered autobiographical. Images of and jokes about fighting parents occur in many Woody Allen films, and Allen is quite public about their autobiographical basis.)[13]

Another example of an obviously fictional but emotionally apt image from Alvy's childhood is the image of Alvy's father directing traffic at a bumper-car concession. Not only is this a perfect image for conveying the idea that his father was not a very distinguished role model in terms of having a meaningful occupation (the one thing people do not need on a bumper-car ride is a traffic director), but it is also expressive of a father who failed miserably at teaching his son impulse control. Near the end of the film when Alvy runs amok in a California parking lot, smashing into several cars, images of Alvy as a child bumping into cars at his father's concession flash on the screen. As if to confirm that this vivid image of Alvy's past is not to be taken literally, Alvy confesses immediately before the images of his father at his bumper-car concession appear on the screen, "You know, I have a hyperactive imagination. . . . I have some trouble between fantasy and reality."

In another telling distortion of the past, Alvy pictures his mother sitting at the kitchen table in Alvy's childhood home, vigorously scraping carrots (read, castrating mother) as she harangues him about his character deficiencies: "You always only saw the worst in people. You never could get along with anyone at school. You were always outta step with the world. Even when you got famous, you still distrusted the world." Interestingly, in this scene Alvy's mother appears as a young woman (the way his mother looked to him as a child), even though she is speaking from the perspective of the present, after Alvy has grown up and become famous. By putting the words of his mother in the present into the mouth of his mother from the past, Allen is suggesting that Alvy has heard the same message over and over again and thus has become fixated on the criticizing, castrating mother of his childhood.[14] (In Allen's next film, *Manhattan,* the main character's work in progress is an expanded version of an earlier short story about his mother entitled "The Castrating Zionist.")

Alvy's fixation on his castrating mother comes up later in the film when Alvy complains that even as a kid, "I always went for the wrong women. . . . When my mother took me to see *Snow White,* everyone fell in love with Snow White. I immediately fell for the Wicked Queen." Allen then cuts to a cartoon image of Disney's wicked queen from *Snow White,* but with Annie's face and voice. (See figure 62.) Here, we are not being shown an image of the way Alvy experienced the wicked queen in *Snow White* when he was a child, but as he perceives her as an adult, now with the face of Annie. Alvy's making Annie, who has none of the qualities of the wicked queen, into such an imago reveals that Alvy has projected or transferred the frustrating qualities of his mother onto both Annie and the wicked queen. Here, the distinction between life and fiction totally breaks down, because both the people in life (Annie) and fantasy images on the screen

Figure 62. Annie as the wicked queen in *Snow White.* (*Annie Hall,* 1977, Metro-Goldwyn-Mayer Studios.)

(the sexualized image of the wicked queen) are shown to be distorted by the fantasies we construct about each.

Allen not only demonstrates the way our experience of the present is distorted by our experiences in the past, but also the reverse—the way our knowledge in the present can reshape and reconfigure memories from the past. In a flashback from Alvy's grade-school days, for example, after a teacher scolds him for kissing a little girl, humiliating him in front of the entire class, suddenly we hear Alvy's adult voice answering the accusation: "Why, I was just expressing a healthy sexual curiosity." The camera pans over to reveal a grown-up Alvy sitting in the back of the classroom, authoritatively contradicting all charges against him. He goes on to counter the teacher's obnoxious ploy of invidiously comparing him with one of his classmates ("Why couldn't you have been more like Donald. Now, there's a model boy.") by directing Donald to reveal what he became when he grew up. "I run a profitable dress company," Donald replies. To underline the point that Alvy turned out better than his classmates, a number of other children also report on their boring or dubious futures— "I'm president of the Pinkus Plumbing Company"; "I sell tallises"; "I used to be a heroin addict. Now I'm a methadone addict"; "I'm into leather." Allen then cuts to a television screen that shows Alvy appearing masterfully funny on the *Dick Cavett Show*. By mixing Alvy's past with these glimpses into the future Allen provides little Alvy with an ally (his adult self) who defends him against the narrow-minded, puritanical teacher who was blind to his special qualities and talents. He also literalizes the fantasy many of us have that if we could only relive our childhoods, knowing what we know now, we would not have had to suffer so much.

Just as Alvy rewrites his past by bringing his adult self in as an ally against his overbearing teacher, in another flashback he inserts into his past the famous media critic Marshall McLuhan. Here his purpose is to take revenge on a pretentious Columbia media professor who irritates him with his know-it-all pontificating about Fellini and the theories of Marshall McLuhan as Alvy is standing in line at the movies with Annie to see *The Sorrow and the Pity*. When the professor protests that he has a right to his opinion because he teaches media studies at Columbia, Alvy summons McLuhan from behind a large movie poster. McLuhan tells the professor: "You—You know nothing of my work. . . . How you ever got to teach a course in anything is totally amazing." Alvy, after all, is narrating his story and he can conjure up anyone he wants in order to prove a point. Speaking directly to the film audience, he says: "Boy, if life were only like this!" Again we are reminded that what we see of Alvy's life is often a fantasy. He tells us his past as it felt, as it is remembered, as it is wished, through a creative rewrite of the script of his life.

Near the end of *Annie Hall* Alvy literally does rewrite the script of his life. Soon after the scene in which we see Alvy and Annie break up at a health-food restaurant on Sunset Boulevard in Los Angeles, we see Alvy, now a playwright, watching a rehearsal of his play in which this very same scene is reenacted. An actor who looks like Alvy and an actress who resembles Annie are arguing, using the exact words we have just heard uttered by Alvy and Annie. But the scene in the play ends very differently from the scene we have just witnessed in *Annie Hall*. In the film, Annie refuses to go back to New York with Alvy, and drives away from him in anger and disgust, leaving him at the curb ranting about the hollowness of award ceremonies in Hollywood, thus undercutting Annie's pride in all the awards for which her new boyfriend has been nominated. Alvy then gets into his car and begins smashing into the other cars in the parking lot, ending up in jail. In Alvy's play-within-the-film the scene is quite different. In contrast to Alvy in "real" life, the actor playing Alvy is in total control of his emotions. He says, philosophically (if a bit flatly):

Figure 63. The mirrored mise-en-scène underlines Allen's postmodern skepticism about the capacity of art or language to reveal an essential reality. (*Annie Hall*, 1977, Metro-Goldwyn-Mayer Studios.)

"You know, it's funny, after all the serious talks and passionate moments that it ends here . . . in a health-food restaurant on Sunset Boulevard. Goodbye, Sunny." At this point Sunny/Annie does not drive away, but cries, "Wait. I'm—I'm gonna . . . go with you. I love you." "Tsch, whatta you want? It was my first play," Alvy says in another direct address to the film audience, apologizing for the forced and implausible happy ending. Unable to make things turn out well for himself in life, Alvy does so in art.

At one point in this scene, Allen does not photograph the actors reading his play directly, but instead shows us only their reflections in a large mirror with Alvy listening to them in the foreground in front of the mirror. (See figure 63.) Here the mirrored mise-en-scène underlines Allen's postmodern skepticism about art's, or language's, capacity to reveal an essential reality. Everything is a reflection of a reflection. The actors are only fragments in the mirror of Alvy's mind, just as the characters in *Annie Hall* are only fragments in the mirror of Allen's mind, in an infinite regression. In *Annie Hall*, we are repeatedly reminded that nothing is real.

At the same time, Alvy's happy ending to his play is carefully constructed by Allen to be a foil to the much more "realistic" or plausible
ending of the film *Annie Hall*. While the scene in which "Sunny" declares her love for the Alvy stand-in may give an audience a momentary
jolt of happiness, because we are conditioned to want couples who have
separated to get back together, everything we have learned about Alvy
in the film suggests that his relationship with Annie is impossible. After
all, he defines himself in the film's present as being someone who would
never join a club that would accept him as a member. If he did get Annie back, we can infer, he would quickly lose interest in her again. If
they married and moved in together, she would be as suffocating to him
as he would be to her. Woody Allen also broached the theme of recip-
rocated love bringing not fulfillment but suffocation in a darkly comic
way in *Love and Death*. Boris pursues the rejecting Sonia throughout
the film, but when he is finally rewarded with her love, instead of being
jubilantly happy, he tries to hang himself. Whether Allen is suggesting
that Alvy is too neurotic to love, and all the psychoanalysis in the world
cannot help, or whether he is positing a malignant mechanism in the human psyche that dooms even the best relationships to failure, is hard to
determine. The answer seems to be both. Yet we do not feel utterly dismal at the end of *Annie Hall* because Allen gives us the possibility of finding a kind of salvation, not in life, but in art. The pleasure of watching a
brilliantly executed film about an inevitable breakup somehow mitigates
the sadness of the ending in the same way that De Sica's technique in
telling his story makes the loss of the bicycle bearable at the end of *The
Bicycle Thief*.

While Alvy's happy ending for his play is facile and implausible,
Allen's *Annie Hall* ends, if not happily, at least artfully. As Alvy begins
to relate how after their breakup he and Annie did meet again, the voice
of Annie singing "Seems Like Old Times" is softly heard on the sound
track. Alvy relates that Annie has moved back to New York and has taken
her new boyfriend to see *The Sorrow and the Pity*, the film that Alvy was
always dragging her to see because of the importance and seriousness of
its message. He calls this "a personal triumph," presumably because it
suggests that Alvy is still alive in her mind: she has internalized his values. She has also left the shallow viciousness of Los Angeles to return
to New York, another indication that Alvy's values have affected her
life choices.

In keeping with the postmodern attitudes of skepticism and irony, *Annie Hall*, like so many of Allen's films, is less about love than about its

loss or impossibility. But since this is a Woody Allen film whose main character is a stand-up comedian, *Annie Hall* does end with a joke. In the film's final monologue, Alvy relates the story of a man who goes to a psychiatrist complaining about his crazy brother who thinks he is a chicken. When the doctor asks, "Why don't you turn him in?" the man answers, "I would, but I need the eggs." Alvy compares the illusory eggs to the illusory hope people hold out that despite the irrational, crazy, absurd nature of relationships, maybe the next one will actually work out. Without that illusion, life would be too sad and lonely to endure. The implication is that all of us are like the man in the joke, who is clearly as crazy as his brother. We all need the eggs—the fictions or illusions which make life bearable. The bad news at the end of *Annie Hall* is that all we have to go on are illusions. Only in fictions (Alvy's play) do relationships end happily ever after. The good news is that life itself can be thought of as a work of art. Memories, the only traces left of lived experience, can be rearranged, rethought, and reinterpreted in the montage of our minds, as Allen/Alvy demonstrates brilliantly and entertainingly throughout *Annie Hall*. If the postmodern philosophers are right, and our lives are merely a compendium of fragmentary multiple fictions, Woody Allen's art seems to tell us that at least we are free to rearrange the parts until we come up with a better picture.

11

Political Cinema

Spike Lee's *Do the Right Thing*

WAKE-UP CALL

Spike Lee's 1989 film *Do the Right Thing* seems a contradiction in terms: an entertaining Hollywood film with a disturbing political message. Intended by Lee as a wake-up call to America (the film's narrative begins with Señor Love Daddy [Samuel Jackson], a radio DJ, urging his listeners to "Waaaake up"), the film implies that underneath a thin surface of affability between blacks and whites in America lurks a mutual hatred, resentment, and distrust that makes outbreaks of violence between them inevitable. The film's action takes place on the hottest day of summer in the Brooklyn neighborhood Bedford-Stuyvesant, the heat serving as a catalyst to bring simmering racial tensions to a roiling boil. The film culminates in a violent race riot in which African Americans loot and burn Sal's Famous Pizzeria, the only white-run business on the predominantly African-American block. The riot is set off by the death of Radio Raheem (Bill Nunn), a young African-American man who dies when a white policeman uses unnecessary force (a fatal choke hold) to restrain him from an attack on Sal (Danny Aiello), the owner of the pizzeria. Radio Raheem attacks Sal in retaliation for Sal's having demolished Radio Raheem's boom box with a baseball bat. After Radio Raheem dies, voices in the crowd call out the names of Michael Stewart and Eleanor Bumpers, evoking the memory of two 1988 real-life instances in which black people died because of the use of unnecessary force by the police.[1]

By setting *Do the Right Thing* in a white-owned Italian pizzeria and having Sal attack Radio Raheem's boom box with a baseball bat, Spike Lee also alludes to the Howard Beach incident in Queens, New York, which occurred when three black men whose car had broken down in an all-white Italian neighborhood stopped at a pizza parlor to eat and make a phone call. When they left they were chased by a gang of white youths carrying baseball bats who screamed racial insults at them and ordered them out of the neighborhood. One of the black men escaped, one was caught and beaten, and the third, Michael Griffith, a West Indian immigrant, panicked and ran out into an expressway. He was hit by a car and killed. None of the white youths was convicted of causing Griffith's death because the defense depicted the black men as troublemakers with police records, making the incident seem like a street fight rather than a hate crime.

As Spike Lee has stated in an interview, the deaths of Michael Stewart and Eleanor Bumpers at the hands of the white police and the failure of the courts to punish those who had caused the death of Michael Griffith in the Howard Beach incident epitomize the racist oppression under which blacks live in America. "There's a complete loss of faith in the judicial system," he comments, "And so when you're frustrated and there's no other outlet, it'll make you want to hurl [a] garbage can through a window."[2] These considerations motivated him to make a political film about a race riot, told from an African-American perspective, that would raise consciousness about racism in America and pose the question of how black people should respond to racial inequality and physical oppression. Is violent retaliation the way? At the end of the film, Lee juxtaposes two statements, one by Martin Luther King and one by Malcolm X. King writes that "Violence as a way of achieving racial justice is both impractical and immoral." Malcolm X states: "I am not against using violence in self-defense. I call it intelligence." Lee gives Malcolm X the last word.

Interestingly, in this regard, the destruction of Sal's Famous Pizzeria at the end of *Do the Right Thing* does not occur as a spontaneous outpouring of wrath by the crowd. It is deliberately instigated by Mookie, who works for Sal and is the character Spike Lee plays in the film. After witnessing Radio Raheem's death at the hands of the police, the crowd is angry but not violent. Then Mookie, who has been standing by the side of Sal and his two sons, abruptly changes sides. He walks across the street, picks up a garbage can, empties its contents onto the street, walks back across the street to Sal's Famous Pizzeria and hurls the garbage can through the front window. This action arouses the onlookers from their stunned quiescence. Following Mookie's lead, they loot, trash, and set the pizza parlor on fire. In the published script of the film, Lee writes "Mookie hurls the garbage can through the plate glass window of Sal's Famous Pizzeria. That's it. All hell breaks loose. The dam has been unplugged, broke. The rage of a people has been unleashed, a fury. A lone garbage can thrown through the air has released a tidal wave of frustration."[3]

The film generated enormous controversy when it was released. Some reviewers felt the film was an incendiary call for a black uprising and predicted race riots (which never happened) following the film's release in the summer of 1989. One reviewer quipped, "Let's hope it doesn't open in a theater near you." The majority of reviewers, however, admired the cinematic brilliance and originality of the film, and praised Spike Lee's sympathetic, humorous, even-handed portrayal of its black, white, and Korean characters. But many of even the most admiring critics had problems understanding why Spike Lee had Mookie, the character he plays, set off the race riot. Was Spike Lee implying that Mookie did the right thing? Was Spike Lee advocating violence?

According to Lee, only white viewers of the film had to ask. The African-American viewers he spoke to were never in doubt.[4] In numerous interviews and commentaries on his film, Spike Lee clearly states that he intended viewers to understand that Mookie did the right thing in starting the riot in order to express outrage at Radio Raheem's death at the hands of the white police. As he writes in a final word at the end of the companion volume to *Do the Right Thing*, "Am I advocating violence? No, but goddamn, the days of twenty five million Blacks being silent while our fellow brothers and sisters are exploited, oppressed, and murdered, have to come to an end. Racial persecution, not only in the United States, but all over the world, is not gonna go away; it seems it's getting worse (four years of [George Herbert Walker] Bush won't help). . . . Yep, we have a choice, Malcolm or King. I know who I'm down with."[5]

While Spike Lee clearly agrees with Malcolm X that violence in self-defense is a justified form of protest, and intends audiences to feel that Mookie did the right thing in sparking the attack against Sal's Pizzeria, Spike Lee did not make *Do the Right Thing* as a strident racial agitprop film that celebrates violence. The production designer Wynn Thomas remarks on the special care he took in making Sal's Famous Pizzeria a cut above the way actual pizza parlors in poor neighborhoods look, in order to create an environment people would like on an unconscious level, and hence would regret seeing destroyed.[6] The power of *Do the Right Thing* and its effectiveness as political cinema lies not in its making an airtight case that Mookie did the right thing, but in its success in opening up a dialogue between the positions of Martin Luther King and Malcolm X. A photograph of Martin Luther King and Malcolm X smiling and shaking hands that reappears throughout the film and is its final image works powerfully on our imaginations, preparing us to read the written statements of the two men which appear at the end of the film in the spirit of "both/and" as opposed to "either/or." *Do the Right Thing* is best understood as a vehicle not for solving the dilemma that Malcolm X and Martin Luther King's opposing views create, but for making us contemplate two opposing views together, and thereby forcing our minds into new pathways of understanding.

DIALECTICAL FORM

The film is structured throughout as a constant play of opposite modalities clashing against one another. In *Do the Right Thing*, Spike Lee returns to the dialectical methods of Sergei Eisenstein in the 1920s, who, inspired by the writings of Hegel and Marx, created a cinema that involves a constant juxtaposition or clash of opposites (a thesis and an antithesis), the goal being the creation of a new synthesis or higher consciousness in the mind of the viewer. Spike Lee's method was the same as Eisenstein's, to confront the viewer with a constant stream of conflicting images and viewpoints. For Lee, the goal was to liberate his audience from fixed stereotypical images of the conflict between black and white Americans and to open their minds to a more subtle awareness of racism in American society and the danger that racism poses to us all.

Spike Lee begins *Do the Right Thing* with a shock. What we think (because of all the film's advance publicity) is going to be a tense urban racial drama that explodes in violence begins with what looks like a number from a film musical. Rosie Perez performs a dance (under the film's credits) to the pounding rhythms of Public Enemy's rap song "Fight the Power." Rosie Perez plays the role of Tina, Mookie's girlfriend, in the film, but here she functions not as a character in the narrative but as a pure symbol of the creative and destructive energy of black youth.

The surprising opening number is structured by conflicts on multiple levels. On the most obvious level, the sound track clashes with the image. Angry male voices urging violence in response to racism ("Got to give us what we want! Got to give us what we need!/ Our freedom of speech is freedom of death/ We got to fight the powers that be") are counterpointed by the image of a petite female performing a dance. Yet the dance itself contains its own clash of opposites because it is choreographed as a combination of an aerobic workout session and a fight. The choreography includes multiple shots of Perez punching her fists directly at the audience, at times wearing boxing gloves. Sometimes she looks angry, sometimes she looks sexy, as her pugilistic stances segue into erotic movements. Here, through another clash of opposites, Lee fuses sensual entertainment and political threat. The LOVE and HATE featured so prominently on Radio Raheem's brass knuckles later in the film are symbolically prefigured by Perez's erotic yet angry expressions and dance movements.

Lee cuts this sequence in a way that recalls Eisenstein's use of montage (discussed in chapter 2) to create optical shocks. Eisenstein created these shocks by creating as much contrast as possible between each juxtaposed shot, both in content and on a purely formal level. Shots of Rosie Perez dancing in long shot are abruptly cut together with extreme close-ups of her face or parts of her body. Smooth matches on Perez's movements join together shots in which both her costume and the background against which she is dancing abruptly change. We first see her, for example, in an orange minidress dancing in front of urban brownstone residences but this shot is smoothly connected (by a position-and-movement match) to a shot of her in a blue spandex workout suit, now dancing in front of a deteriorating graffiti-marked building. Shortly thereafter she appears in front of a shop window, now wearing a black-and-white boxing outfit that contrasts with a pair of bright orange boxing gloves. At another moment near the end of the number, an image of Rosie Perez in profile shadowboxing on screen right jump cuts to an image of her performing the same movement on screen left. The abrupt juxtaposition creates a shock, because she seems to be fighting against herself. (This cut prefigures Lee's preoccupation in the film, not only with tensions between members of different races, but also tensions between members of the same race as well as tensions within individuals who are at war with themselves.)

Conflicts are also created through the use of color filters. A red filter occasionally transforms the black-and-white background image before which Rosie Perez is dancing[7] into a sinister image connoting heat and blood. The use of warm red filters to illuminate the background in one shot contrasts with cool blue filters in the subsequent shot. Sometimes Lee mixes reds and blues, creating a conflict of colors (hot and cold tones) within the same shot, a technique similar to Eisenstein's intraframe optical conflict. The formal contrasts of this opening number (long shots with close-ups, movement matches smoothly connecting discontinuous spaces, jump cuts, and color contrasts that create optical jolts) in conjunction with contrasts relating to the content of the images (male voices/female body, dancing/fighting, sex/aggression) creates a visually compelling, fun-to-watch spectacle which at the same time prepares us mentally for a film structured by a clash of opposites that will move its audiences beyond ossified ways of thinking about racial relations in America.[8]

The systematic clash of opposites that informs the filmic treatment of Rosie Perez's dance also informs the mise-en-scène of *Do the Right Thing*. The film was shot on location in Bedford-Stuyvesant, thus grounding it in the physical materiality of the black ghetto. The film's cinematographer, Ernest Dickerson, felt something vital would be missing from the look of the film if they shot the film on constructed sets on a Hollywood back lot. "You wouldn't get those same molecules at a studio"[9] he comments. Yet, despite the location shooting, the look of *Do the Right Thing* has nothing of the gritty realism of a film such as De Sica's *The Bicycle Thief*. This is because the atmosphere of authenticity gained by shooting on location is dialectically countered by the distinctly nonrealistic theatricality and stylization of the film's art design. The facades of many of the buildings on the block on which the film was shot were freshly painted, a huge, colorful "Bedford Stuy Do or Die" mural was added, and the garbage-strewn streets were cleaned up. The drab browns and tans of the urban-desert cityscape were punctuated by bursts of vivid colors, the most striking example being the fire-engine red building before which the three corner men spend most of the day loafing and commenting on life. According to cinematographer Ernest Dickerson, the major motivation for the predominance of warm or even hot colors in the set design (reds, oranges, and yellows) was to imbue the film, whose action takes place on the hottest day of the summer, with a felt sense of heat. But aside from the effect of heating up the atmosphere, the bright colors of the neighborhood take on a metaphorical meaning, connoting life, vitality, and emotional, as opposed to merely physical, warmth. The setting, moreover, is bathed in the glow of old-fashioned carbon-arc lighting, giving the film the look of an MGM Hollywood musical.

Lee was criticized for choosing to shoot in a black ghetto but then prettying it up. In news conferences[10] and interviews he is frequently asked: Where was all the garbage that typically litters the streets? Where were the prostitutes? The drug dealers? The rapists? The guns? Lee justifies his aesthetic choices by claiming that there are enough films already that show black people only in the context of garbage, drugs, sex, and violence and he consciously chose not to add to this store of stereotypes. In an interview he states: "I made that choice because any time you hear people say Bed-Stuy, right away they think of the rapes, murders, drugs. There's no need to show garbage piled high and all that other stuff, because not every single block in Bedford-Stuy is like that. . . . These are hard working people, and they take pride in their stuff just like everybody else."[11]

By deliberately creating an atmosphere that contests stereotypes of the way people live in the black ghetto, Spike Lee is not trying to put one over on his audience by creating false "positive images" of ghetto life. Rather, by creating a mise-en-scène that patently clashes with preconceived ideas, he encourages viewers to confront their stereotypical expectations. I am reminded of Robert Stam's analysis of a moment in Mel Brooks's comedy *Blazing Saddles,* when a group of redneck cowboys start singing "Ole Man River," after which a group of black railroad workers suavely sing "I get no kick from champagne." Like Lee, Brooks was less interested in constructing positive images of sophisticated black workers than in "challenging the stereotypical expectations an audience may bring to a film."[12] Moreover, while the deliberate brightening-up of a dismal reality works to give most of the film a Hollywood escapist feel, it also makes the ending of the film all the more devastating when the candy-colored world erupts into violence and all that conspicuously absent garbage from the streets of Bedford-Stuyvesant reappears with a vengeance in the scenes after the riot.

DIALECTICAL CINEMATOGRAPHY

Spike Lee also creates conflicts in *Do the Right Thing* through self-consciously expressionistic cinematographic effects. These heighten the visual excitement of the action and add intensity to the slowly building plot tensions in a way that is reminiscent of, if not directly influenced by, techniques Eisenstein discussed nearly seventy years earlier in his essays on film form. Eisenstein wrote "Absolute realism is by no means the correct form of perception."[13] By this he means that the representation of objects realistically, according to the proportions proper to them, is not nearly as emotionally expressive as when the artist departs from reality. The greater the disparity or perceived conflict between the expected proportions and the artist's deviation from them, Eisenstein believed, the greater the emotional power of the work of art. Using the portraits of eighteenth-century Japanese artist Sharaku as an example, Eisenstein points out that the proportions are impossible: "The space between the eyes comprises a width that makes mock of all good sense. The nose is almost twice as long in relation to the eyes as any normal nose would dare to be, and the chin stands in no sort of relation to the mouth; the brows, the mouth, and every feature—is hopelessly misrelated." According to Eisenstein, Sharaku "repudiated normalcy" in his representations in order to better express the psychic essence of his subjects.[14]

Eisenstein even claims that the disproportionate depiction of an event is natural to us and has its roots in children's drawings. He points to an example of a drawing by a child of a stove being lit. The firewood, the stove, and the chimney are all represented fairly realistically, but in the center of the picture appear huge zigzag forms which turn out to be matches. "Taking into account the crucial importance of these matches for the depicted process," Eisenstein observes, "the child provides a proper scale for them." Eisenstein connects this process to cinematic form: "Is this not exactly what we of the cinema do temporally . . . when we cause a monstrous disproportion of the parts of a normally flowing event, and suddenly dismember the event into 'close-up of clutching hands' . . . 'extreme close-up of bulging eyes' . . . in making an eye twice as large as a man's full figure?"[15] In his essay "A Dialectical Approach to Film Form," Eisenstein lists additional ways a filmmaker can move beyond a realistic rendition of the world to add psychological expressiveness to the images depicted. Two of his methods are especially evident in the cinematography of *Do the Right Thing*: "Conflict between matter and viewpoint (achieved by spatial distortion through camera-angle)" and "Conflict between matter and its spatial nature (achieved by *optical distortion* by the lens)."[16]

Examples of expressive spatial distortions through the use of extreme camera angle abound in *Do the Right Thing*: numerous shots are taken from extreme high angles, low angles, and Dutch angles (when the cameraman tilts the camera so that the entire image looks askew or off-balance). Lee uses extreme high and low skewed angles for humorous effect when he photographs Da Mayor (Ossie Davis) from the point of view of Mother Sister (Ruby Dee). The camera looks down on him from on high, making him seem small in the frame, the visual expression of Mother Sister's disdain for the old drunk. Correspondingly, Mother Sister is photographed from an extreme low angle to give a heightened sense of her

Figure 64. To increase the sense of menace, Ernest Dickerson shot Radio Raheem's face in a big close-up with an extreme (10mm) wide-angle lens. (*Do the Right Thing,* 1989, Universal City Studios.)

power as a supreme superego figure whose esteem Da Mayor tries to win throughout the film. Later in the film when he gains her respect, the extreme angles on Da Mayor and Mother Sister cease.

The most extreme camera angles in the film are used in the cinematic treatment of Radio Raheem. He is usually shot from both an extreme low angle—making his huge body seem even larger and hence more overpowering and intimidating—and from extremely askew Dutch angles, visual forewarnings of the destabilizing role his presence will play in the film's denouement. Moreover, Lee achieves the effect Eisenstein calls "conflict between matter and its spatial nature (achieved by *optical distortion* by the lens)" when he shoots Radio Raheem's face in a big close-up using an extreme (10mm) wide-angle lens. The effect is to distort his facial features in a way that adds to a sense of his menace. (See figure 64.)

In two separate incidents Lee distorts time in a manner reminiscent of Eisenstein's prolonging the action on the Odessa Steps in *The Battleship Potemkin,* by repeating the same shots. When Mookie visits his girlfriend Tina (Rosie Perez) Lee overlaps the action of her opening her arms to embrace him so that she appears to embrace him twice. When Mookie throws the garbage can through the window of Sal's Pizzeria, the action also appears twice on the screen. First we see it from a perspective outside the shop, and then again from within. In both cases the overlapping editing gives heightened dramatic expressiveness and emphasis to these two important moments in his film. As Charles Musser observes: "Lee intertwines the styles of artifice and realism most forcefully in two privileged moments which twin all the principal oppositions around which the film is built . . . one attached to love, one attached to hate—one to the private world of family, one to the public world of work. It is at such moments that Lee's dialectics work most effectively."[17]

DIALECTICAL CONTENT

Thus far I have been focusing on Spike Lee's dialectics on the level of form. Just as striking are the constant clashes and contradictions he sets up on the level of content—clashes between characters and conflicts within individual characters—all of which bring the viewer to a heightened understanding of the racial tensions that explode into violence at the end of the film. The central clash of opposites in the film is between Mookie and Sal, which culminates in Mookie's instigation of the destruction of the pizzeria. Lee depicts the reasons for conflict between the two men with such nuanced complexity that Mookie's act of violence against Sal seems simultaneously justified and a betrayal of Sal.

Throughout the film there is an edgy tension between the two men (as there is between almost everyone in the film on this hottest day of the summer), but until the last moments of the film, Mookie acts as a keeper of the peace, a protector of Sal's Pizzeria, not an instigator of violence against it. Lee makes it clear that aside from Mookie's official job of delivering pizzas he functions as a go-between for Sal, smoothing over (or trying to smooth over) moments of racial tension that daily flare up between Sal and his customers. Mookie, for example, banishes his friend Buggin' Out (Giancarlo Esposito) from Sal's Pizzeria for one week after Buggin' Out enrages Sal by insisting that Sal include pictures of African Americans on his Wall of Fame, which Sal has devoted exclusively to pictures of Italian-American celebrities. Mookie is also protective toward Sal's sympathetic younger son Vito (Richard Edson), advising him on how to deal with his nasty older brother. As a result, when Mookie suddenly turns against his employers we sit up and take notice. If a chronic complainer like Buggin' Out had set off the violence, the act would not make nearly as strong an impression. It is the clash between who we expect to start the riot and who actually starts it that forces us to think.

This is not to say that Lee depicts Mookie's relation to his white employers as conflict-free. Lee, always dialectical, sets Vito's affability against the openly racist hostility of Pino, Vito's older brother. Pino (John

Turturro) calls Mookie a "nigger" and refers to his father's pizza parlor, with its mostly black customers, as the "Planet of the Apes." Pino warns Vito that no black man can be trusted: "The first time you turn your back, boom, a knife right here." Mookie, moreover, chafes against the drastic limitations of his position in Sal's Famous Pizzeria. He is stuck in a menial, minimum-wage, delivery-boy job with no future. He expresses his resentment by coming into work late and taking too much time delivering pizzas. He goes home to take a shower on his way back from a delivery and later, after delivering a pizza to his girlfriend and mother of his child, he has a leisurely early evening tryst with her. Mookie, moreover, refuses to do chores such as sweeping the floor for Sal even when he has nothing else to do, claiming he is just paid to deliver pizzas.

Sal's tolerance of Mookie's "attitude" combines with Danny Aiello's sympathetic portrayal to make Sal, for the most part, an appealing character. He obviously "gets" the reasons behind Mookie's disaffected laziness and is willing to ignore his lapses. Sal, in fact, is far more tolerant of Mookie's questionable work ethic than Mookie's own sister, who berates him for his "patented two-hour lunches" and insists, "Sal pays you, you should work." In contrast to Pino, who openly attacks Mookie's behavior, Sal seems genuinely affectionate toward Mookie, an affection which makes us feel that the attack on Sal's Pizzeria at the end of the film causes Mookie inner conflict. Moments before he makes his decision to act, we see him holding his head in pain.

But while Lee depicts Sal's affection for and sympathetic treatment of Mookie, he also portrays him as exploitative and latently racist. Not only does Sal pay Mookie low wages, he never acknowledges the important role Mookie plays as a mediator between Sal and the African-American customers he relies upon in order to make a living. (In this light, Mookie's instigation of the violence against the pizzeria can also be read as Mookie's sending Sal a message: if it were not for me this would have happened a long time ago.) Lee depicts Sal's affection toward his black clientele when Sal says that he is proud to have nurtured a generation of black children with his pizza. But almost in the same breath he refers to his customers as "dese people," hence as racial others. Sal's underlying racism explodes into the open when he screams racial epithets at Radio Raheem for playing his music in his restaurant (he calls it "jungle music") and then goes on to destroy the boom box, an action that can be read as a symbolic murder. Prophetically, one of Sal's early lines in *Do the Right Thing* is "I'm gonna kill somebody today." Nevertheless, for all his shortcomings, Lee's depiction of Sal is a far cry from the one-sided villains of propagandistic political melodrama. Sal is constructed with a mixture of conflicting traits. He is affectionate and exploitative, tolerant and racist, a nurturer and a (symbolic) murderer.[18]

The issue that indirectly triggers the race riot at the end of *Do the Right Thing* is Sal's refusal to bow to a demand by the political activist Buggin' Out that he put up pictures of African Americans on his Wall of Fame. But Sal's refusal to give in (which unleashes the violence) is not presented by Lee as an egregious example of Sal's racist intolerance, nor does he treat Buggin' Out's request as necessarily justified. They both have their reasons for their stances and both are, to some extent, valid. Sal tells Buggin' Out that if he wants "brothers up on the Wall of Fame, you open up your own business, then you can do what you wanna do. My pizzeria— Italian Americans up on the wall." Through the conversation of the "Corner Men," the three men who sit around all day drinking beer and discussing life, Lee criticizes African Americans for not starting businesses in their own neighborhoods. One of them deplores the fact that a Korean man and woman who have been in the country for less than a year have started their own business (a fruit and vegetable store) in the neighborhood in a building that had previously been boarded up. "Either dem Koreans are geniuses," he comments, "or we Blacks are dumb."

Yet Lee has Buggin' Out counter Sal's argument with a good argument of his own. "You own this," he acknowledges, "but rarely do I see any *Italian* Americans eating in here. All I've ever seen is black folks. So since we spend *much* money here, we do have some say." As in so much of *Do the Right Thing*, there is not a right or a wrong position, just two conflicting ways of seeing an issue. Sal as owner of the pizzeria has the right to decorate it as he pleases. African Americans who spend money in Sal's restaurant have a right to demand the respect of representation.

By placing the two stances side by side, Lee opens up a dialogue between them and makes us think more deeply about the issues involved. The fact that Sal is so irritated at Buggin' Out for demanding that Sal put "brothers on the wall," to the point that he threateningly takes out his baseball bat (his sons restrain him), suggests that the demand has struck a nerve. Why, we wonder, does this request make him so angry? Why couldn't he oblige his customers by hanging pictures of African-American celebrities alongside Italian Americans on his Wall of Fame? Sal's refusal to include African Americans on his wall perhaps reflects his need to maintain the boundaries of his white identity, almost as if mixing whites and blacks on his wall would be for him a form of symbolic miscegenation. Pino, the openly racist son, admits to feeling humiliated in front of his friends because he works all day among black people, as if something bad might rub off on him. Sal's adamant refusal to accede to Buggin' Out's request hints that Pino's father may well have his boundary issues too.

But Lee puts Buggin' Out's demands under scrutiny as well. We are also made to wonder why it is so important to Buggin' Out that Sal does not have pictures of African Americans on his wall. Most of the people in the neighborhood do not seem to mind and no one except for Radio Raheem and Smiley takes Buggin' Out's proposed boycott of Sal's seriously. In fact, the most sympathetic characters in the film strenuously oppose it. When Buggin' Out tries to enlist Mookie's sister Jade in his campaign to boycott Sal's, for example, she chides him by saying "You can really direct your energies in a more useful way." Jade's comment suggests that Buggin' Out is an injustice collector, a man who homes in on small slights (he also overreacts when a white man accidentally steps on his new white Air Jordans) rather than working for causes in the community in which he can effect real changes.

Although Buggin' Out's demand is not treated as a serious issue worth fighting for by most of the characters in the film, it nevertheless triggers the violence that occurs at the end. Buggin' Out, who has earlier in the day been banished from the pizzeria, returns to renew his demands, now backed up by the intimidating physical strength of Radio Raheem and the moral support of Smiley (Roger Smith), a man with a severe speech impediment who peddles a photograph of Martin Luther King and Malcolm X standing together in friendship and accord. The combination of the late hour (it is the end of a very long day), the intense heat which has not let up, even at night, and Sal's being confronted simultaneously by Buggin' Out's demand and Radio Raheem's blaring music creates a kind of critical mass. Sal explodes in anger. When Buggin' Out keeps repeating his demands and Radio Raheem refuses to turn off his radio, Sal reaches for his bat and before anyone can stop him "kills" the radio, after which Radio Raheem tries to kill him in turn. The white police then come and kill Radio Raheem and Mookie instigates the race riot, which, as Spike Lee has stated, he intends audiences to interpret as a fully justified protest against Radio Raheem's death at the hands of the white police.

SPIKE LEE'S REFUSAL OF MELODRAMA

D. W. Griffith's *The Birth of a Nation*, like *Do the Right Thing*, was also a political film which intended to justify the use of violence. Griffith sought to justify the Ku Klux Klan's violence against blacks who came to power during the post–Civil War Reconstruction period. The rioting black soldiers whom the Klan rides in to subdue are melodramatically presented as purely evil in their single-minded determination to sexually possess white women. The Klansmen who demolish the power of the blacks are characterized as noble and purely good, the saviors of many damsels in distress. When the Klan triumphs, there is a clear-cut victory of good over evil within the racist terms set up by the film's narrative. In 1915, white audiences stood up and cheered at the film's climax. In Spike Lee's *Do the Right Thing,* when the people of Bedford-Stuyvesant rise up to fight the power by destroying Sal's Pizzeria, much more complicated emotions are aroused because of Lee's refusal to divide his characters up into the categories of good and evil. Thus Sal, the "villain" of the piece, as we have seen, is depicted as both racist and tolerant, while Radio Raheem, the film's victim and martyr, is depicted as an intimidating, intrusive, even scary bully.

Lee depicts Radio Raheem as a threatening, even terrifying figure. He intimidates a group of Puerto Ricans who are obliged to turn off their salsa music in deference to his superior strength (and the superior volume on his boom box), frightens the Korean store owner, and in general seems to irritate everyone in the film (including Buggin' Out) by his unrelenting repetition of the song "Fight the Power," played at a nerve-jangling high volume on his boom box. As I mentioned above, his threatening actions are made to seem even more sinister through the extreme camera angles and distorted lenses through which he often appears. By means of subtle editing techniques, Lee makes Radio Raheem's appearances in the film seem sudden and unexpected. The best instance of this is when he appears at Sal's with Buggin' Out just before his violent clash with Sal. We never see him walk in the door. Suddenly he is just there, standing in the middle of the room like an apparition in a nightmare. His brass knuckles, which spell out the words LOVE and HATE, are scarily reminiscent of the psychotic minister played by Robert Mitchum in *The Night of the Hunter* (Charles Laughton, 1955) who similarly displays the words "love" and "hate" on the knuckles of his right and left hands.

Spike Lee's choice of Radio Raheem as the victim whose death sets off violence against Sal's Pizzeria is another instance of the dialectical logic which structures so much of the film. If the victim had been someone depicted more sympathetically, the reaction of the audience (to Mookie's setting off the riot in response) would have been automatically more sympathetic as well. It is easy to get audiences to react in outrage when a sympathetic character is killed, as D. W. Griffith knew well when

Figure 65. The image of Radio Raheem's feet off the ground is doubly disturbing because of its connotations of a lynching. (*Do the Right Thing*, 1989, Universal City Studios.)

he had the renegade ex-slave Gus cause the death of the darling of *The Birth of a Nation*, Flora, the little pet sister. By making a scary bully also a victim, Spike Lee makes us ponder the implications of Radio Raheem's death. Why, in the logic of the film, did he have to die? Why did Mookie have to protest his death by attacking Sal's?

Radio Raheem becomes the victim of the white police, Lee implies, not in spite but because of his intimidating strength. The white powers that be in this country, Lee suggests, are so frightened of the specter of the black man fighting back that they use unnecessary force on any black person who might do so successfully. The message repetitiously intoned on Radio Raheem's boom box, after all, is "Fight the Power," which is also the theme song and underlying message of *Do the Right Thing*. A motif that runs through the film is that unless people, no matter what their race, fight back against harmful power, they will be annihilated. Thus Mookie throughout the film tries to convince Vito to stand up to his abusive brother. In the scene in which Radio Raheem buys batteries at the store owned by the Korean couple, his abusive behavior to the store owner halts abruptly when the man starts screaming back, using the same expletives as Radio Raheem was shouting at him. Surprised, Radio Raheem breaks out laughing. But when Radio Raheem fights back against white power, he is killed.

Spike Lee has deliberately made the victim of the white police resemble the black bogeyman white people fear they will meet on a dark street: Radio Raheem is a white stereotype of a black thug. Lee may even be daring members of the audience to feel secretly relieved that Radio Raheem is killed. At the same time, he clearly presents Radio Raheem's death as the result of the white policeman's rage against and fear of the strong black man. The powerful close-up of Radio Raheem's feet dangling several inches off the ground as he is being strangled to death is an unforgettable metaphor for the helplessness and vulnerability of even the most powerful black man in the face of institutionalized white power. The image is doubly disturbing because it resembles a lynching.[19] (See figure 65.) Through the dialectical strategy of making the bully the victim Lee may have relinquished his ability to tap the stock responses of outrage common in political melodramas, but the end result is that he allows his audience to grapple with the meaning of Mookie's response to Radio Raheem's death on a higher level of consciousness. Though not all critics agree that Spike Lee has made a convincing case that Mookie did the right thing, much ink has been spilled in discussing the issues the film raises. Richard Sklar said of Spike Lee's film: "In the twenty-first century, the Hollywood film from 1989 most likely to be screened, discussed, argued over, is *Do the Right Thing.*"[20] So far, he is right.

12

Feminism and Film Form
Patricia Rozema's *I've Heard the Mermaids Singing*

All of the films I have considered thus far have been made by male directors. What difference might it make—in a film's style, content, or representation of women—when a woman directs? To consider this question, I turn to an exceptional film written and directed by a woman, the Canadian director Patricia Rozema's *I've Heard the Mermaids Singing*. The film, made on a tiny budget, had limited distribution by Miramax and is rarely seen now outside of college film courses, but it was the surprise hit at the Cannes Film Festival in 1987, and winner of the Prix de Jeunesse for the best first feature film that year. The film was subsequently voted one of the ten best Canadian films ever made by one hundred international critics, filmmakers, and scholars.[1] Rozema's offbeat, innovative style and the psychological themes she explores in her film reflect a keen consciousness of the issues raised by feminist critics regarding the way women have been represented in films directed by men.

FEMINIST FILM CRITICISM

Most feminist approaches to film share a common assumption: the ways women are represented in mainstream commercial films reflect, justify, reinforce, and naturalize what Molly Haskell in her pioneering book *From Reverence to Rape* calls "The Big Lie" of patriarchy, that women are inferior to men and rightly occupy a subordinate place in culture. Feminist film critics work to raise our consciousness about the negative images of women in film in order to denaturalize these images, to expose them as cultural constructs, not mirror reflections of the way women really are.

The first feminist film critics took a sociological approach to the subject, exemplified by two books that came out simultaneously in the early 1970s, Marjorie Rosen's *Popcorn Venus* (1973) and the above-mentioned *From Reverence to Rape* (1974), by Molly Haskell. Both Rosen and Haskell persuasively demonstrate that women on the screen are often nothing more than cultural stereotypes of women—the flapper, the vamp, the virgin, the Madonna, the femme fatale, the gold digger, the hooker with a heart of gold. Moreover, despite the fact that the rise of the Hollywood film industry coincided with the crest of the first wave of feminism in America, when more and more women were entering the labor force, attending college, earning doctorates, and entering the professions, most movies still ended in marriage, which was presented as the only real fulfillment of the heroine's heart's desire. Marjorie Rosen in *Popcorn Venus* asks, "Why did screen heroines covet 'winning the love of another' above all else? Why did they not value themselves? Their work? An independent future? Or dedication beyond that of their hearts?" Hollywood, she concludes, was determined to "squash feminine self determination."[2] The result was the depiction of deplorably bad role models for those women in the audience who aspired to more than the most conventional, male-centered definitions of what a woman is and what a woman wants.

The sociological approach greatly contributed to an awareness of how restricted images of women in film often were, but it was limited. Academic feminist critics, influenced by semiology, the study of how meaning is produced in communication systems such as language, literature, and film, suggested a more sophisticated and nuanced approach. For these critics, the argument that women are presented as negative stereotypes or poor role models in film does not go far enough toward explaining how Hollywood films reinforce the idea of women's inferiority. What really matters is not so much the type of woman the fictive character in the film represents, but what she comes to signify within the whole textual system of the film's narrative. Hollywood, for example, can easily, and often did, serve up a strong, ambitious career woman—the kind Katharine Hepburn is famous for playing and the kind of woman Rosalind Russell plays in *His Girl Friday*. Yet at the same time, the image of the strong woman is undercut by subtle and not so subtle narrative effects. As I argued in my analysis of *His Girl Friday* in chapter 4, Rosalind Russell's Hildy, for all her talent as a newspaper reporter, remains distinctly inferior to Walter Burns. He knows from the start what is best for her, and the film brings her around to his point of view. In the end, she depends on him to rescue her from an inappropriate marriage and to teach her what she really wants—to be a newspaper reporter and remarried to him. Thus despite the positive image of Hildy as an ace reporter, she remains *his* girl Friday.

An even better example of how a seemingly progressive Hollywood film has it both ways—presents a smart ambitious woman but ultimately contains and undercuts her—is George Cukor's *Adam's Rib* (1949). Here Katharine Hepburn plays Amanda, a feminist lawyer who successfully defends a woman on trial for shooting her husband point-blank when she catches him with another woman. Amanda wins the case by pleading that the woman is a victim of society's double standard. If a *man* had committed the same crime, that is, shot his unfaithful wife, she argues, society would sympathize with him and set him free. From a purely sociological perspective, *Adam's Rib* appears to be a subversive film.

So, what's wrong with this picture? If you look at the film from the perspective of how meaning or gender ideology is produced in the text, it is apparent that *Adam's Rib* is profoundly negative in its attitude toward its bright, ambitious heroine, proving that even if the heroine seems progressive, the movie need not be. Although Amanda convinces the jury and wins the case, the film's narrative is constructed in such a way that the spectator feels the jury is wrong. This point is not subtle. My son, who was seven years old when we watched the film together, said right after the jury's verdict was announced, "They made a mistake, didn't they, Mommy?"

The film's plot is constructed in such a way that we never doubt that Amanda is wrong-headed in her defense of the outraged wife. The first sequence of the film shows us the crime. We see an emotionally distraught, hysterical woman (Judy Holliday in her best dumb blond mode) stalking her husband and compulsively eating. When she catches him in his love nest with another woman, she shoots at him point-blank, failing to kill him only because of her incompetence. She doesn't know how to use the gun and she closes her eyes when she shoots. This account, which the film presents as the "real" event—it is presented not as a flashback through a character's point of view but from the perspective of an omniscient narrator—is distorted by Amanda's reconstruction of it during the trial. She coaches the defendant to tell the story in a way that makes it seem as if she was just trying to scare her husband, not kill him. Since the audience has seen the "truth," it is clear that Hepburn wins her case only by lying. Amanda also literally turns the courtroom into a circus when, in order to prove that women are equal to men (a point that has nothing substantive to do with the case), she instructs one of her witnesses, a female circus "strong man," to lift up her husband (Spencer Tracy), the prosecuting attorney in the case, who is made to look ridiculous as he dangles helplessly over the courtroom.

Hence, despite the characterization of the film's heroine as a smart, ambitious, successful lawyer, the deeply conservative ideological subtext of the film asserts that putting women in positions of power is dangerous to our legal system and society. It means chaos over order, lying over the truth, and the humiliation of men. Man-killers will be set loose on society. Like the title *His Girl Friday*, the very title *Adam's Rib* reflects a condescending attitude toward women. The title refers to Amanda, Adam's wife, reducing her to the body part the biblical Adam had to sacrifice for the sake of Eve's creation. In this light, Amanda can be read as a modern-day Eve moving onward and upward in her ruination of the male sex. From the way she humiliates (ribs) her husband and compulsively competes with him in a man's world, it is not too hard to guess what part of his anatomy she is after next.

CINEMA-SPECIFIC APPROACHES TO WOMEN IN FILM

Thus far we have been discussing the way meaning is constructed through narrative strategies that undermine or qualify seemingly progressive images of women in film. But, since this kind of analysis can apply not only to film but to literature and drama as well, academic feminist film critics went beyond considerations of the ways female characters appear within film plots to address the way women's inferior secondary position in culture was inscribed in the use of the film medium itself. Drawing upon and extending the theories of French psychoanalytic film theorist Christian Metz, feminist film theorists came up with even more subtle and sophisticated tools of analysis to demonstrate how film's unique means of representation and specific appeal help construct or naturalize denigrating ways of looking at women.

Christian Metz theorizes that the primal pleasure of cinema lies in its satisfaction of a primal urge—our *scopophilia*, or love of looking. In the live theater, Metz observes, we watch actors who are aware of and hence implicitly give consent to our presence. At the cinema, the actors on the screen are in a time and space radically elsewhere. Even when looking directly into the lens of the camera, the actors can never really return our gaze. Hence we can look at them to our heart's content, but they can never see us looking. At the root of cinema's appeal, Metz believes, is a license for a lawless looking, a guiltless, because safe, voyeurism.[3] The very first cinema spectators viewed moving pictures through Edison's Kinetoscope, a peephole device, which foregrounded the voyeuristic appeal of the images. As Alfred Hitchcock made evident in *Rear Window* (1954), the rectangle of the cinema screen is like a window on the world through which we often peer at the private lives of people with prurient fascination. At the cinema we are all peeping Toms.

The voyeuristic pleasure offered at the cinema, however, is distinctly inflected by gender. (Even my use of the term "peeping Tom" genders the peeper male.) The thrust of much feminist film criticism, influenced by Laura Mulvey's formative essay, "Visual Pleasure and Narrative Cinema," has been that most mainstream films assume a male spectator and play to male pleasure by visually objectifying and eroticizing the women on the screen.[4] Whatever happens to be the heroine's function in the plot, a necessary component of her appeal is usually sexual: her appearance pleases the man on the screen and the men in the audience who identify with the camera's eroticizing gaze. Often the narrative action is suspended as the woman on the screen becomes primarily an erotic object to be looked at.

In *Coma* (Michael Crichton, 1978), for example, the heroine (Genevieve Bujold) is a physician in a major hospital who lives with her fiancé, who is also a doctor. Soon after she conducts major surgery, we see her at home arguing with him over whose turn it is to get dinner. As the two quibble, the man is standing fully clothed at the bathroom door gazing at the woman, who is standing stark naked in the shower. (See figure 66.) Later in the film, as the heroine perilously searches the ventilation system of the hospital for clues that will expose a crime that led to her friend's death, she is obliged to remove her pantyhose to achieve a more secure footing, an action captured by a voyeuristic camera looking up from below. Feminist film critics argue that the apparatus of the cinema extends and intensifies an enduring tradition in Western art, a tradition which the art historian John Berger sums up in his famous dictum: "Men act and women appear."[5] These conventions of looking in

Figure 66. The man stands, fully clothed, gazing at the woman, who is stark naked in the shower. (*Coma,* 1978, Turner Entertainment.)

film, which give activity to male characters and passivity to female characters, are replicated on the level of a film's plot. Male characters are traditionally the heroes, the doers, the rescuers, or even the psychotic killers, whereas the women are traditionally the hero's reward, the rescuee, or the victim.[6]

In "Visual Pleasure and Narrative Cinema," Mulvey uses psychoanalysis as a political tool to investigate the psychic roots of why women are eroticized and disempowered in mass-media representation. At the root of the problem, she argues, is the male child's castration anxiety when he discovers that his mother lacks a penis. This, according to Freud, is a momentous discovery because it signals to the little boy that he could lose his too. The trauma of the boy's discovery of his mother's "lack," Freud believed, helps to catapult him out of his mother's sphere into an identification with his father (who has the valued penis) as well as into the cultural place of power and privilege which having the penis signifies in a patriarchal culture. But traces of castration anxiety forever remain in the boy's unconscious, making women ambivalent figures in the male psyche. They are objects of erotic desire but also of scorn and contempt (they lack something the boy has) and also fear and dread (they remind the boy of what he has to lose). Mulvey's main point is that for men, women signify castration, a disturbing idea which forever threatens to break through into consciousness and thereby interfere with their erotic pleasure.

In the medium of film, Mulvey goes on to argue, men have found a perfect system of representation which allows them both maximum erotic pleasure and the disavowal of their castration anxiety. In the large majority of mainstream films, Mulvey notes, the point of view or the gaze is predominantly filtered through the eyes of a male character. That is, we see the action through a male's eyes, and what he is looking at is often the figure of a sexy woman, as in the example of the woman in the shower observed by her fiancé in *Coma*. This eroticizing gaze, according to Mulvey, gives the male spectator who identifies with the male character on the screen a feeling of power, control, and heightened virility, counteracting male fear of women's lack. Women are also made nonthreatening in films through plots in which women are dominated, investigated, found guilty, and disempowered. The logic here is: "*She* is lacking, humiliated, guilty, weak—not me."

A final filmic strategy to counteract the threat of women's lack is to deny or disavow it by an extreme idealization of women on the screen. Only ravishingly beautiful women with perfect bodies and regular features become film stars, and these women are made even more perfect through an arsenal of special lenses and lighting techniques. The ultra-perfection of the female star, Mulvey theorizes, exists to disavow her imperfection, the lack of a penis, which makes her threatening to male viewers. In addition, costumes of female stars often include oversized hats, spike-heeled shoes, long black stockings or gloves, or flowing scarves, all of which, Mulvey suggests, are fetishistic phallic stand-ins, objects that symbolize the penis and reassure the male viewer that there is nothing about these women to fear and dread. The camera can play a role in disavowing the woman's lack by isolating parts of the woman's body in close-up shots, focusing on just her hands, her legs, her feet, or her breasts—all of which, like the fetish objects which adorn her body, stand in for the missing penis. The bodies of women on film tend to be seen in pieces, the camera focusing in on close-ups of body parts much more than it does in photographing the bodies of men, which are more likely to be seen in medium or full shots. The special (or specialized) treatment reserved for women in film demonstrates conclusively for Mulvey that films are cut to the measure of male desire.

Although it was criticized from a number of perspectives,[7] "Visual

Figure 67. Scantily clad chorus girls perform suggestive dances with giant bananas positioned at their crotches. (*The Gang's All Here,* 1943, Twentieth-Century Fox Films.)

Pleasure and Narrative Cinema" was enormously influential, because it made viewers acutely aware of the prevalence of the male gaze in the cinema and the ways in which women, much more than men, were fetishized on the screen. One only needs to look at "The Lady in the Tutti Frutti Hat" number from Busby Berkeley's musical *The Gang's All Here* (1943), in which scantily clad chorus girls perform suggestive dances with giant bananas positioned at their crotches, to know that Mulvey was onto *something.* (See figure 67.)

Mulvey's article remains important because at the end she raises the issue of how women filmmakers can create alternative conventions to liberate cinema from male-centered practices of representation. At the conclusion of "Visual Pleasure and Narrative Cinema," she recommends the overthrow of the whole system of voyeuristic pleasure as the basis of narrative film:

> There is no doubt that this [the disappearance of filmic devices that invite voyeuristic pleasure] destroys the satisfaction, pleasure and privilege of the "invisible guest," and highlights how film has depended on voyeuristic active/passive mechanisms. Women, whose image has continually been stolen and

used for this end, cannot view the decline of the traditional film form with anything much more than sentimental regret.[8]

Patricia Rozema's *I've Heard the Mermaids Singing* is an especially appropriate film to discuss in the context of Mulvey's call for a counter-cinema, because in a number of ways it does what Mulvey suggests. It subverts most male-centered conventions of female representation by refusing the voyeuristic pleasure of objectifying or fetishizing women and it also interferes with the male-active, female-passive dynamics of most mainstream films. At the same time, however, *Mermaids* is visually appealing, emotionally complex, and fun to watch, whether or not one is consciously aware of the conventions it is subverting.

I'VE HEARD THE MERMAIDS SINGING AS COUNTERCINEMA

The title *I've Heard the Mermaids Singing* is a quotation from T. S. Eliot's "The Love Song of J. Alfred Prufrock." In the poem, Prufrock is an alienated, painfully self-conscious ("Do I dare to eat a peach?"), middle-aged bachelor who senses beauty in the world but can never capture or create it. In the poem he laments, "I have heard the mermaids singing, each to each / I do not think that they will sing to me."[9] He is an outsider in the realms of love and art. Despite the gender, age, and class difference between Prufrock and Polly (Sheila McCarthy), the film's protagonist, Polly shares not only the first initial of Prufrock's name but his sad predicament. Still unmarried at age thirty-one, she refers to herself as a spinster. An orphan (her parents died when she was twenty-one), she supports herself by being a temporary part-time worker for a Person Friday agency, which places women in low-level positions, despite the politically correct update of the agency's name. Her real passion and pleasure in life, however, is photography. The walls of her small apartment are thick with her photos, images she has captured on film of things that she loves. Her problem is that she has no one other than herself with whom to share her rich internal world.

If this were a mainstream film, Polly's lack would most likely be filled by the narrative. She would find a man and the world would at last recognize her talent. Yet though Polly gains neither recognition nor a partner, the film has a genuinely feel-good ending, albeit not in the conventional Hollywood mode. Rozema was able to challenge mainstream film conventions because she was not aiming her film at a mass-market audience. In an interview she confides that "I hoped for the respect—very secretly and quietly—of Margarethe von Trotta, Wim Wenders, Woody Allen, or Bill Forsyth."[10]

PLOT SYNOPSIS

Polly's story, which is framed by a videotaped image of herself narrating her tale as if she were directly addressing the film audience, begins when her temporary agency sends her to assist Gabrielle St. Pères (Paule Baillargeon), the curator and owner of a small art gallery. Gabrielle is an attractive, wealthy, articulate, sophisticated older woman whom Polly greatly admires. Despite Polly's clerical inadequacies, the curator (the name by which Polly refers to Gabrielle throughout the film) enjoys Polly's presence and makes her position permanent. Polly's happiness is somewhat tempered by the return of Mary (Ann-Marie McDonald), a young artist and Gabrielle's ex-lover. But since Polly defines her love for the curator as platonic—"I just loved how she talked and wanted her to teach me everything"—she manages to coexist with Mary, still happy to have her job and to bask in the daily presence of her beloved mentor.

At her birthday party, the curator, having obviously had too much to drink, confides to Polly that she is depressed because she knows she will forever fail to achieve her greatest desire in life, which is to create one immortal and enduring painting. Recently, when she tried to sign up for an adult art course (the sort where housewives learn landscape painting), she was devastated when the instructor refused to admit her, deeming her work "simple minded." But when Polly sees the curator's work, she is dazzled by its beauty. "I didn't even have to pretend to like it," she tells us. When the curator falls into a drunken sleep, Polly takes one of her paintings home. Inspired by its beauty and feeling herself a kindred spirit (Polly too is insecure about the value of her work), she decides to send Gabrielle some of her photographs. "I kind of thought she just might like them," she says. To make the undertaking less risky, she mails the photographs to the gallery under a pseudonym.

While the curator is out sick, Polly, behind her back, displays her painting at the gallery. An art reviewer sees the painting and writes a rave review. The same day that the review appears in the newspaper, Polly's photographs arrive in the mail. After giving them a cursory glance, the curator dismisses them as "completely simple minded," and "the trite made flesh." When Polly asks if the photographs at least show potential, the curator replies that the photographer is going nowhere and "She just doesn't have it." Devastated, Polly burns her photographs and then, in a final act of self-loathing, pushes her beloved camera off a ledge. Later, she refuses solace from Mary who, happening upon one of Polly's photos (but not knowing its creator) questions the curator's harsh judgment.

Because of the curator's meteoric rise in the art world, she spends less and less time in the gallery and Polly is left desolate and alone. One night Polly gets drunk in the gallery in the presence of the curator's luminous work. Hearing Gabrielle enter the gallery with Mary, Polly hides behind a bench and overhears their conversation. It turns out that Mary, not the curator, is the real artist. The curator, afraid to show her own work even to her clerk, had shown Polly Mary's paintings, allowing her to surmise they were her own. When Polly exhibited them the next day under Gabrielle's name and they were enthusiastically received, Mary and Gabrielle decided to continue the deception. Mary despises the pretentiousness of the art world and has no desire to play the role of celebrated artist. "I paint, you talk," she says.

Gabrielle discovers Polly hiding and invites her to go along with the deception. But Polly's realization that Gabrielle is a fake at last enables her to unleash her long-pent-up rage at the curator's crushing dismissal of her beloved photographs. She flings a cup of scalding tea in the curator's face and, for the first time in a long while, feels wonderful. Then, she impulsively steals the gallery's surveillance camera and returns to her apartment. We understand in retrospect why Polly has been taping her confession into a video camera. She is trying to explain why she has to leave town ("before they send me to prison or sue me") to the person who will be making the arrangements to sell her furniture and rent out her apartment. "There it is," she says to the video camera, "That's what happened." The credits begin to roll.

However, to the surprise of those who have begun to leave the theater, the film is not yet over. The credits are intercut with the film's continuing action. There is a knock at the door and we see (from the point of view of the video camera) Mary and Gabrielle (with a bandaged face) enter Polly's apartment. Polly apologizes to the curator for hurting her. When Mary points out to Gabrielle that the photographs she so harshly dismissed were Polly's, the curator apologizes in turn. This sounds a little flat in the telling, but it marks a moment of powerful reconciliation. As the credits continue, Polly's voice-over says, "C'mon, I'll show you some more." In the final shot of the film, Polly opens a door which now magically leads out into a richly colored forest into which she invites Mary and Gabrielle. Before Polly joins them, she runs back inside, smiling triumphantly, and turns off the video camera. This signals the real end of the film.

EXPLORING WOMEN'S DESIRES

If we look at plot alone, the differences between *I've Heard the Mermaids Singing* and the films directed by the male directors discussed in this book are already manifest. *Mermaids* focuses on the concerns and desires of its female protagonist, while the protagonists of the previous films, from *The Birth of a Nation* to *Do the Right Thing,* focus on the concerns and desires of males.[11] At least five of the plots of the male-directed films I have considered involve the oedipal dynamic of two men vying for the love of a woman, reflecting the male child's rivalry with the father for the love of the mother. In the plot of *Mermaids* an oedipal triangle also exists, but all three of its members are women—Polly and Mary both love Gabrielle. What marks *Mermaids* as female-directed is not so much the fact that the plot is about women, but the depth with which it explores the dynamics of female psychology, specifically the inner worlds of women who compete with their sisters for the favors of their mothers, a theme rarely treated in mainstream cinema, but an important and resonant one for many female spectators.

The curator, an older woman whose job, as her name suggests, is caretaking, is like a mother with two daughters. She thinks one is beautiful, but the other is not. She thinks one is talented, and the other is not. Mary is the kind of daughter who fulfills the narcissistic needs of a depressed mother by allowing the mother to participate vicariously in her talent. The film makes this fantasy literal, as Gabrielle takes the credit for Mary's paintings. In this light, Gabrielle's excessive denigration of Polly's photographs can be understood as the loathing of the depressed mother for the daughter who reflects her self-doubt and vulnerability, rather than her grandiosity. Note that Gabrielle uses the same words in judging Polly's photos as the art instructor has used to dismiss *her* work, calling them "simple minded."

The film can also be read as a feminist fairy tale, a playful, slightly tongue-in-cheek reworking of the Cinderella story. Polly, like Cinderella, is an orphan who has to do all the drudge work at the gallery, unlike the favored "sister" Mary, whom Gabrielle thinks is too talented to work. But unlike Cinderella, Polly is neither beautiful nor even good at being a drudge. And no prince comes to her rescue. Rather Cinderella reconciles with the evil stepmother and stepsister and the three of them live happily ever after. Polly needs no prince to redeem her. The happy ending comes when she learns to value herself and discovers kindred spirits with whom to share her work. This is exactly the kind of film heroine Marjorie Rosen called for in her 1973 book *Popcorn Venus*.

Just as *8 1/2* presents the conflicts and confusions of a male artist from the inside out, *Mermaids* presents the conflicts, difficulties, and inhibitions of a female artist. From this perspective, *Mermaids* can be read as a meditation on the difficulty women have in gaining confidence in a world in which they are defined as defective. Polly is the cosmic opposite of Guido in *8 1/2*. He suffers from too much adulation while she suffers from too little. An ex-boss, Polly tells us, once called her "organizationally impaired." The curator echoes Polly's male boss's judgment of her as fundamentally lacking when she says that the creator of Polly's photographs "just doesn't have it." Part of Polly's problem, which is the same problem of all women in a male-privileged culture, is having internalized these harsh judgments of herself as defective or impaired.

The character in the film who most ostensibly has "it," of course, is the curator. According to Rozema, in her original conception of the script the curator was a male. She changed the gender, she explains, because "I found that I seemed to be making an anti-masculine-authority statement, and all I wanted was an anti-authority message."[12] But while Gabrielle is a woman, she appears to be psychologically male-identified in the sense that she is a woman who has made it in a man's world and internalized male values. She owns an art gallery, has plenty of money, and trades on her power and mastery of words. This becomes evident when she convinces a client that a trite painting hanging in her gallery is trendy and profound. She even has an attractive, younger, female lover.

Gabrielle is also male-identified in her adherence to absolute, universal standards of value. She wants to create a work of art that is "undeniably, universally good," aligning her with the absolutist values of patriarchal culture which itself is based on the idea of the phallus as a universal symbol of all that is powerful, complete, and good. This system, which empowers men and denigrates women, is upheld by the authoritarian patriarchal institutions of church and state. It is no coincidence that Gabrielle's gallery is named "The Church Gallery." As Rozema remarks, "I wanted to point out the parallel paths of organized art and organized religion, because neither can exist without the assumption of absolute authority and infallibility of the reigning leaders. When in fact, the history of religion as well as art is a study of trends, fashions, and cycles."[13] Gabrielle's belief in an absolute standard of value which defines her as deficient (she unquestioningly accepts the authority of the male teacher who calls her work "simple minded") emotionally devastates her. She passes on this sad legacy to Polly, whom she emotionally devastates in turn. The film's happy ending involves Polly's triumphant recovery from her acceptance of Gabrielle as an ultimate authority.

To Gabrielle's absolutist way of thinking, Rozema counterposes a relativistic philosophy. Polly voices this viewpoint in a fantasy sequence in which she imagines herself, poised and wise, lecturing to Gabrielle. Polly's lesson is that no one has direct communication with some ultimate truth or knowledge. Truth is relative, and ultimately subjective. There is no one right way. When Gabrielle asks Polly how her relativistic philosophy applies to relationships, Polly (whose name reflects her philosophy) draws on Freud's concept of *poly*morphous perversity, which holds that all children are born open to a range of sexual preferences. There is no one right way to be. It is only society that pushes us to conform to set ways of expressing our sexuality. Since social norms are not based on any universal truths, Polly believes, one should actively cultivate rather than repress polymorphous inclinations, which she believes are natural and not perverse.

As Polly is intoning her wisdom to an enthralled Gabrielle (reversing their usual roles), Rozema pulls back the camera to reveal that Polly is walking on water. But, despite the authority these words are given by likening Polly to Christ, Rozema immediately reminds us that Polly's truth, too, is relative and subjective. When Gabrielle wonders how Polly has suddenly become so wise and articulate, Polly answers, "It is, after all, *my* vision." Rozema's belief in the importance of relativity and subjectivity, that there is no one right way, is reflected in the witty way she represents Gabrielle's (though actually Mary's) paintings. They are seen as luminous blank screens, and thus ripe for the projection of subjective responses based not on one universal standard of merit but on individual values. Rozema's relativistic vision has profound feminist implications. By undermining the idea of phallocentric universal standards of truth, Rozema empowers women who no longer need to be defined as deficient, just different.

DEPARTURES FROM MAINSTREAM CINEMA STYLE

Rozema's relativism is built into the very infrastructure of her film. Beginning with the opening credit sequence, she undermines the mainstream film convention that aligns the spectator with an all-seeing camera eye (the eye of God) with access to an unmediated reality unfolding on the screen before us. The reality in *I've Heard the Mermaids Singing* is mediated from the very beginning. The opening credits of the film are intercut with video images of Polly narrating the film's story before a video camera that she herself has set up. The bad quality of the video image makes us acutely aware that we are watching an image, not reality, and foregrounds the fact that we are seeing the events through one person's eyes. Then, even the authority of the pseudodocumentary window-on-the-world "reality" of the video image is undercut by being placed in dialogue with the film's credits. Here Rozema broadcasts loud and clear that what we are seeing is a constructed fiction, made to seem like reality, not real life.

When Rozema cuts from the video image of Polly narrating to a visualization of the events of her story, the film becomes more conventional. The film stock is standard 35mm color film, the kind used to give an illusion of unmediated reality in most mainstream films, and, in fact, we do get drawn into the fiction in these portions of the film, identifying with Polly in all her painful predicaments. Yet Rozema keeps undermining this illusion by continually cutting to Polly's fantasy visions of impossible actions in which she is flying, climbing up the side of a huge skyscraper, or walking on water. These visions are photographed in black and white with a grainy film stock, calling attention to the film medium. The juxtaposition of three kinds of film stock in one film—videotape, 35mm color film, and grainy black-and-white film stock—renders every "reality" we witness in the film relative. Rozema manages to have it both ways. Much of the film is in the style of mainstream cinema with the viewer an "invisible guest" looking in. At the same time her juxtaposition of multiple film stocks (and the constant use of freeze-frames whenever Polly snaps a picture) makes us aware of the artifice of this seeming reality and hence aware of the fact that we are always seeing her (Rozema's) vision and not some ultimate truth.

Rozema departs most noticeably from the conventions of mainstream cinema in *I've Heard the Mermaids Singing* with her creation of a radically different kind of film heroine. Polly's very appearance goes counter to the way heroines look in mainstream films. A birdlike little person with flaming red hair that sticks up, she could never be mistaken for a star. Nor does the camera idealize her through the use of flattering lights and lenses. Just the opposite. The poor-quality video image in which she appears throughout much of the film is harsh and unflattering. Even the

Figure 68. Polly's appearance counters the way heroines look in mainstream films. (*I've Heard the Mermaids Singing,* 1987, Miramax Films.)

position of her head is awkwardly decentered in the frame. (See figure 68.) Nor is she given star visual treatment in the body of the film. Mostly she looks awkward and unattractive, especially in comparison with the more conventionally beautiful Gabrielle and Mary. By the end of the film, however, she becomes extremely appealing to look at. This is not because Rozema has begun to photograph her in a more flattering way, but simply because we have gotten to know and like her. Thus Rozema demonstrates that women need not be fetishized or idealized to be attractive, appealing film heroines.

Not only is Polly not idealized, she is not objectified in this film by appearing as the passive object of the camera's (male) gaze. As I noted earlier, when we first see Polly, she is setting up a camera to film herself. At least within the fiction of the film's narrative, she is in control of the visual apparatus, simultaneously the subject and object of the camera's look. The form of the surveillance camera in the gallery wittily mirrors this theme. The camera is placed inside a TV monitor where the head should be on a bust of a nude woman. (See figure 69.) Hence the nude body cancels out its objectification by itself becoming all-seeing. Nor in

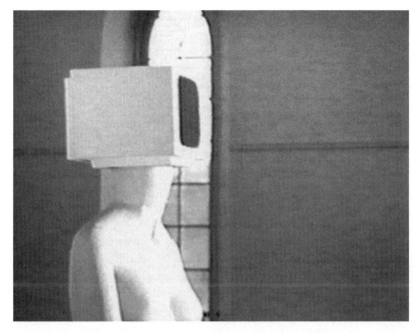

Figure 69. The camera is placed inside a TV monitor where the head should be on the bust of a nude woman. (*I've Heard the Mermaids Singing*, 1987, Miramax Films.)

Mermaids does the audience have the illusion that we are "uninvited guests" peering at someone who is unaware that we are watching them. Instead, Polly directly addresses her words to the camera and hence, it would appear, to the film audience. She knows we are out there. Occasionally she even addresses us directly.

RETHINKING CINEMATIC VOYEURISM

Perhaps the most innovative aspect of *I've Heard the Mermaids Singing* is the way it self-consciously plays with the concept of cinematic voyeurism. Mulvey, as you will recall, decreed in her conclusion to "Visual Pleasure and Narrative Cinema" that in order to be nonsexist, films must eliminate the pleasures of voyeurism. Rozema, it would appear, is too much of a relativist to sanction such extreme measures. Voyeurism abounds in Rozema's film, but it is a different brand of voyeurism than that found in mainstream cinema. A major difference, of course, is that in *I've Heard the Mermaids Singing* the voyeur is a woman—not a peeping Tom but a peeping Polly. In scene after scene Polly engages in illicit looking, sometimes combined with illicit listening. She secretly watches the curator and Mary kiss when she turns on the surveillance camera in the Church Gallery. She snaps pictures of a couple making love until they discover her watching. She listens at the door as the curator mesmerizes a client with her words, talking him into buying her art. She stands outside the window watching Mary and Gabrielle together on the night of Gabrielle's birthday party. Finally, hidden under a bench in the gallery, she overhears the conversation between Mary and Gabrielle that reveals that Gabrielle has deceived her about the paintings.

Polly can certainly be defined as a voyeur, but she is a voyeur with a difference. The kind of voyeurism Mulvey wanted to ban from women's cinema was the controlling, objectifying sort, in which women are reduced to the status of sex objects for the delectation of male viewers. Polly's voyeurism derives from curiosity, the curiosity of a young child who wants to know what adults do together when they are alone, a curiosity that transcends gender. Something about the charged atmosphere between Mary and Gabrielle when Mary first appears at the gallery sends Polly rushing to the surveillance camera to find out more about just what is going on between them in the next room. She watches Gabrielle and Mary kiss with the wide-eyed fascination of a small child discovering sex for the first time. Part of Polly's astonishment, to be sure, comes from the fact that two women are kissing. In mainstream male-directed films such as *Personal Best* (Robert Towne, 1982) and *The Hunger* (Tony Scott, 1983), the camera lingers over scenes of women making love to make them as titillating as possible. Rozema refuses to provide this kind of voyeuristic satisfaction. Mary and Gabrielle move out of the monitor's range at the moment they begin to kiss. But even as Rozema denies us voyeuristic pleasure, she humorously makes us aware of our prurient desires by showing Polly peering beyond the edge of the monitor frame hoping to see more. (See figure 70.) Polly, who is munching crackers as she watches the love scene on the monitor screen, recalls the spectators in the audience munching popcorn as we too watch the cinematic screen in guilty fascination. In this brilliant and funny scene, voyeurism is not eliminated but foregrounded, contemplated, laughed at, and acknowledged as natural.

Rozema then juxtaposes the scene of Polly watching Gabrielle and Mary making love with images of Polly taking pictures of a young couple making love in the woods. The juxtaposition of the two incidents suggests a cause-and-effect relationship. Polly, odd woman out, is trying to master her hurt feelings by actively seeking images of couples making love and joining in vicariously with her camera. Polly is not taking pictures

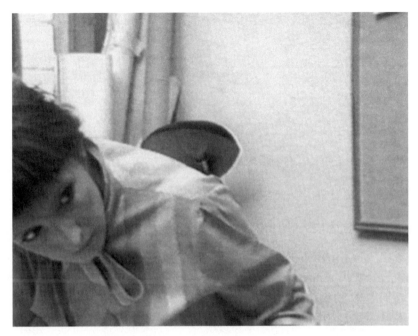

Figure 70. Rozema humorously makes us aware of Polly's (and our) prurient desires by showing her peering beyond the edge of the monitor frame, hoping to see more. (*I've Heard the Mermaids Singing,* 1987, Miramax Films.)

to gain some kind of sadistic control over objects in the world but to provide a kind of solace for herself. She becomes even more sympathetic when the couple spots her taking pictures and she lamely tries to pretend she is bird-watching.

A final way that sexual voyeurism is played with and transformed in *Mermaids* is the brief scene just after Polly sees Gabrielle and Mary kissing. Presumably from Polly's point of view, the camera begins at Gabrielle's feet and slowly moves up her body, almost as if the camera were caressing her. This frankly sexual gaze from the point of view of a woman is rarely seen in mainstream films, and Rozema is consciously playing against the convention in so many mainstream films of the sexualized female body seen from the point of view of a male character. Interestingly, the shot is accompanied by Polly's voice-over disavowing that her love for the curator is sexual. "I don't think I wanted kissing and hugging and all that stuff," she says. "I just loved her." But here a picture is worth a thousand words—Polly's inhibited desire is expressed by how she sees, not by what she says. Although she will later express the idea in a fantasy

Figure 71. A quote from Dziga Vertov's *The Man with a Movie Camera.* (*I've Heard the Mermaids Singing,* 1987, Miramax Films.)

Figure 72. A similar shot from *The Man with a Movie Camera.* (*The Man with a Movie Camera,* 1929, Film Preservation Associates.)

sequence that gender is irrelevant in matters of the heart, that is, that desire naturally follows love irrespective of the gender of the loved one, it
is made clear by the counterpoint of word and image that Polly's sexual
liberation lags behind her philosophical one.

Yet *I've Heard the Mermaids Singing* is not primarily about sex. It is
equally about looking. While the film plays with the conventions of sexual voyeurism, Polly's voyeuristic impulses are seen as a natural continuum of her more generalized love of looking, the passion that has led to
her hobby of photography. She likes to take pictures of things she loves—
and not just images of people making love in the woods (though, of course,
that too). Polly's passion encompasses a wide variety of subjects—from
majestic skyscrapers to mothers holding babies. A film like *Mermaids* illustrates through its parade of stunning and surprising visual images, especially as they appear in Polly's fantasy visions of strange urban landscapes and waves crashing against cliffs, that the pleasures of looking
need not involve sexual voyeurism to enthrall and engage us.

Patricia Rozema makes it clear in her film that women filmmakers do
not have a monopoly on nonsexualized visual aesthetics. The scene in
which Polly climbs a ladder to the top of a grain silo to take a picture
(see figure 71) is a quotation from Dziga Vertov's self-reflexive silent film
masterpiece *The Man with a Movie Camera* (1928). (See figure 72.) Rozema's homage to Vertov suggests she feels an aesthetic kinship with him.
Vertov's camera's gaze in *The Man with a Movie Camera* is by no means
the sadistic, controlling, objectifying gaze deplored by Mulvey, but a playful, self-reflexive one that celebrates the capacity of cinema to reveal the
world in a new and revolutionary way. This too is Rozema's goal. By including in her film an homage to Dziga Vertov's *The Man with a Movie
Camera,* Rozema, a woman with a movie camera, proclaims that in the
best of all worlds, gender is irrelevant in the creation of cinematic art.
In this ideal world, whether a man or a woman is behind the movie camera makes no difference at all. But until that time comes, I am grateful
for films like Patricia Rozema's *I've Heard the Mermaids Singing.*

13

Epilogue
Digital Video and New Forms of Narrative in Mike Figgis's *Timecode*

As I conclude this book on the art of narrative film techniques, I am aware that the medium I have been writing about may well be on the verge of becoming extinct, a casualty of a new technology which threatens to replace it—digital video. Since we are only at the beginning of a new technological age, the question of how new electronic ways of creating moving images will ultimately affect our moviegoing experience and the form future films will take is impossible to predict. It is true that at the time of this writing, films shot with digital cameras and then transferred to 35mm film and projected on the big screen lack the beauty, illusion of depth, and luminosity of live-action footage shot with 35mm film. Reviewers of digital films seem to work overtime in coming up with clever ways to describe how lifeless and charmless digital images can be, especially when the film is shot by a digital camera and then transferred to film. In a review of the film *Sordid Lives* (Del Shores, 2000) for example, the reviewer writes: "The transfer from digital video to 35mm lends the film the vaguely underwater look of a sunken sitcom."[1] For now the consensus seems to be that films shot in digital video are simply not as visually satisfying as those shot on film. However, Lev Manovich makes the interesting point in *The Language of New Media* that digitally created images are potentially superior to celluloid images in the amount of information they can convey about their represented objects. They only appear less satisfying because they have been dumbed down, and the amount of information they convey about the object subtracted. This is so they will resemble celluloid images (the standard by which we measure the reality effect) and hence *seem* more real.[2] In any case, while digital images may well lack the beauty of celluloid images in the present, experts in the field claim that it is only a matter of time before we will be unable to tell the difference between movies shot in 35mm and movies shot with a digital camera.

Whatever the present limitations of digital images, the commercial success of digitally animated computer-generated films such as Pixar's *Toy Story* (1995) and *Toy Story 2* (1999), and *Star Wars—Episode 1, The Phantom Menace* (George Lucas, 1999) suggests that these images are at least good enough to trigger strong emotional reactions from the audience if the stories the films tell are well-structured and compelling. While the colors in Lars Von Trier's digitally shot (and transferred to 35mm film) *Dancer in the Dark* might be less vibrant and the texture of the images less nuanced than they would be if the film had been shot and projected in 35mm, the emotions expressed through the face and singing voice of Icelandic pop artist Björk (as a blind woman who sacrifices her life so that her son can get an operation that will save his eyesight) make the film as moving as any film I have ever seen in any medium.

Even the most passionate proponents of the superiority of celluloid-based images over new electronic media have to admit that digital technology has numerous advantages over film technology, not the least of which is that making movies on digital video costs less than making them on film. One can shoot on digital video for a very small fraction of what it costs to shoot on 35mm film, and this does not take into account the additional expense of developing the film and making copies. Additionally, movies made on digital video are easier to edit. Most celluloid films are now transferred to digital form in order to facilitate editing. With sophisticated editing software one can edit images on a computer with the same ease that one can arrange and rearrange the words in sentences or paragraphs using a word processor. The process of creating special effects digitally, while not necessarily less labor-intensive than doing special effects on film, has the potential to be more spectacular and convincing. Finally, once film theaters are equipped with digital video projectors, the distribution of movies in the theater will be cheaper and easier. No longer will heavy cans of 35mm film need to be physically transported to theaters all over the world, nor will the quality of the film image deteriorate because of the stress on film prints being repeatedly run through scratch-inducing film projectors. Once films are digitized and theaters are retooled, movies can be beamed into theaters directly from satellites. The digital revolution might be just as momentous for the cinema as was the coming of sound.

Despite the fact that few theaters are equipped with digital projectors and the number of commercial feature films shot on digital video remains small, a few filmmakers are experimenting with the possibilities of digital technology for opening up new forms of narrative expression. Mike Figgis's *Timecode* is an interesting case in point. Released in the year 2000, it was the first American studio film shot entirely in digital video.[3] Rather than using digital technology to create imaginary beings or spectacular special effects, Figgis exploited the potential of the new medium to tell a story in a radical new way.

Figgis shot *Timecode* in real time with four synchronized digital cameras, each assigned to photograph the action of one of the four simultaneously occurring segments of the plot. The script was "composed" on music paper in a string quartet format (one line for each of the four plot actions), with each bar representing one minute of time. The film's twenty-eight actors and four camera operators were given the general outline of the plot and could improvise within that structure, but they were equipped with synchronized watches so that they could keep their appointments with predetermined moments in the plot. Since the film was shot in real time, the running time (ninety-three minutes) exactly corresponds to the time it took to shoot the film.

As might be expected, shooting the film in four simultaneous takes in real time was a risky venture. Any number of mistakes could be made by the camera operators or the actors. Mistakes that occur in films made in the traditional way can be corrected by reshooting a scene. One mistaken action in a film shot in real time in long, unbroken takes cannot be corrected unless the entire take is done over. On the other hand, films shot in bits and pieces take weeks, months, or sometimes years to complete. *Timecode,* because its action takes place in real time, took only ninety-three minutes to shoot. Thus it was possible for Figgis to shoot the entire film in the morning, break for lunch, watch the footage with the actors and crew, and then reshoot the film on the same day, fixing mistakes and incorporating new ideas. According to Figgis, it took fifteen tries before he was satisfied with the results. The DVD version of *Timecode* (put out by Columbia Tristar Home Video) includes not only the final release version of the film but Figgis's first attempt, allowing viewers to compare the two.

The innovative way in which *Timecode* was shot (in real time in one take with four cameras) is matched by the unique way the action is presented on the screen. The film appears on a screen divided into four quadrants, each of which presents the footage of one of the four cameras. As a result we see all four segments of the film's plot simultaneously. The viewer is repeatedly reminded that the actions are simultaneous by the frequent appearance of clocks, cell-phone conversations between characters located in separate spaces, and the plot device of having earthquakes occur from time to time, which shakes up the action in each of the four quadrants simultaneously. (Since Figgis obviously could not count on the occurrence of actual earthquakes, he had his camera operators create the impression of earthquakes at appointed times by means of jerky movements of their handheld cameras. The players were instructed to act accordingly.)

Timecode could only have been made with the new digital technology for a number of reasons. In the first place, photographing a feature-length narrative in real time, in one long take, unbroken by edits or cuts, is technically impossible in the film medium, since the film camera has the capacity to hold only enough film for an uninterrupted ten-minute take. The digital camera, in contrast, can shoot up to two hours without interruption. (Video technology also makes it possible for directors to shoot in long uninterrupted takes lasting up to two hours, but the inferior quality of the VHS video image, while sufficient for television distribution, is not suitable for commercial distribution on the big screen.) Even if film cameras were capable of shooting prolonged actions without interruption, the film and developing costs would make Figgis's kind of experimentation impossible. Working in the expensive medium of 35mm film would have mitigated against the actors' and camera operators' freedom to improvise and experiment because mistakes would simply have been too costly. It is too hard to take risks if too much money is at stake. Though Figgis had to pay his actors to go through fifteen versions of *Timecode*, at least the cost of tape and equipment was negligible.

Having discussed the technical factors that made *Timecode* possible to make, we can now look at the new kind of narrative experience Figgis's experiment in digital media offers the spectator. *Timecode* begins with narrative information appearing only in the upper right quadrant of the screen, while screen credits and random images appear in the other three quadrants. In this way Figgis allows the audience to acclimate to the new style of narrative. A woman whose name we later learn is Emma (Saffron Burrows) is telling her therapist about a dream in which her husband, Alex (Stellan Skarsgard), is bleeding to death from a wound and she is helpless to stop the blood. As the woman continues to discuss the problems with her marriage, the action of the quadrant on the upper left portion of the screen appears. Lauren (Jeanne Tripplehorn) approaches a car, deliberately lets the air out of one of its tires, and retreats to her limousine. Soon after, the owner of the sabotaged car, Rose (Salma Hayek), discovers the flat tire and somewhat grudgingly accepts a ride to Los Angeles in Lauren's limousine. While this action occurs, the bottom quadrants of the split screen are filled in. They focus on action in various spaces of an office building that houses the Red Mullet film production company.

As the plot evolves, we learn more about the characters and how they are related to one another. Alex, the wounded man described in the dream, is the depressed alcoholic head of Red Mullet Productions. Rose is an aspiring actress who is having an affair with Alex, hoping to get a part in one of his films. Lauren is Rose's possessive lover who has lured her into her limousine by means of the flat tire so that she can put a listening device in her purse and hence keep her under constant surveillance. At the end of the film, as the result of her discovery of Rose's affair with Alex (by means of her eavesdropping), Lauren shoots Alex in a fit of jealous rage. Alex ends up dying in a pool of blood, making Emma's dream at the film's beginning prophetic.

Although it might seem that an action unfolding in four separate quadrants on the screen would be utterly confusing and hard to follow, several factors keep viewers oriented. First of all, Figgis employs the sound track to help focus our attention on important plot elements. We never hear the dialogue from all four quadrants simultaneously. Rather, the volume of the sound shifts from one quadrant to another, cueing us into which quadrant of the action we should focus on. Secondly, the action is carefully composed so that events important to the plot take place in only one, or at most two, of the quadrants at one time. Until she murders Alex at the end, Lauren's action is confined to the upper left quadrant of the screen. Mostly she stays put in her limousine, accusing Rose of being unfaithful or, after she puts the bug in Rose's purse, reacting to what she hears through her headphones. Emma, Alex's wife, whose actions primarily occupy the upper right quadrant of the screen, announces to Alex that she is leaving him, and then spends a lot of time walking from place to place, leafing through books in a bookstore, or in fatuous conversation with Cherine (Leslie Mann), an aspiring actress who has auditioned for a part at Red Mullet Productions and, it turns out, was once Emma's lover.

The more crucial actions take place in the bottom two quadrants of the screen. These are devoted to the action of Rose's sexual tryst with Alex, and then Rose's miraculous (unrelated) discovery by a director who gives her an audition for the leading role in a sleazy Red Mullet production, *The Bitch from Louisiana*. She gets the part. As the tacky title of the film within the film suggests, aside from being an experiment in film narrative, *Timecode* is a satire on a rubbish-producing Hollywood production company. The bottom quadrants contain scenes in which Red Mullet executives pitch potential Red Mullet films. In order to make the point that this studio manufactures crap, Figgis has one of its executives seriously pitch a film entitled *Time Toilet* about a janitor who discovers that a toilet is actually a portal to the past and can hence send twentieth-century excrement back into important moments in history, such as the assassination of Lincoln.

Because the top quadrants of the screen are less demanding of our attention, we can concentrate on the more significant action taking place on the bottom half of the screen. At some of the most crucial points in the plot, two cameras focus on the same action in the bottom quadrants, which the audience sees from two slightly different camera perspectives. The overlapping view of the same action, aside from offering some purely aesthetic effects which I discuss later, also gives certain moments of *Timecode* doubled emphasis, to insure that the viewer does not miss something important. This being said, *Timecode* nevertheless involves more active participation and attention, and calls for more tolerance for confusion from the spectator, than is demanded in conventionally constructed film narratives. But for those who are willing to make the effort (and even better, to see the film repeatedly), the delights of watching a narrative in real time on a split screen are manifold. The DVD version of the film does more than simply offer the viewer an opportunity to watch the film multiple times; it also has a special feature which the viewer can use to remix the film's sound. Thus we can go through the entire film choosing which quadrant we wish to hear. *Timecode*'s digital construction makes possible an unprecedented form of audience interactivity. Through our ability to remix the sound, we can modify our experience of the film with each viewing.

Probably the most obvious pleasure derived from *Timecode*'s presentation of four slices of the narrative action simultaneously is the heady feeling of omniscience we get as spectators. The use of crosscutting in the conventional film narrative affords us a kind of omniscience as well, but one that is more limited. In conventional crosscutting, the action unfolds linearly, one image at a time. In *The Birth of a Nation,* for example, while Flora is going alone to the well while (unbeknownst to her) Gus is in pursuit, we see first Flora and then Gus in alternating images, one at a time on the screen. Although we are given the illusion of omniscience because we know more than Flora does, we are in fact totally at the mercy of the director, who gets to choose what we see of the actions, and in what order we see them. Figgis's use of four synchronized cameras to record the actions of the plot simultaneously in real time, combined with his split-screen presentation, allows the spectator to view all the actions of the plot simultaneously. Thus in *Timecode,* when Alex is having a tryst with Rose and unbeknownst to him a studio executive is trying to discover where he is, spectators can switch their attention at will back and forth between the two quadrants of action. Because of the spatial, as opposed to the linear, montage in *Timecode,* we get to "edit" what we see ourselves. Even though Figgis's sound track does guide our attention, as I noted earlier, because of *Timecode*'s spatial montage our attention can never be completely coerced. Godlike, we can transcend human limitations in time and space to perceive at a glance actions taking place simultaneously in real time in four separate places.

Figgis doubles our pleasure in the unprecedented omniscience he gives us by creating a plot that revolves around a jealous lover, a woman who has a desperate desire to know what is going on in places where she cannot be present, but who has only a limited means of satisfying her desire. In order to keep an "eye" on Rose, she bugs Rose's purse. But Lauren can only *hear* what Rose is doing, while the viewer can both see and hear what Rose does. We also have the power to watch Lauren's reactions as she listens in on Rose's life. The complex spectatorial fun of *Timecode* reaches a climax, as it were, when Rose and Alex are making love behind a screen upon which the studio executives are watching screen tests featuring various couples who are quite vocally making love. Because the screen is transparent, we can see the images of the couples having sex on both sides of the screen in the bottom two quadrants of the film. The spectator can delight in reading Lauren's face (in the upper left quadrant) as she listens, puzzled, to the sounds emanating from the screen (of people making love) which presumably (and as it turns out, temporarily) block her ability to know that Alex and Rose are in fact making love.

Figgis's experimental technique allows his audience to have a great deal of fun at Lauren's expense because our voyeuristic capacities are so superior to hers. He also allows us to feel superior to the movie executives who do not have our knowledge that just on the other side of the screen on which images of couples are engaging in sex is a "real" couple making love which we can watch while they cannot. But even as Figgis gives the film audience an erotic charge by putting us in a superior position of voyeuristic surveillance and by madly multiplying images of sex which we can watch to our heart's content unobserved, he also makes us hyperaware of our own perverse pleasure in voyeurism by confronting us—a movie audience watching sex on the screen—with the image of a movie audience within the film simultaneously watching images of sex on the screen—the movie executives. By turning the screen momentarily into a kind of mirror for the audience, Figgis confronts us with our own perverse voyeuristic desires.

In addition, Figgis makes us self-conscious about looking by occasionally focusing the camera, usually in the bottom right quadrant of the screen, on the image of two huge eyes, which appear to be painted on one of the buildings in the vicinity of Red Mullet Productions. The effect is that the screen is looking back at us, putting us under a kind of surveillance. Interestingly in this regard, the first image we see of the Red Mullet production headquarters is the screen of a surveillance monitor split into four quadrants revealing disparate spaces of the building (elevators, stairwells, the lobby, and the reception area) which we see simultaneously in real time, mirroring the split screen we are watching in the theater. By means of these self-reflecting images—eyes which look back at us as we are watching them, images of surveillance cameras that remind us of how we too are often being watched—Figgis undercuts the spectator's illusion of voyeuristic supremacy even as his four screens increase our voyeuristic capacity. (See figure 73.)

At the end of *Timecode,* through another kind of mirroring device, we are made to confront our ghoulish fascination with screen violence. As Alex lies dying in an ever increasing pool of blood, Ana Pauls, the young director who has come to pitch an experimental film to Red Mullet Productions, calmly photographs the spectacle with her digital camera, thereby mirroring the actions of the digital cameraman who is recording the actions of the film we are watching. Not surprisingly, the experimental film Ana has come to pitch is a film shot with no editing in real time, a film whose form, therefore, exactly mirrors *Timecode*'s. We see a framed image of Alex dying (in Ana's viewfinder) within the framed screen image of Alex dying. Here Figgis doubles his images of death just as he has doubled his images of sex, in order to call our attention to the attraction of filmmakers and audiences alike to morbid

Figure 73. Figgis undercuts the spectator's illusion of voyeuristic supremacy even as his four screens increase our voyeuristic capacity. (*Timecode,* 2000, Screen Gems.)

images of screen violence. Through such pointedly self-reflexive moments in *Timecode,* Figgis continuously implicates its audience in the dubious desires that make Red Mullet Productions a successful company, desires which Figgis (whose own production company is called Red Mullet) simultaneously satisfies and parodies.

Timecode offers a fascinating synthesis of the pleasure of a mainstream film narrative with that of the radically self-reflexive postmodern experimental film. While it tells a conventional Hollywood story involving a love triangle, with lots of sex and violence, and gives the audience an unprecedented illusion of omniscience by allowing us to observe multiple elements of the plot simultaneously, the novelty of the film's experimental form is always something of a distraction, taking precedence over our absorption in the narrative and identification with the characters. The film deliberately pits the reality effect of a film shot in real time, with the actors giving naturalistic improvisational performances, against stereotypical character types and a hackneyed plot. The effect is quintessentially postmodern in that Figgis appears to be saying simultaneously that what you are seeing is for real *and* that it is all totally ridiculous.

Aside from this postmodern play on the boundaries between reality and fantasy, *Timecode* also has an intriguing aesthetic dimension. At times we can forget altogether about the plot and focus on the fascinating effects of seeing multiple actions taking place simultaneously in real time. Thus, the spatial juxtaposition of an image of Rose and Lauren sitting in the back seat of the limousine in the upper left quadrant of the screen, juxtaposed with an image in the bottom left quadrant of the limousine, seen from the outside, pulling up in front of the building that houses Red Mullet Productions, is oddly satisfying, aside from any plot implications, simply because we know that two cameras are capturing the same moment in time from different perspectives, one from the inside and one from the outside of the same car. In another instance involving the limousine, we see the reflection of the lower half of Cherine's face in the upper right quadrant of the screen in the mirrorlike surface of Lauren's limousine window. Simultaneously, in the upper left quadrant, we see Lauren inside the limousine looking out at Cherine through the window. (The window has a mirrored tint, so that the occupant of the car can look out but those on the outside cannot see in.) When Lauren partially lowers her window to speak to Cherine, we see, in the upper right quadrant of the screen, Lauren's eyes (as seen looking out of the car window) combined with the *reflection* of Cherine's nose and mouth. Here Figgis achieves a composite image of two women, an effect reminiscent of the famous moment in Ingmar Bergman's *Persona* (1966) when the faces of two women merge into one. (See figure 74.) Such images offer a purely formal satisfaction that comes from being shown a familiar world in an unfamiliar way.

At certain privileged moments, the formal design of *Timecode* serves the narrative. Because two cameras are shooting simultaneously from inside and outside of Lauren's car, when Rose finally opens the door to leave its confining space, she steps not just out of the car but also into a new quadrant of the split screen, moving from the upper left quadrant to the lower left quadrant. Here the effect is oddly exhilarating because she is liberated from Lauren (for the moment) both on the level of narrative and on the level of the formal design of the film. She has literally moved into her own space.

Another instance in which the spatial configuration of the images in the four quadrants serves the narrative occurs just after Rose and Alex (occupying the bottom right quadrant) have made love and are sharing the birthday cake Rose has brought Alex. Lauren, Rose's jealous lover, and Emma, Alex's discontented wife, appear in the top left and top right quadrants of the frame. Thus we can either shift our attention

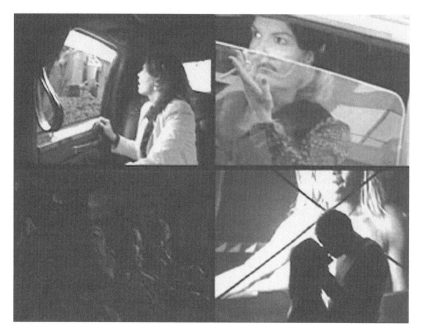

Figure 74. In the upper right quadrant Figgis creates a composite image of two women, an effect reminiscent of the composite face in Ingmar Bergman's *Persona*. (*Timecode*, 2000, Screen Gems.)

back and forth between the couple and Lauren, who is reacting to everything they say (because they are bugged), or we can "cut" our attention to Emma (who, we remember, has forgotten Alex's birthday) as she wanders numbly through the stacks of a bookstore.

In the example I alluded to above when comparing spatial montage to conventional crosscutting, the juxtaposition of Rose and Alex in the room behind the screen and the image of the studio executive who is searching for Alex creates suspense as we wonder whether Alex and Rose will be discovered. But unlike the way the action proceeds in a traditional film in which the director has control over what we see and when, in *Timecode* the viewer is free to decide which of the four quadrants to watch and in which order. If we are alert and proactive, we can find many moments of irony, drama, and suspense throughout the film because of the intricate ways the images in the quadrants relate to one another, in form and content. There are multiple ways of finding significant connections (both formal and plot-based connections) between the actions of the various quadrants. What is important is that we are given a choice.

To the extent that *Timecode*'s experimental form gives the viewer greater freedom of choice over what to focus on, it adds a new wrinkle to an old debate in film theory: which is the best way to present an action in film—in long takes or short shots (that is, montage)? As discussed in chapter 3, the "realist" film theorist André Bazin disagreed with the position of "expressionist" film theorists such as Sergei Eisenstein who argued that editing, or montage, was the foundation of film art. Bazin preferred the style of filmmakers such as William Wyler, Orson Welles, Jean Renoir, Robert Flaherty, and the Alfred Hitchcock of *Rope*,[4] because they curtailed their use of editing, relying mostly on the moving camera, long takes, and composition in depth to explore the dramatic possibilities of letting actions on the screen unfold seamlessly in real time and space. Bazin especially praised the early style of Jean Renoir who, he writes, looked "beyond the resources provided by montage and so uncovered the secret of a film form that would permit everything to be said without chopping the world up into little fragments, that would reveal the hidden meanings in people and things without disturbing the unity natural to them."[5] Montage, according to Bazin, is too manipulative: it imposes the director's meaning on a filmed event in too obvious or overt a manner. Bazin was also wary of montage techniques because they often distort the natural relationship between an object or character and its context in order to construct false or misleading temporal and spatial relationships.

Figgis calls attention to Bazin's critique of montage in *Timecode* by having the experimental film director Ana Pauls announce that "montage has created a fake reality." She claims that her film will capitalize on the capacity of digital video to create "a film without one single cut. No editing. Real time." She is, as mentioned above, describing a film, very much like *Timecode,* whose revolutionary style allows us to contemplate exactly what happens when the realist dream of creating an entire feature film without cuts is actually fulfilled.

From this perspective, *Timecode* reveals that the dichotomy between the montage style and that of the long take is a false one. Although there are no literal cuts in *Timecode,* there is a great deal of camera movement that achieves many of the same effects as cutting. The moving camera in each of the four quadrants is highly selective, directing the viewer's attention to details of the mise-en-scène or to close-ups of faces in a way that achieves the same effect as editing.

When a dramatic event occurs in the film, for example, a pan to the reaction on a character's face elicits almost the same response as a cut to the same reaction would have done. I suspect that Mike Figgis, by beginning *Timecode* with Emma in close-up telling her therapist about a dream in which the central image is a cut (the word she repeatedly uses to refer to Alex's bleeding wound), is making an in-joke, announcing from the start that there is no such thing as a film without a cut. A narrative told in real time in one long take can be every bit as manipulative of our attention as a narrative told with heavy editing. André Bazin's dream of cinema's potential to present a world with the seamless unity and ambiguity of reality through the use of long takes is revealed in *Timecode* to be an illusion.

As we have seen, however, *Timecode* in some respects is in fact less manipulative than most mainstream films. Although our attention is very much directed by the camera's point of view within each quadrant, we can nevertheless see all four quadrants simultaneously. As a result, we have far greater freedom to choose which actions to focus on than we have in a conventionally edited film. This is what makes *Timecode* both demanding and exciting. The spatial montage of *Timecode,* not its use of the long take in real time, fulfills Bazin's wish for a film form that gives the viewer a freedom to interpret the filmic world in a way that is often foreclosed by linear montage.

Perhaps the ubiquity of computer screens in our lives, which demand that we switch our attention back and forth between multiple windows, to say nothing of the split-screen capacities of televisions which allow viewers to watch the action on two or more channels simultaneously, may be developing a hunger in the spectator for more complexity on the cinema screen as well, a hunger that *Timecode* satisfies. Lev Manovich in *The Language of New Media* predicts that the next generation of cinema will increasingly add multiple "windows" or split screens to its language. But the relatively poor box-office reception of *Timecode* suggests that Mike Figgis's experiment in presenting an *entire* film in a split-screen format is still far ahead of its time.[6] While its box-office take the first week it appeared on screens was respectable,[7] the film disappeared from the screen after only two weeks in Berkeley, California, a place where one would imagine there would be a large audience for experiments in film form. Clearly, audiences, no matter how acclimated they have become to computers with multiple windows and the split-screen capacities of their television sets, are not yet craving multiple frames on movie screens.

The traditional cinema with one screen has not yet exhausted its creative possibilities and perhaps it never will. But Mike Figgis's grand experiment with the capabilities of digital cinema is a successful failure.

Those who give the film their full attention and the multiple screenings it deserves will find aesthetic delight in the way its four streams of seamlessly interacting images attain the formal beauty of a musical fugue, thus conveying narrative information in a subtle and challenging new way. *Timecode* provides us with a preview of one possible way the language of the cinema may evolve in the digital age of the moving image.

Notes

CHAPTER 1. THE BEGINNINGS OF FILM NARRATIVE

1. For details of Griffith's early life and career as an actor, I have drawn from Richard Schickel, *D. W. Griffith: An American Life* (New York: Simon and Schuster, 1984), 15–93.

2. Griffith's play, *The Fool and the Girl,* based upon his experience in California picking hops when he could not get steady work as an actor, played briefly in Washington in 1907 to mixed but mostly scathing reviews. See Schickel, *Griffith,* 85–7. Griffith's one published poem, "The Wild Duck," appeared in a weekly magazine in January 1907. Schickel prints the entire poem, 82–4.

3. I am indebted to chapter 1, "Theory and History: Narrative Discourse and the Narrator System," in Tom Gunning, *D. W. Griffith and the Origins of the American Narrative Film* (Urbana: University of Illinois Press, 1994), 10–30, for this elegant way of schematizing Griffith's contribution to film narrative.

4. Karel Reisz and Gavin Millar, *The Technique of Film Editing* (New York: Hastings House, 1968), 24.

5. Attempts at matches existed well before Griffith began making films. Direction matches, which are defined later in this chapter, appear at the end of Georges Méliès's *A Trip to the Moon* (1903). Méliès, however, did not develop the match cut systematically in his films, as Griffith did.

6. As David A. Cook points out in *A History of Narrative Film* (New York: W. W. Norton, 1996), Griffith did not invent the maintenance of screen direction. The rise of multishot film narratives prior to Griffith's appearance on the

scene, and especially the popularity of chase films, demanded that the direction of characters' movements be maintained consistently from shot to shot, so that characters in a chase would not seem to be bumping into each other. Griffith can be credited with refining the system—although, as Cook points out, he struggled with the problems of maintaining a consistent screen direction in films made as late as 1909–1910 (63–4).

7. Again, Griffith was not the first director to use the point-of-view shot. At the turn of the century, short films such as the Pathé frères' *Through the Keyhole* or G. A. Smith's *As Seen Through a Telescope* included rudimentary point-of-view shots. A character would look through a telescope or keyhole and the next shot would present what the character saw—a lady's ankle or a couple embracing—through a circular or keyhole shaped matte. But in these films, the device was used for isolated moments of titillation. Griffith transformed these devices into ways to add dramatic emphasis to complex narrative events. Tom Gunning makes a distinction between an earlier cinema of attractions and Griffith's narrative-centered cinema (*D. W. Griffith and the Origins of the American Narrative Film*, 42).

8. Richard Barry, "Five-Dollar 'Movies' Prophesied," quoted in "Introduction," *Focus on* The Birth of a Nation, ed. Fred Silva (Englewood Cliffs, N.J.: Prentice-Hall, Inc., 1971), 10. First published in *Editor* 40 (April 24, 1915): 409.

9. The forest setting was in fact remote from the sets of the Cameron home, which were shot in the Reliance-Majestic Studios located on Sunset Boulevard in Los Angeles. According to Richard Schickel, Griffith filmed the encounter between Gus and Flora in the mountainous terrain of Big Bear Lake, California, after a great deal of scouting for a location with the right atmosphere for this scene. See Schickel, *Griffith*, 225–6.

10. The Soviet filmmaker and theorist Sergei Eisenstein has written a persuasive article claiming that many of Griffith's film techniques, including the close-up and crosscutting, have their origins in the fiction of Charles Dickens. See Eisenstein's "Dickens, Griffith, and the Film Today," in *Film Form,* ed. and trans. Jay Leyda (New York: Harcourt, Brace & World, Inc., 1949), 195–255.

11. Christian Metz, *The Imaginary Signifier: Psychoanalysis and the Cinema,* trans. Celia Britton et al. (Bloomington: Indiana University Press, 1982).

12. In Dixon's *The Clansman,* Gus is literally guilty of raping, not Ben Cameron's sister, but his ex-sweetheart. The rape is described in the following language: "A single tiger-spring, and the black claws of the beast sank into the soft white throat and she was still" (Thomas Dixon, Jr., *The Clansman: An Historical Romance of the Ku Klux Klan* [Norbone, Mo.: Salon Publishing Company, n.d.], 304). Also quoted by Everett Carter, "Cultural History Written with Lightning: The Significance of *The Birth of a Nation*," in Silva, ed., *Focus on* The Birth of a Nation, 139.

13. Russell Merritt, "Dixon, Griffith, and the Southern Legend: A Cultural Analysis of *The Birth of a Nation*," *Cinema Journal* XII (Fall 1972): 26–45.

14. Quoted, among other places, in Richard Schickel, *Griffith,* 270.

15. It is not surprising that Wilson saw *The Birth of a Nation* as reflecting

historical truth, given that Griffith in several title cards from *The Birth of a Nation* quoted directly from Wilson's book *A History of the American People.*

16. Everett Carter, "Cultural History Written with Lightning," 136.

17. Everett Carter, "Cultural History Written with Lightning," 138–9.

18. The term *projection* comes from the discourse of psychoanalysis. It refers to a psychological process in which individuals disavow troublesome aspects about themselves (envy, aggressive wishes, perverse sexual desires) and imagine that these impulses are coming from other people.

19. Michael Rogin notes in "'The Sword Became a Flashing Vision': D. W. Griffith's *The Birth of a Nation*," *Representations* 9 (Winter 1985), that many of the marauding armed blacks in *The Birth of a Nation* were played by white men wearing blackface, and these were often the same extras who also donned sheets and played the parts of the Klan members. This production detail, Rogin argues, exposes a kinship between the rapists and avengers. He writes: "The obviousness of blackface, which fails to disguise, reveals that the Klansmen were chasing their own negative identities, their shadow sides" (181).

20. Thomas R. Cripps, "The Reaction of the Negro to the Motion Picture, *The Birth of a Nation*," in Fred Silva, ed., *Focus on* The Birth of a Nation, 113.

21. Peter Noble, "The Negro in *The Birth of a Nation*," in Fred Silva, ed., *Focus on* The Birth of a Nation, 130–1.

CHAPTER 2. THE ART OF MONTAGE

1. Quoted in Marie Seton, *Sergei M. Eisenstein* (New York: A. A. Wyn, 1952), 86.

2. For background on Eisenstein I have drawn on Yon Barna's biography *Eisenstein*, trans. Lise Hunter (Bloomington: Indiana University Press, 1973).

3. Quoted in Barna, *Eisenstein*, 36.

4. Quoted in Barna, *Eisenstein*, 74.

5. V. I. Pudovkin, *Film Technique and Film Acting*, ed. and trans. Ivor Montagu (New York: Grove Press, 1958), 168.

6. Quoted in Jay Leyda, *Kino: A History of the Russian and Soviet Film* (New York: Collier Books, 1960), 165.

7. Quoted in Barna, *Eisenstein*, 53.

8. Sergei Eisenstein, *Film Form: Essays in Film Theory*, ed. and trans. Jay Leyda (New York: Harcourt, Brace & World, 1949), 7–8.

9. According to Eisenstein, he drew from other massacres which actually took place during the revolutionary year of 1905 for his depiction of the massacre on the Odessa Steps (Barna, *Eisenstein*, 98).

10. Eisenstein, *Film Form*, 38.

11. Eisenstein expands on these ideas in "A Dialectic Approach to Film Form" in *Film Form*, 45–63.

12. Eisenstein, *Film Form*, 170–1.

13. Eisenstein further developed the practice of cutting away from the film's literal action to symbolic images that comment on the action in his next film,

October. He terms this technique "intellectual montage." Eisenstein discusses intellectual montage in "The Cinematic Principle and the Ideogram" and "A Dialectic Approach to Film Form," in *Film Form.*

14. Leyda, *Kino,* 199.

15. Eisenstein, *Film Form,* 35.

CHAPTER 3. EXPRESSIONISM AND REALISM IN FILM FORM

1. Like Griffith and Eisenstein, Murnau worked in the theater before he came to the cinema. He began as an actor in Max Reinhardt's theater school, but eventually became more interested in directing. After serving as a flyer in World War I, he came to Berlin and founded a film company. For detailed background on Murnau's early life, theatrical career, and the films he made prior to *The Last Laugh,* see Lotte Eisner's *Murnau* (Berkeley: University of California Press, 1973).

2. Lotte H. Eisner, *The Haunted Screen: Expressionism in the German Cinema and the Influence of Max Reinhardt* (Berkeley: University of California Press, 1973), 10.

3. William Nestrick, *Film Study Extract:* The Cabinet of Dr. Caligari (Mount Vernon, N.Y.: Macmillan Films, 1975), 9–10.

4. Film historians such as David Cook refer to *The Last Laugh* not as an expressionist film but as a *Kammerspiel,* a term that translates as "intimate theater" (*A History of Narrative Film,* 3rd. ed. [New York: W. W. Norton & Company, 1996], 117). But as Cook and other historians acknowledge, Carl Mayer, the co-scriptwriter of *The Cabinet of Dr. Caligari,* wrote the script for *The Last Laugh* during the height of expressionism and the film retains many expressionist qualities.

5. Many of Murnau's techniques were inspired by the ideas of his cameraman Karl Freund, with whom he closely collaborated.

6. Quoted in Lotte Eisner, *Murnau,* 65.

7. Because the film has no titles, the identity of this woman is uncertain. Commentators refer to her variously as the doorman's aunt or housekeeper.

8. This title, announcing a totally implausible happy outcome, was tacked on by the studio bosses because they felt the original sad ending in which the doorman finally accepts his defeat was too downbeat for export to American audiences.

9. Lotte Eisner, *Murnau,* 67.

10. Lotte Eisner, *Murnau,* 67.

11. High-key lighting evenly illuminates a scene with no dramatic shadows and low contrast between dark and light areas of the shot.

12. Other filmmakers Bazin celebrated for their realist aesthetic include Orson Welles, Jean Renoir, Eric von Stroheim, Yosujiro Ozu, and Vittorio De Sica.

13. André Bazin, *What Is Cinema?* ed. and trans. Hugh Gray (Berkeley and Los Angeles: University of California Press, 1967), 13.

14. Rudolph Arnheim, *Film As Art* (Berkeley: University of California Press, 1969), 9.

15. V. F. Perkins argues in *Film as Film* that expressionist conceptions of film

art were influenced by the fact that the birth of cinema coincided with the heyday of Postimpressionism in the arts, a period in which descriptive imitations of natural forms were denigrated. Photography's ability to mechanically reproduce images of the world was seen as a limitation that had to be overcome if film were to be taken seriously as high art. See "The Sins of the Pioneers," in *Film as Film: Understanding and Judging Movies* (Middlesex, England: Penguin Books, 1972), 9–27.

16. André Bazin, *What Is Cinema?* 15.

17. André Bazin, *What Is Cinema?* 27.

18. I noticed this detail for the first time when I viewed the film again before writing this chapter.

19. The shooting ratio of *The Adventurer* was about 100 to 1. That is, for every one foot of film that showed up in the finished product, he shot one hundred feet of film. My source for these production details was Gerald Mast, *The Comic Mind: Comedy and the Movies* (Indianapolis, Ind. and New York: The Bobbs-Merrill Company, 1973), 67.

20. André Bazin, *What Is Cinema?* 147.

CHAPTER 4. THE CONVERSION TO SOUND AND THE CLASSICAL HOLLYWOOD FILM

1. Béla Balázs, *Theory of the Film: Character and Growth of a New Art* (New York: Dover Publications, 1970), 44.

2. Rudolph Arnheim, *Film as Art* (Berkeley: University of California Press, 1969), 227.

3. René Clair, *Cinema Yesterday and Today*, trans. Stanley Appelbaum (New York: Dover Publications, 1972), 139.

4. This manifesto, titled "Statement," is reprinted in Elisabeth Weis and John Belton, eds., *Film Sound: Theory and Practice* (New York: Columbia University Press, 1985), 83–5.

5. V. I. Pudovkin, *Film Technique and Film Acting*, ed. and trans. Ivor Montagu (New York: Grove Press, 1976), 192.

6. André Bazin, *What Is Cinema?* ed. and trans. Hugh Gray (Berkeley and Los Angeles: University of California Press, 1967), 28.

7. See chapter 2, "Editing and the Sound Film," in Karel Reisz and Gavin Millar, *The Technique of Film Editing* (New York: Hastings House, 1968), 41–5.

8. Reisz and Millar, *The Technique of Film Editing*, 45.

9. David Bordwell and Kristin Thompson, *Film Art: An Introduction*, 6th. ed. (New York: McGraw-Hill, 2001), 294–5.

10. See chapter 1, " Projections of Sound on Image," in Michel Chion, *Audio-Vision: Sound on Screen*, ed. and trans. Claudia Gorbman (New York: Columbia University Press, 1990), 3–24.

11. In a dissolve, the ending of one shot is briefly superimposed over the beginning of the next shot.

12. I am indebted to Gerald Mast's detailed and insightful discussion of *His Girl Friday* in *Howard Hawks, Storyteller* (New York: Oxford University Press, 1982).

13. Howard Hawks has commented: "If you'll ever listen to some people who are talking, especially in a scene of any excitement, they all talk at the same time. All it needs is a little extra work on the dialogue. You put a few words in front of somebody's speech and put a few words at the end, and they can overlap it. It gives you a sense of speed that actually doesn't exist. And you can make the people talk a little faster." (Quoted in Bordwell and Thompson, *Film Art: an Introduction,* 354.)

14. André Bazin, "La politique des auteurs," in *The New Wave,* ed. Peter Graham (New York: Doubleday, 1968), 143, 154.

15. David Bordwell, Janet Staiger, and Kristin Thompson, *The Classical Hollywood Cinema: Film Style and Mode of Production to 1960* (New York: Columbia University Press, 1985), 4.

16. Bordwell and Thompson also use *His Girl Friday* to exemplify classical Hollywood narrative techniques in *Film Art: An Introduction,* 384–8.

17. Bordwell et al., *Classical Hollywood Cinema,* 3–4.

18. Three-point lighting involves a key light or primary source of illumination, a fill light (to fill in shadows cast by the key light), and a backlight, illumination coming from behind objects that outlines or highlights their contours.

19. The exact quotation is "The power of the dead is that we think they see us all the time." Don Delillo, *White Noise* (New York: Penguin Books, 1985), 98.

20. David Bordwell and Kristin Thompson make this point in *Film Art: An Introduction,* 355. However, they incorrectly designate the time at the beginning of the first scene as 12:57 rather than 12:35. It is 12:57 at the end of the scene.

21. Shot/reverse shot indicates the practice of alternating shots of two characters in conversation. The characters are shot so that their glances appear to converge, and often we see each character from over the shoulder of the other.

22. Peter Wollen persuasively makes this argument in *Signs and Meaning in the Cinema* (Bloomington: Indiana University Press, 1969), 81–94.

23. The screwball comedy was a Hollywood genre that flourished from 1934 to 1942. Usually set against a background of opulence and wealth and featuring devil-may-care anarchic and eccentric protagonists, the popularity of the genre is often seen as offering escape, in a form of manic defense, against the grim years of the Depression and the anxiety about the coming of World War II. Critics have never been very precise in defining just what constitutes a screwball comedy beyond its conveying a general impression of zaniness. Howard Hawks defined the screwball comedy in the context of remarks on *Bringing Up Baby.* "There were no normal people in it," he said. "Everyone you met was a screwball." Howard Hawks, interview by Peter Bogdanovich, *Movie* 5: 11.

24. Gerald Mast, *Howard Hawks, Storyteller* (New York: Oxford University Press, 1982), 226.

25. Although there are some notable exceptions in the roles Katharine Hepburn plays opposite Spencer Tracy and Joan Crawford's role in *Mildred Pierce,* most of the beautiful unconventional women of classical Hollywood film are femmes fatales or pathologically evil.

26. Molly Haskell, *From Reverence to Rape: The Treatment of Women in the Movies,* 2nd. ed. (Chicago, Ill.: The University of Chicago Press, 1973), 126.

27. Stanley Cavell, *Pursuits of Happiness: The Hollywood Comedy of Remarriage* (Cambridge, Mass.: Harvard University Press, 1981), 171.

CHAPTER 5. EXPRESSIVE REALISM

1. See Roy A. Fowler, "*Citizen Kane*: Background and a Critique," in *Focus on* Citizen Kane, ed. Ronald Gottesman (Englewood Cliffs, N.J.: Prentice Hall, 1971), 78.

2. Quoted in Fowler, "*Citizen Kane*," 79.

3. In a two-part *New Yorker* article entitled "Raising Kane" (February 20 and 27, 1971), reprinted in *The* Citizen Kane *Book* ([Boston, Mass.: Little, Brown and Company, 1971], 1–84), Pauline Kael argues that Herman Mankiewicz, upon whose script *Citizen Kane* was based, should be considered the real author of the film. But since Welles collaborated heavily on the script and was the one who directed the actors and determined what was original about the visual look of the film, I am not persuaded by Kael's argument. See Robert L. Carringer, *The Making of* Citizen Kane (Berkeley: University of California Press, 1985), for a balanced account of the dispute over the authorship of the film.

4. Pauline Kael, "Raising Kane," 41.

5. Quoted in Pauline Kael, "Raising Kane," 43.

6. Quoted in Pauline Kael, "Raising Kane," 44.

7. André Bazin, "The Evolution of the Language of Cinema," in *What Is Cinema?* ed. and trans. Hugh Gray (Berkeley and Los Angeles: University of California Press, 1967), 37.

8. Laura Mulvey first made me aware of the play between an omniscient point of view and a restricted narration (i.e., narration limited to the point of view of a particular character in the fiction) in *Citizen Kane* in a lecture she delivered at Berkeley in 1991. She has formalized her ideas in her excellent book *Citizen Kane* (London: British Film Institute, 1992).

9. For a lucid discussion of the issues involved in interpreting *Citizen Kane* and for a convincing argument that the sled does adequately explain Kane's life, see Noel Carroll's "Interpreting *Citizen Kane*" in *Perspectives on* Citizen Kane, ed. Ronald Gottesman (New York: G. K. Hall & Co., 1996), 254–67.

10. For a detailed technical discussion of the recent changes in the technology of lighting, lens construction, and film stock that enabled Toland to create the deep-focus images that Welles required, see Gregg Toland's essay "How I Broke the Rules in *Citizen Kane*" in Ronald Gottesman, ed., *Focus on* Citizen Kane, 73–7.

11. André Bazin, *What Is Cinema?* 36. Bazin also praises, among others, Jean Renoir, William Wyler, Roberto Rossellini, and Vittorio De Sica for using deep-focus photography and long takes, but singles out Welles's usage as "most spectacular and, by virtue of his very excesses, the most significant" (37).

12. A dissolve is the superimposition of the end of one shot onto the begin-

ning of the next, so that the two images briefly overlap. In a lap dissolve, the superimposition of the two shots lingers, often to make a symbolic point about the relation of the two shots.

13. Edgar Allan Poe, "The Haunted Palace," in Edward H. Davidson, ed., *Selected Writings of Edgar Allan Poe* (Boston, Mass.: Houghton Mifflin Company, 1956), 32–3.

14. The snow dome is originally Susan's possession. It can be seen on Susan's dressing table on the night Kane meets her.

15. A wide-angle lens has a short focal length (less than 30mm in 35mm filming). It gives a wider angle of vision than a "normal" (50mm) lens and skews a scene's perspective by distorting straight lines near the edges of the frame and by exaggerating the distance between the foreground and background planes of the shot.

16. An especially good one is Robert L. Carringer's *The Making of* Citizen Kane.

17. See Rick Altman, "Deep-Focus Sound: *Citizen Kane* and the Radio Aesthetic," in Ronald Gottesman, ed., *Perspectives on* Citizen Kane, 94–121.

18. See Bernard Herrmann, "Score for a Film," in Ronald Gottesman, ed. *Focus on* Citizen Kane, 69–72. This article is also anthologized in Ronald Gottesman, ed., *Perspectives on* Citizen Kane.

19. Bernard Herrmann, "Score for a Film," 70.

20. Bernard Herrmann, "Score for a Film," 70.

CHAPTER 6. ITALIAN NEOREALISM

1. For the following summary of the history and style of Italian neorealism I have drawn upon a number of sources, including Peter Bondanella, *Italian Cinema: From Neorealism to the Present* (New York: Ungar, 1983), Bert Cardullo, *What is Neorealism? A Critical English Language Bibliography of Italian Cinematic Neorealism* (Lanham, Md.: University Press of America, 1991), David A. Cook, *A History of Narrative Film* (New York: W. W. Norton, 1996), Pam Cook, ed., *The Cinema Book: A Complete Guide to Understanding the Movies* (New York: Pantheon, 1985), and Pierre Leprohon, *The Italian Cinema*, trans. Robert Greaves and Oliver Stalleybrass (New York: Praeger, 1972).

2. Pierre Leprohon, *The Italian Cinema*, 98.

3. Quoted in Maya Deren, *An Anagram of Ideas on Art, Form and Film* (New York: Alicat Book Shop Press, 1946), no p. n. Reprinted in VeVe A. Clark, et al., eds., *The Legend of Maya Deren: A Documentary Biography and Collected Works*, vol. 1, part 2 (New York: Anthology Film Archives, 1988), 585.

4. The Italian name of the film is *Ladri di Biciclette,* which translates as "Bicycle Thieves," but in English the title is always *The Bicycle Thief.*

5. André Bazin, "Bicycle Thief," in *What Is Cinema?* vol. 2, ed. and trans. Hugh Gray (Berkeley: University of California Press, 1971), 49.

6. As occurred often in films which used nonprofessional actors, Ricci's voice had to be dubbed in by a professional actor because the dialect of the man who portrays him would not have been understood by most of the people of Italy.

7. André Bazin, *What Is Cinema?* vol. 2, 56.

8. André Bazin, *What Is Cinema?* vol. 2, 51.

9. The term "Macguffin" derives from a tale about a nonexistent device for trapping lions in the Scottish Highlands, where there are no lions. Hitchcock adopted the term for the unimportant plot objectives in his films. See Donald Spoto, *The Dark Side of Genius: The Life of Alfred Hitchcock* (New York: Da Capo Press, 1993), 145.

10. André Bazin, *What Is Cinema?* vol. 2, 54.

11. Pam Cook makes this point in her section on Italian neorealism in *The Cinema Book*, 37.

CHAPTER 7. AUTEUR THEORY AND THE FRENCH NEW WAVE

1. The term *new wave* today connotes liberal or progressive politics, especially because of the association of the French New Wave with Jean-Luc Godard's leftist political films. However, the moniker "nouvelle vague," which translates as "new wave," was originally given to the generation of apolitical young people in France in the late 1950s whose values and way of life contrasted with the politically engaged, idealistic youth of the immediate postwar years. See Kristin Thompson and David Bordwell, *Film History: An Introduction* (New York: Mc-Graw-Hill, 1994), 521.

2. Quoted in James Monaco, *The New Wave: Truffaut, Godard, Chabrol, Rohmer, Rivette* (New York: Oxford University Press, 1976), 5.

3. Sarris coined this term in his book *The American Cinema: Directors and Directions 1929–68* (New York: Dutton, 1969), and it caught on, even though the French author policy (to which I will subsequently refer as auteur theory) was not, strictly speaking, a systematic film theory.

4. François Truffaut, "A Certain Tendency of the French Cinema," in *Movies and Methods*, ed. Bill Nichols (Berkeley: University of California Press, 1976) 224–37.

5. For a comprehensive treatment of the benefits and critiques of auteur theory, see John Caughie, ed., *Theories of Authorship* (London: Routledge & Kegan Paul, 1981). For a concise overview of the issues, see Caughie's introduction, 9–16, and Edward Buscombe, "Ideas of Authorship," 22–34.

6. Quoted in John Caughie, ed., *Theories of Authorship*, 26.

7. For a discussion of how mass media reinforces cultural ideology see Louis Althusser, "Ideology and Ideological State Apparatuses," in *Lenin and Philosophy and Other Essays*, trans. Ben Brewster (New York: Monthly Review Press, 1970), 127–9.

8. I discuss feminist film theory in much greater detail, taking into account aspects of style as well as content, in chapter 12.

9. Roland Barthes's article "The Death of the Author" is anthologized in Caughie, ed., *Theories of Authorship*, 208–13.

10. In 1953 the French government began to subsidize high-quality short films and in 1959, the year *400 Blows* was made, an advance on receipts system was

created which helped finance first features on the basis of promising scripts. Kristin Thompson and David Bordwell, *Film History: An Introduction*, 521.

11. I am indebted to Annette Insdorf's biography *François Truffaut* (Cambridge: Cambridge University Press, 1994) for details of Truffaut's life, especially chapter 6, 173–7.

12. Quoted in Monaco, *The New Wave: Truffaut, Godard, Chabrol, Rohmer, Rivette*, 6.

13. François Truffaut with Helen G. Scott, *Hitchcock*, rev. ed. (New York: Simon and Schuster, 1984), 17.

14. A "swish pan" occurs when the movement of the panning camera is so rapid that the image is blurry.

15. Quoted in Monaco, *The New Wave: Truffaut, Godard, Chabrol, Rohmer, Rivette*, 25.

CHAPTER 8. HOLLYWOOD AUTEUR

1. Eric Rohmer and Claude Chabrol, *Hitchcock*, trans. Stanley Hochman (New York: Frederick Ungar Publishing Co., 1979), 152.

2. François Truffaut with Helen G. Scott, *Hitchcock*, rev. ed. (New York: Simon and Schuster, 1984), 20.

3. *Easy Virtue* is available in DVD format (Los Angeles, Calif.: Delta Entertainment Corp., 1999).

4. Strictly speaking this is a title, not a line of dialogue, because *Easy Virtue* is a silent film.

5. Truffaut, *Hitchcock,* 51.

6. For Eric Rohmer and Claude Chabrol, *The Wrong Man* confirms the Catholic doctrine of original sin, which holds that no matter how innocent we may believe ourselves to be, we are in fact guilty. This is implied throughout their chapter on *The Wrong Man* (*Hitchcock,* 145–52).

7. Truffaut, *Hitchcock,* 43.

8. For this observation, I am indebted to Tom Ryall, *Alfred Hitchcock and the British Cinema* (London: Athlone, 1996).

9. Truffaut, *Hitchcock,* 167.

10. Quoted in Donald Spoto, *The Dark Side of Genius: The Life of Alfred Hitchcock* (New York: Da Capo Press, 1993), 285.

11. Spoto, *The Dark Side of Genius*, 299–300.

12. In *The Women Who Knew Too Much: Hitchcock and Feminist Theory* (New York: Routledge, 1989), a feminist reading of Hitchcock's films, Tania Modleski argues that Hitchcock is much more identified with and sympathetic to the plights of his women heroines than is generally acknowledged.

13. Truffaut, *Hitchcock,* 171.

14. Alfred Hitchcock, "Direction (1937)," in *Focus on Hitchcock,* ed. Albert J. LaValley (Englewood Cliffs, N.J.: Prentice-Hall, Inc., 1972), 35.

15. An even more stunning example of Hitchcock's use of pure cinema to give visual emphasis to the key occurs at the beginning of the next sequence of the

film. The camera photographs the party at the mansion, beginning high above the staircase. It then gradually descends, moving closer and closer to Alicia (who is greeting guests with Sebastian), until all that appears in the frame is a huge close-up of Alicia's hand, which clasps the crucial key.

16. Truffaut, *Hitchcock*, 282.

17. Hitchcock said this at a press conference in 1947.

18. Franz Kafka wrote this in a letter to Oskar Pollak, January 27, 1904. In Franz Kafka, *Letters to Friends, Family, and Editors*, trans. Richard and Clara Winston (New York: Schocken, 1977), 16.

CHAPTER 9. THE EUROPEAN ART FILM

1. For an excellent extended discussion of art-film narration, see David Bordwell's chapter "Art Cinema Narration" in *Narration in the Fiction Film* (Madison: The University of Wisconsin Press, 1985), 205–33). I have applied many of Bordwell's insights about art-film narration to my discussion of *8 1/2*.

2. This quote by Horst Ruthrof appears in Bordwell, *Narration in the Fiction Film*, 208.

3. Fellini is quoted in Peter Bondanella, *The Cinema of Federico Fellini* (Princeton: Princeton University Press, 1992), 71.

4. Scenes like this, and scenes with the monumental prostitute Saraghina, have made Fellini subject to criticism from those who deplore the exploitation of women within the film by the character Guido Anselmi and the voyeuristic ogling of women by Fellini's camera. His apologists (with whom I tend to agree) insist that his film is about the social and psychological foundations of sexism and that Fellini's portrait of Guido as head of a harem is in fact a self-deprecating parody. It is clearly presented as the fantasy of a middle-aged man who fears the loss of his potency and hence needs to lord it over servile, nubile women.

5. Quoted in Peter Bondanella, *The Cinema of Federico Fellini*, 164–5.

6. Christian Metz, "Mirror Construction in Fellini's *8 1/2*," in *Film Language*, trans. Michael Taylor (New York: Oxford University Press, 1974), 234.

7. Fellini cleverly disarms criticism of his film by having Daumier, an unattractive character, criticize it so harshly. As Robert Stam notes in *Reflexivity in Film and Literature: From Don Quixote to Jean-Luc Godard* (New York: Columbia University Press, 1992), the incorporation of criticism of the work into the fictional world is a hallmark of many modernist self-conscious or self-reflexive works. See Stam's comments in this regard on *8 1/2*, 155.

8. Quoted in Suzanne Budgen, *Fellini* (London: British Film Institute, 1966), 85–6.

9. Suzanne Budgen, *Fellini*, 50–1.

10. Sigmund Freud, "The Most Prevalent Form of Degradation in Erotic Life," in *Sexuality and the Psychology of Love*, ed. Philip Rieff (New York: Collier Books, 1963), 58–70.

11. Karel Reisz and Gavin Millar, *The Technique of Film Editing* (New York: Hastings House, 1968), 216–7.

12. This information was given to me in the 1970s by Furio Colombo, a personal acquaintance of Fellini's.

CHAPTER 10. FILM AND POSTMODERNISM

1. Jon Mattox, "Post Modernism or post–Post Modernism?" 1995, http://jonmattox.com/grids/ideas/postmodernism.html (accessed August 17, 2003). The quotation is attributed to multimedia artist and author Barbara Krieger.

2. By having a black prostitute refer to her "black" hole, reducing herself to her race and sexual anatomy, the joke also has a racist and sexist subtext.

3. Allen uses some of the modernist techniques associated with Fellini in *Stardust Memories,* but *Stardust Memories* is a parody of *8 1/2.*

4. Nancy Pogel, *Woody Allen* (Boston, Mass.: Twayne, 1987).

5. In *Fantastic Voyage* (Richard Fleischer, 1966), human beings are miniaturized and injected into the bloodstream of a terminally ill patient in order to combat the problem that is threatening the patient's life.

6. This is a term Charles Jencks coins in *What Is Post-Modernism?* (New York: St. Martin's Press, 1987), 7, to describe the eclecticism of postmodern constructs.

7. *An American Family,* produced by Craig Gilbert and directed by Alan and Susan Raymond, aired for twelve weeks beginning January 11, 1973.

8. Woody Allen, *Four Films of Woody Allen* (New York: Random House, 1982), 3.

9. Eric Lax, *Woody Allen: A Biography* (New York: Vintage Books, 1992), 10.

10. John Baxter, *Woody Allen: A Biography* (New York: Carroll and Graf, 1999), 245.

11. Sigmund Freud, *Introductory Lectures on Psycho-Analysis*, ed. and trans. James Strachey (New York: W. W. Norton, 1996), 138–53.

12. Quoted in John Baxter, *Woody Allen,* 242–3.

13. Eric Lax quotes Allen's musings on the "totally contentious" relationship of his parents all throughout childhood. "They did everything except exchange gunfire" (*Woody Allen,* 16). "When I went to school in the morning I never knew if I was coming home to both parents" (*Woody Allen,* 43). It is tempting to connect Allen's concerns as a child about the possible breakup of his parents' marriage with the childhood fear he gives to Alvy in *Annie Hall* that the universe was going to break apart.

14. In *8 1/2,* Fellini gets a similar effect by doing the opposite. As I noted in the previous chapter, Guido's mother appears in a flashback to his early childhood as an old woman, even though she would still have been a young woman at the time Guido is remembering.

CHAPTER 11. POLITICAL CINEMA

1. Michael Stewart was apprehended by police for writing graffiti in a New York subway station and then killed when police used a choke hold to restrain him, similar to the one that causes Radio Raheem's death in the film. Eleanor

Bumpers was a mentally deranged black woman whom police were called in to subdue. They kept firing bullets at her until she was dead, even after they had already disarmed her by shooting at her hand which held a knife. Among other sources, this information appears in Amy Taubin, "Fear of Black Cinema: *Do the Right Thing*," *Sight and Sound* 12, no. 8 (2002): 27.

2. Quoted in Marlaine Glicksman, "Spike Lee's Bed-Stuy BBQ: Spike Lee Interviewed," *Film Comment* 25, no. 4 (1989): 14.

3. Spike Lee with Lisa Jones, *A Companion Volume to the Universal Pictures Film* Do the Right Thing (New York: Simon & Schuster, 1989), 48–9.

4. Lee states this in the supplementary commentary on disk 2 of the DVD version of *Do the Right Thing*, The Criterion Collection, 2001.

5. Spike Lee, *Companion Volume*, 282.

6. Wynn Thomas's comments appear in the unpaginated insert of photographs included in the above-cited companion volume. The comment that they were "trying to create an environment people are going to like on an unconscious level" occurs in the commentary included in the Criterion DVD version of the film.

7. Rosie Perez dances in front of gigantic slides hung in a studio and illuminated by banks of colored lights.

8. Other critics have read this opening number in a very different way, criticizing Lee for perpetuating stereotypical notions of woman as the erotic object of the male gaze. The independent filmmaker Zeinabu Irene Davis, for example, writes: "It is clear that Rosie Perez is a good dancer, but the length of those opening credits and her profiles (particularly towards the end of the sequence) prove only to be another tits and ass visual postcard." See Zeinabu Irene Davis, "Black Independent or Hollywood Iconoclast?" *Cineaste* 17, no. 4 (1990): 37.

9. From Dickerson's commentary in the supplementary material section on the Criterion Collection DVD.

10. The Criterion DVD of *Do the Right Thing* includes the news conference which followed the film's screening at the Cannes Film Festival.

11. Quoted in Marlaine Glicksman, "Spike Lee Interviewed," 16.

12. Quoted in Robert Stam and Louise Spence, "Colonialism, Racism and Representation: An Introduction," in Bill Nichols, ed., *Movies and Methods,* vol. 2 (Berkeley: University of California Press, 1985), 641.

13. Sergei Eisenstein, *Film Form: Essays in Film Theory,* ed. and trans. Jay Leyda (New York: Harcourt Brace & World, 1949), 35.

14. Eisenstein, *Film Form,* 33.

15. Eisenstein, *Film Form,* 34.

16. Eisenstein, *Film Form,* 54.

17. Charles Musser, "L-O-V-E AND H-A-T-E," *Cineaste* 17, no. 4 (1990): 38.

18. I find it interesting that Officer Long, the policeman who murders Radio Raheem by means of the fatal choke hold, is played by Rick Aiello, Danny Aiello's son, symbolically (albeit nondiegetically) linking Sal by blood to the crime.

19. I am indebted to Maria St. John for this observation.

20. Robert Sklar, "What is the Right Thing?: A Critical Symposium on Spike Lee's *Do the Right Thing,*" *Cineaste* 17, no. 4 (1990): 32.

CHAPTER 12. FEMINISM AND FILM FORM

1. Since *I've Heard the Mermaids Singing* Rozema has made four more feature films: *The White Room* (1990), *When Night Is Falling* (1994), *Mansfield Park* (1999), and *Happy Days* (2002). A collection of Patricia Rozema's works is available on DVD from Alliance Atlantis Home Video, 2003.

2. Marjorie Rosen, *Popcorn Venus: Women, Movies and the American Dream* (New York: Avon Books, 1973), 105.

3. These issues are discussed in "The Passion for Perceiving," in Christian Metz, *The Imaginary Signifier*, trans. Celia Britton et al. (Bloomington: Indiana University Press, 1982), 58–68.

4. Mulvey's article originally appeared in *Screen* 16, no. 3 (Autumn 1975), but was reprinted in numerous anthologies of feminist film theory and criticism. My subsequent references to the article are from Constance Penley, ed., *Feminism and Film Theory* (New York: Routledge, 1988), 57–68.

5. John Berger, *Ways of Seeing* (London: British Broadcasting Corporation and Penguin Books, 1975), 47. In *Ways of Seeing,* Berger writes of the way representations of men and women in Western painting have divided up certain attributes according to gender. Images of men connote power or the promise of power; images of women are seen and judged as sights, objects of erotic contemplation. Berger believes women are depicted in quite different ways from men, "not because the feminine is different from the masculine—but because the 'ideal' spectator is always assumed to be male and the image of the woman is designed to flatter him" (64).

6. I say traditionally because these methods of representation have obviously changed since the 1970s (when most of the pioneering feminist criticism was written), as the film industry responded to feminist critiques and the public's desire to see women play more active roles. Nevertheless, to quote Elizabeth Cowie in her extended article on *Coma,* a woman character can be written as "strong" while "as an actant within the narrative she is 'weak.'" ("The Popular Film as a Progressive Text—A Discussion of *Coma,*" in Penley, ed., *Feminism and Film Theory,* 125.)

7. Mulvey's article was controversial from the start, criticized as male-centered in its perspective because it did not explain or theorize in a very satisfactory way why women, if they were so objectified and disempowered in movies, nevertheless made up such a large proportion of the film audience. Women's pleasure in cinema, according to Mulvey, resulted from their narcissistic identification with the eroticized women on the screen, and their masochistic pleasure in the women's objectification and/or victimization. With feminist friends like this, one might well inquire, who needs enemies? Mulvey was also criticized for being heterosexist. All her theorized male spectators went to the movies to ogle women. She never took the male homosexual spectator into account. Nor did her theory acknowledge the pleasure lesbians might have in looking at the bodies of women on the screen.

Moreover, as many critics pointed out, and Mulvey herself later acknowledged in an article entitled "Afterthoughts on 'Visual Pleasure and Narrative Cinema,'" in Penley, ed., *Feminism and Film Theory,* 69–79, women are not confined to same-sex screen identifications. Women can feel empowered identifying with the active males on the screen. Other critics, most notably Gaylyn Studlar, emphasized that male spectators, too, identify not just with the male characters but also with the women on the screen. The point is that movies provide more than sadistic pleasure for men by presenting the spectacle of female suffering. Men can also derive masochistic pleasure by identifying with the suffering woman. Studlar points to the prevalence of films, notably those by Joseph von Sternberg, in which men are victims of powerful women. Thus it is not only women on the screen who are punished and humiliated. See Gaylyn Studlar, *In the Realm of Pleasure: Von Sternberg, Dietrich, and the Masochistic Aesthetic* (Urbana and Chicago: University of Illinois Press), 1988.

8. Mulvey, "Visual Pleasure and Narrative Cinema," 68.

9. T. S. Eliot, "The Love Song of J. Alfred Prufrock," *Major Writers of America II,* ed. Perry Miller (New York: Harcourt, Brace and World, 1962), 770–3.

10. Quoted in Karen Jaehne, *"I've Heard the Mermaids Singing:* An Interview with Patricia Rozema," *Cineaste* 16, no. 3 (1988): 22.

11. Possible exceptions are *His Girl Friday* and *Notorious,* both of which divide attention between the male and female protagonists. Despite the title of Woody Allen's *Annie Hall,* this film is told from the perspective of Alvy Singer, not Annie.

12. Jaehne, "An Interview with Patricia Rozema," 23.

13. Jaehne, "An Interview with Patricia Rozema," 23.

CHAPTER 13. EPILOGUE

1. Wesley Morris, review of *Sordid Lives, The San Francisco Chronicle,* June 15, 2001.

2. Lev Manovich, *The Language of New Media* (Cambridge, Mass.: The MIT Press, 2001), 199–204.

3. At *Timecode*'s premiere it was projected on a digital video projector, but since most theaters do not yet have digital projectors, it had to be transferred onto 35mm film for release in theaters. Figgis had the clout to make such an experimental film because of the enormous success of his *Leaving Las Vegas* (1995).

4. In *Rope,* as in *Timecode,* real time equals screen time, but, because Hitchcock was shooting with 35mm film, the effect of the events on the screen taking place in an unbroken time continuum had to be faked. Some of the individual takes in the film are unusually long, however, lasting up to ten minutes.

5. André Bazin, "The Evolution of the Language of Cinema," in *What Is Cinema?* ed. and trans. Hugh Gray (Berkeley and Los Angeles: University of California Press, 1967), 38.

6. The use of split screens, of course, is not new to the cinematic medium. In 1927, Abel Gance experimented with spectacular split-screen effects in the climax of *Napoleon.* Earlier in *Napoleon,* during a snowball fight, the screen is

split into twelve segments. More recent directors who experiment with split-screen effects in parts of their films include Brian DePalma in *Dressed to Kill* (1980), Stephen Frears in *Grifters* (1990), and Darren Aronofsky in *Requiem for a Dream* (2000). Mike Figgis experiments with them not only in *Timecode*, but also in *Miss Julie* (2000), and *Hotel* (2001), the latter an experiment in form similar to *Timecode*.

7. According to the figures given at http://boxofficeguru.com (accessed August 20, 2003), *Timecode* in its limited release to only seven theaters averaged $13,307 per theater site, an impressive amount for such an experimental film.

Glossary

THE SHOT

Narrative films are made up of a series of *shots*. Also referred to as a *take*, a shot is defined as an uninterrupted run of the camera. Shots can be manipulated in many ways. The following terms, grouped under the headings of Editing, Shot Duration, Shot Type, Camera Movement, Camera Angle, Camera Lens, Lighting, Composition, Symbolism, and Sound, provide definitions of some of the most common techniques by which shots can be ordered and arranged for expressive effect in narrative films.

EDITING

MATCHES, OR TECHNIQUES OF CONTINUITY EDITING

Continuity editing is a system of joining shots together to create the illusion of a continuous and clear narrative action. When a scene is broken up into a sequence of shots for the purpose of achieving greater dramatic emphasis in mainstream narrative films, the shots are usually reconnected smoothly so that viewers do not notice the cut or lose their orientation in screen space. This is often achieved by using *matches* or *match cuts*. Some of the common kinds of match or continuity cuts are defined below. For a comprehensive discussion of the techniques of continuity editing, see chapter 14, "Editing the Picture," in Karel Reisz and Gavin Millar, *The Technique of Film Editing*, from which I have drawn the following definitions.

259

MOVEMENT MATCH In a movement match, a movement or gesture of a character begun in one shot appears to be seamlessly continued or completed in the next shot. As a result, the viewer focuses on the movement and not on the cut. If movements from one shot to the next are not matched, that is, if the same action is repeated in adjacent shots or if a portion of the action is omitted from one shot to the next, the effect will be a noticeable jerk and the action will lose its illusion of seamless continuity. Another form of movement match occurs when the camera moves (tracks or pans) in the same direction at the same rate from shot to shot. Here the movement match is on the camera movement.

DIRECTION MATCH In a direction match, the direction in which a person or object is moving is consistent across the splice. If, for example, a character exits frame right in shot 1, he or she must enter from frame left in shot 2. If the direction is not matched, it will appear that the character has suddenly turned around and is moving in the opposite direction.

EYELINE MATCH The glances of characters in separate shots seem to meet. In order to create this illusion, the direction of their glances must be consistent. For example, if the character on the left looks in the direction of screen right, the character on the right should look in the direction of screen left.

SHOT/REVERSE SHOT A technique usually used to photograph two characters in conversation. Rather than photographing them in a *two shot*, that is, a shot in which two characters are shown together in the frame, the shots alternate between the two characters. First we see one character and then we see the second character from the reverse angle. Over-the-shoulder framings are common in shot/reverse shot editing: that is, the camera alternately photographs one character from over the shoulder of another, with a shoulder prominent in the foreground of each shot.

AXIS MATCH The angle from which the camera shoots the action remains the same from shot to shot. For example, if the first shot is a long shot and the second a medium shot, the camera moves forward without changing the angle from which the action is photographed. If the angle changes slightly, it will appear that elements in the background of the shot have shifted slightly, and the continuity will not be perceived as smooth. If there is a marked change in camera angle (in which the camera moves through 90 degrees) the shot will be perceived as smooth because the background will be markedly different and not create a confusing "jump" in the position of background objects.

POSITION MATCH The position of an object or person remains in the same area of the frame from shot to shot. In a cut from pursuer to pursued, for example, the pursued person would appear in the same area of the frame as the pursuer.

GRAPHIC MATCH Any juxtaposition of graphically similar images, such as a cut from a spinning umbrella to a spinning train wheel. Vivid visual effects can also be achieved by deliberately contrasting graphics from one shot to the next so that, for example, a composition emphasizing vertical lines clashes in the next shot with a composition emphasizing horizontal lines.

RHYTHMIC MATCH Any juxtaposition of images with actions moving at similar rates or speeds. In the above example, the umbrella and wheel would be spinning at the same rate.

JUMP CUT A continuity mismatch in which the rules of continuity are violated, often resulting in the disorientation of the spectator. In jump cuts the characters seem to jump around in space against a constant background or the background suddenly changes while the characters remain in the same position. Jump cuts are sometimes deliberately created by directors who wish to call attention to the medium. Creators of experimental or art films often deliberately violate the rules of continuity cutting. Examples of the deliberate use of jump cuts can be found in Jean-Luc Godard's *Breathless* (1959).

OPTICAL TRANSITIONAL DEVICES

These devices, often created in an optical printer, give a certain amount of pizzazz to transitions between shots. They are used to give dramatic or visual emphasis to marked ellipses in time and space, although they can be employed to enhance the technical smoothness of the transition between shots as well. Optical devices can also help to regulate the pacing of the film and can be used to emphasize symbolic associations between conjoined or adjacent shots. Common optical transitional devices include:

IRIS-IN A shot, found most often in silent films, that opens from darkness in an expanding circle of light. In an *iris-out*, the opposite happens.

FADE-IN A shot that begins in darkness gradually brightens. In a *fade-out*, the shot gradually darkens until the screen goes black.

DISSOLVE A dissolve is the superimposition of the end of one shot onto the beginning of the next, so that the two images briefly overlap. In a *lap dissolve*, the superimposition of the two shots lingers, sometimes (as often happens in *Citizen Kane*) to make a symbolic point about the relation of the two shots.

WIPE In the simplest form of this technique, a vertical line appears to travel across the screen, removing (wiping out) as it travels the content of one shot, while simultaneously replacing it with the content of the next. Wipes can also be made using horizontal lines, diagonal lines, spirals, or circular shapes.

CONVENTIONS OF SHOT CONTINUITY

Developed early on in narrative film history, these are editing techniques that work to increase the spectator's mental participation in the action of the film.

POINT-OF-VIEW (POV) OR EYELINE SHOT A POV shot is the shot that immediately follows a shot in which we see a character looking at something offscreen or beyond the borders of the frame. The camera is positioned where the character's eyes would be. Viewers are cued mentally to construct the shot as if they were viewing it from the point of view of a character in a film. The use of POV shots can establish powerful identifications between the spectator and the characters on the screen. Mentally, we merge with the on-screen characters, seeing the world as they do, from their point of view. Usually, POV shots are from the viewpoint of a protagonist with whom we are supposed to identify, but complicated effects can be achieved when the point-of-view shot is seen through the eyes of villains or monsters. Since POV shots create a strong illusion of being spatially contiguous or in close proximity to the person who is looking, they can achieve interesting effects when they regard objects we know are literally far away. For a disconcerting or surreal effect, a person standing in front of the White House can look offscreen and in the next shot appear to "see" an image of the Eiffel Tower. Soviet theorists called this effect "creative geography."

REACTION SHOT A shot following a POV shot, revealing the reaction of the character from whose point of view we were looking.

CROSS-CUT A cut to another scene or line of action that is usually (but not always) spatially remote from the original line of action, but which seems to be happening simultaneously in time. A common use of the cross-cut that never seems to go out of fashion is alternating shots of an imperiled person with shots of another person coming to the rescue, generating in the viewer's mind the question: Will the rescuer get there in time? One or more lines of action are often crosscut to create dramatic irony (in which the film viewer is given information of which the characters are unaware) or otherwise to "thicken" the plot.

CONTRAST CUT Cutting back and forth between two contrasting actions so that one action strengthens audience response to the other. Shots of a starving man contrasted with shots of a glutton, for example, will increase the impact of both shots, making the former seem more pathetic and the latter more disgusting.

ASSOCIATIONAL CUT A cut made for symbolic purposes to an object which often is not present in the world of the film's story (its *diegesis*). Pudovkin referred to these as symbolic cuts, and Sergei Eisenstein called the technique intellectual montage. In *October* (1928), Eisenstein cuts from a vain, ambitious dictator to shots of a gilded, mechanical peacock. In the cult film *Harold and Maude* (Hal Ashby, 1972), after a psychiatrist asks Harold how he feels about his mother, there is a cut to a huge medicine ball crashing into a brick building.

FLASHBACK, FLASH FORWARD A cut which takes the action to a prior or future time in the plot.

SHOT DURATION

The length (duration) of the shot can determine the rhythm or pace of the film, short shots traditionally being used in scenes of violence, and long shots being associated with more lyrical moments. Shots that end slightly before the viewer has had a chance to take in all they contain can instill an atmosphere of nervous, anxious excitement; films that cut after the average viewer has comprehended the content of the image tend to seem calming, contemplative, or in some cases, boring.

SHOT TYPE

Also called *distance of framing*, *camera distance*, or *shot scale*, this category describes the camera's proximity to the main focus of interest in the shot, which is usually, but not always, a human figure.

CLOSE-UP (CU) A shot taken very close to the subject, so that it fills most of the frame. In the case of a person, it usually includes the head and the upper part of the shoulders, or another portion of the body. In a close-up of a small animal, such as a squirrel, the entire body of the animal would fill the frame.

BIG CLOSE-UP (BCU) In relation to a human face, just the face (without hair or shoulders) or part of a face (the eyes only; the mouth only). In relation to an object, a detail only.

MEDIUM CLOSE-UP (MCU) A shot framing the human subject from the level of midchest.

MEDIUM SHOT (MS) A shot framing the human figure from the waist up. When more than one person appears in the shot, it is referred to as a medium-two shot or medium-three shot, etc., depending on the number of people in the shot. This applies to the next two definitions as well.

MEDIUM-LONG SHOT (MLS) Also referred to as *plan American*, this type of shot frames the human body from the knees up.

FULL SHOT (FS) A person's body appears in its entirety, approximately equal to the height of the screen.

LONG SHOT (LS) The human character appears shorter than the height of the screen and a fair amount of the setting is encompassed within the frame of the shot.

EXTREME LONG SHOT (ELS) The human subject is tiny in relation to the size of the screen.

ESTABLISHING SHOT Usually, a long shot used near the beginning of a sequence to establish the setting or the position of people or objects so that the viewer remains oriented when the sequence is later broken down into a series of closer shots. An extreme long shot is often used as an establishing shot, introducing a landscape or the city in which the subsequent action takes place.

CAMERA MOVEMENT

PAN, OR PANORAMA SHOT The camera rotates from a fixed position along a horizontal plane: The camera can *pan right*, *pan left*, or all the way around in a circle, in a *360-degree pan*.

SWISH PAN A very fast pan that makes action appear blurred.

TILT The camera rotates from a fixed position through a vertical plane. The camera can tilt up or down.

TRAVELING SHOT As opposed to the fixed position of the pan, in a tracking or traveling shot, the camera and whatever it is mounted on (a dolly, a track, an automobile, etc.) moves as it photographs the action. In relation to the action, the camera can track backward, forward, to the left, or to the right.

CRANE SHOT A shot taken from a crane specially constructed for the camera: a moving vehicle with a long boom on which the camera can be mounted and suspended far above ground level. Crane shots can be very dramatic, permitting high-angle tracking and panning shots and moving up and down in relation to the action.

CAMERA ANGLE

The viewpoint or angle from which the camera films the subject.

STRAIGHT ON, OR EYE-LEVEL The camera is located at eye-level in relation to the subject.

HIGH ANGLE, OR ANGLE DOWN The camera is positioned above the subject and shoots down at it.

LOW ANGLE, OR ANGLE UP The camera is positioned below the subject.

DUTCH ANGLE The camera is tilted so that the frame is not parallel to the horizon.

CAMERA LENS

Lenses can alter the perceived magnification, depth, perspective, and scale of objects in the shot.

NORMAL LENS Produces an image with perspective that seems comparable to that seen by the human eye.

WIDE-ANGLE LENS Gives a wider angle of vision than a normal lens. Also skews a scene's perspective, by distorting straight lines near the edges of the frame, and by exaggerating the distance between the foreground and background planes of the shot. The movement of objects coming toward the camera is exaggeratedly fast.

FISH-EYE LENS An extreme wide-angle lens that distorts the image so that straight lines appeared bent or bowed at the edge of the frame.

TELEPHOTO LENS Enlarges or magnifies distant planes, making them seem close to the foreground planes. Has the effect of flattening the space between planes, foreshortening or squashing them together. Objects moving toward the camera appear to make little progress.

ZOOM LENS A lens that can be changed gradually during a shot, going from a wide angle to telephoto or vice versa.

DEEP FOCUS All objects from close foreground to distant background are seen in sharp definition.

SOFT FOCUS The foreground is in sharp focus while the background appears diffuse and hazy. Also refers to the blurred or hazy effect achieved by shooting slightly out-of-focus or through gauze or Vaseline, so that the sharpness of the film image definition is reduced. Can have a glamorizing effect.

RACK FOCUS A shot during which the focus changes, bringing certain objects into and out of focus.

LIGHTING

In addition to the lighting techniques whose definitions appear below, choices about the direction of the light source—whether it is overhead; sidelighting; underlighting; backlighting; or *angel light* (exaggerated backlighting which creates a halo of light around a subject's head)—can have a profound effect on the impact of a shot.

THREE-POINT LIGHTING A lighting style associated with the classical Hollywood style. The shot is lit with three different kinds of light: a *key light* (the brightest and primary source of lighting for the image, this casts the dominant shadows), a *fill light* (which "fills in" to eliminate or soften shadows created by the key light), and a *backlight* (illumination coming from behind the objects photographed, outlining or highlighting the contours of the figure).

HIGH-KEY LIGHTING Bright, even illumination with low contrast and few conspicuous shadows. Associated with comedies, classical musicals, and light entertainment.

LOW-KEY LIGHTING General low level of illumination with high-contrast atmospheric pools of light. The effects of low-key lighting are often enhanced by dark costumes and sets. Associated with mysteries, thrillers, and film noir.

COMPOSITION

Composition describes the significant graphic characteristics of the shot. Do horizontal, vertical, or diagonal lines dominate? Are there interesting combinations of lines? What is the location of the actor in relation to the ensemble of the shot? Are characters or objects arranged symmetrically or in unstable asymmetrical formations? What are the vertical or horizontal divisions of the frame? Is there significant framing within the frame?

SYMBOLISM

Any element within the shot that seems to stand for more than its literal definition, because of either cultural or unconscious symbolic associations. In D. W. Griffith's *The Birth of a Nation,* a racist film obsessed with the fear of miscegenation, fences proliferate, standing for social barriers and internal restraints that are being overthrown. When in Hitchcock's *Notorious* a woman steals a key from her husband's key ring and gives it to another man, who uses it to penetrate the secrets of the husband's wine cellar, most people intuit that sometimes a key is not just a key. In the act of theft the woman has unmanned her husband. Color can be (and often is) used for symbolic effect in narrative films, as are shadows and patterns of light in the setting.

SOUND

The sound in film can be divided into three categories: speech, noise, and music. Each of these elements can be related to the image track in the following ways:

DIEGETIC SOUND   In a narrative film, the *diegesis* of the film refers to the world of a film's story. Thus, diegetic sound is sound whose source comes from within the imaginary world of the fiction.

NONDIEGETIC SOUND   Sound coming from the space outside the narrative—whose source is neither visible on the screen nor implied by the present action. Nondiegetic sound is added by the director for dramatic effect. Examples would be mood music or an omniscient narrator's voice. Silence can also be nondiegetic.

INTERNAL-DIEGETIC SOUND   Sound coming from the mind of a character (an interior monologue of the character's inner thoughts) that we can hear but the other characters cannot. Internal-diegetic sound can also refer to distortions of sound heard by a character that reflect that character's state of mind. For example, in the case of a character going mad, the sound track may be distorted (e.g., too loud, or with strange echoes). Finally, internal-diegetic sound can represent sound hallucinations (the character hears voices no one else in the story hears). Internal-diegetic silence is used to depict moments of concentration so intense that the sounds of reality disappear.

METADIEGETIC   The source of the sound is diegetic, but it is distorted to heighten the dramatic effect for the spectator, and is not necessarily connected to the internal state of a character. For example, a scream might be presented in high volume and electronically distorted, not to reflect the consciousness of an on-screen character, but to shock the audience.

ON-SCREEN SOUND   The source of the sound is present within the frame of the shot.

OFFSCREEN SOUND   In the case of diegetic sound, the source of the sound comes from beyond the frame. Nondiegetic sound is offscreen by definition.

PARALLEL   Sound which complements the image: hands clapping to the sound of applause, romantic music during a love scene, scary music during an ominous scene.

COUNTERPOINT   Sound which goes counter to the image: a merry tune played over a somber funeral procession, a man speaking with a woman's voice.

SONIC TEXTURE   Significant variations or effects achieved through the loudness of the sound track, or characterization achieved through voice pitch, timber, or dialect.

Bibliography

Allen, Woody. *Four Films of Woody Allen.* New York: Random House, 1982.

Althusser, Louis. "Ideology and Ideological State Apparatuses." In *Lenin and Philosophy and Other Essays,* trans. Ben Brewster. New York: Monthly Review Press, 1970.

Altman, Rick. "Deep-Focus Sound: *Citizen Kane* and the Radio Aesthetic." In *Perspectives on* Citizen Kane, ed. Ronald Gottesman, 94–121. New York: G. K. Hall & Co., 1996.

Arnheim, Rudolph. *Film as Art.* Berkeley: University of California Press, 1969.

Balázs, Béla. *Theory of the Film: Character and Growth of a New Art.* New York: Dover Publications, 1970.

Barna, Yon. *Eisenstein.* Trans. Lise Hunter. Bloomington: Indiana University Press, 1973.

Barthes, Roland. "The Death of the Author." In *Theories of Authorship,* ed. John Caughie, 208–13. London: Routledge & Kegan Paul, 1981.

Baxter, John. *Woody Allen: A Biography.* New York: Carroll and Graf, 1999.

Bazin, André. "Bicycle Thief." In *What Is Cinema?* vol. 2, ed. and trans. Hugh Gray, 47–60. Berkeley: University of California Press, 1971.

———. "The Evolution of the Language of Cinema." In *What Is Cinema?* Ed. and trans. Hugh Gray. Berkeley and Los Angeles: University of California Press, 1967.

———. "La politique des auteurs." In *The New Wave,* ed. Peter Graham. New York: Doubleday, 1968.

———. *What Is Cinema?* Ed. and trans. Hugh Gray. Berkeley and Los Angeles: University of California Press, 1967.

Berger, John. *Ways of Seeing*. London: British Broadcasting Corporation and Penguin Books, 1975.

Bogdanovich, Peter. Interview with Howard Hawks. *Movie* 5 (n.d.).

Bondanella, Peter. *The Cinema of Federico Fellini*. Princeton: Princeton University Press, 1992.

———. *Italian Cinema: From Neorealism to the Present*. New York: Frederick Ungar Publishing Co., 1983.

Bordwell, David. *Narration in the Fiction Film*. Madison: The University of Wisconsin Press, 1985.

Bordwell, David, Janet Staiger, and Kristin Thompson. *The Classical Hollywood Cinema: Film Style and Mode of Production to 1960*. New York: Columbia University Press, 1985.

Bordwell, David, and Kristin Thompson. *Film Art: An Introduction*, 6th ed. New York: McGraw-Hill, 2001.

Budgen, Suzanne. *Fellini*. London: British Film Institute, 1966.

Cardullo, Burt. *What Is Neorealism? A Critical English Language Bibliography of Italian Cinematic Neorealism*. Lanham, Md.: University Press of America, 1991.

Carringer, Robert L. *The Making of* Citizen Kane. Berkeley: University of California Press, 1985.

Carroll, Noel. "Interpreting *Citizen Kane*." In *Perspectives on* Citizen Kane, ed. Ronald Gottesman, 254–67. New York: G. K. Hall & Co., 1996.

Carter, Everett. "Cultural History Written with Lightning: The Significance of *The Birth of a Nation*." In *Focus on* The Birth of a Nation, ed. Fred Silva. Englewood Cliffs, N.J.: Prentice-Hall, Inc., 1971.

Caughie, John, ed. *Theories of Authorship*. London: Routledge & Kegan Paul, 1981.

Cavell, Stanley. *Pursuits of Happiness: The Hollywood Comedy of Remarriage*. Cambridge, Mass.: Harvard University Press, 1981.

Chion, Michel. *Audio-Vision: Sound on Screen*. Ed. and trans. Claudia Gorbman. New York: Columbia University Press, 1990.

Clair, René. *Cinema Yesterday and Today*. Trans. Stanley Appelbaum. New York: Dover Publications, 1972.

Cook, David. *A History of Narrative Film*. New York: W. W. Norton, 1996.

Cook, Pam, ed. *The Cinema Book: A Complete Guide to Understanding the Movies*. New York: Pantheon, 1985.

Cowie, Elizabeth. "The Popular Film as a Progressive Text—A Discussion of *Coma*." In *Feminism and Film Theory*, ed. Constance Penley, 104–40. New York: Routledge, 1988.

Cripps, Thomas R. "The Reaction of the Negro to the Motion Picture, *The Birth of a Nation*." In *Focus on* The Birth of a Nation, ed. Fred Silva. Englewood Cliffs, N.J.: Prentice-Hall, Inc., 1971.

Davis, Zeinabu Irene. "Black Independent or Hollywood Iconoclast?" *Cineaste* 17, no. 4 (1990): 36–7.

Delillo, Don. *White Noise*. New York: Penguin Books, 1985.

Deren, Maya. *An Anagram of Ideas on Art, Form, and Film.* In *The Legend of Maya Deren: A Documentary Biography and Collected Works,* vol. 1, part 2, ed. VeVe A. Clark, et al. New York: Anthology Film Archives, 1988. Originally appeared as a stand-alone volume (New York: Alicat Book Shop Press, 1946).

Dixon, Thomas, Jr. *The Clansman: An Historical Romance of the Ku Klux Klan.* Norbone, Mo.: Salon Publishing Company, n.d.

Eisenstein, Sergei. "The Cinematic Principle and the Ideogram." In *Film Form: Essays in Film Theory.* Ed. and trans. Jay Leyda. New York: Harcourt, Brace & World, 1949.

———. "A Dialectic Approach to Film Form." In *Film Form: Essays in Film Theory.* Ed. and trans. Jay Leyda. New York: Harcourt, Brace & World, 1949.

———. "Dickens, Griffith and the Film Today." In *Film Form: Essays in Film Theory.* Ed. and trans. Jay Leyda. New York: Harcourt, Brace & World, 1949.

———. *Film Form: Essays in Film Theory.* Ed. and trans. Jay Leyda. New York: Harcourt, Brace & World, 1949.

Eisner, Lotte H. *Murnau.* Berkeley: University of California Press, 1973.

———. *The Haunted Screen: Expressionism in the German Cinema and the Influence of Max Reinhardt.* Berkeley: University of California Press, 1973.

Eliot, T. S. "The Love Song of J. Alfred Prufrock." In *Major Writers of America II*, ed. Perry Miller, 770–3. New York: Harcourt, Brace and World, 1962.

Fowler, Roy A. "*Citizen Kane*: Background and a Critique." In *Focus on Citizen Kane*, ed. Ronald Gottesman. Englewood Cliffs, N.J.: Prentice-Hall, Inc., 1971.

Freud, Sigmund. *Introductory Lectures on Psycho-Analysis*, ed. and trans. James Strachey. New York: W. W. Norton, 1966.

———. "The Most Prevalent Form of Degradation in Erotic Life." In *Sexuality and the Psychology of Love,* ed. Philip Rieff, 58–70. New York: Collier Books, 1963.

Glicksman, Marlaine. "Spike Lee's Bed-Stuy BBQ: Spike Lee Interviewed." *Film Comment* 25, no. 4 (1989): 12–8.

Gottesman, Ronald, ed. *Focus on Citizen Kane.* Englewood Cliffs, N.J.: Prentice-Hall, Inc., 1971.

———. *Perspectives on Citizen Kane.* New York: G. K. Hall & Co., 1996.

Graham, Peter, ed. *The New Wave.* New York: Doubleday, 1968.

Gunning, Tom. *D. W. Griffith and the Origins of the American Narrative Film.* Urbana: University of Illinois Press, 1994.

Haskell, Molly. *From Reverence to Rape: The Treatment of Women in the Movies,* 2nd ed. Chicago, Ill.: The University of Chicago Press, 1973.

Herrmann, Bernard. "Score for a Film." In *Focus on Citizen Kane*, ed. Ronald Gottesman, 69–72. Englewood Cliffs, N.J.: Prentice-Hall, Inc., 1971.

Hitchcock, Alfred. "Direction (1937)." In *Focus on Hitchcock*, ed. Albert J. LaValley. Englewood Cliffs, N.J.: Prentice-Hall, Inc., 1972.

Insdorf, Annette. *François Truffaut.* Cambridge: Cambridge University Press, 1994.

Jaehne, Karen. "*I've Heard the Mermaids Singing:* An Interview with Patricia Rozema." *Cineaste* 16, no. 3 (1988): 22–3.

Jencks, Charles. *What is Post-Modernism?* London and New York: St. Martin's Press, 1987.

Kael, Pauline. *The Citizen Kane Book.* Boston, Mass.: Little, Brown and Company, 1971.

Lax, Eric. *Woody Allen: A Biography.* New York: Vintage Books, 1992.

Lee, Spike. *Do the Right Thing, Disc 2: The Supplement.* DVD. The Criterion Collection, 2001.

Lee, Spike, and Lisa Jones. *A Companion Volume to the Universal Pictures Film* Do the Right Thing. New York: Simon and Schuster, 1989.

Leprohon, Pierre. *The Italian Cinema.* Trans. Robert Greaves and Oliver Stalleybrass. New York: Praeger, 1972.

Leyda, Jay. *Kino: A History of the Russian and Soviet Film.* New York: Collier Books, 1960.

Manovich, Lev. *The Language of New Media.* Cambridge, Mass.: The MIT Press, 2001.

Mast, Gerald. *The Comic Mind: Comedy and the Movies.* Indianapolis, Ind. and New York: The Bobbs-Merrill Company, 1973.

———. *Howard Hawks, Storyteller.* New York: Oxford University Press, 1982.

Mattox, Jon. "Post Modernism or Post–Post Modernism?" 1995, http://Jonmattox.com/grids/ideas/postmodernism.html (accessed August 17, 2003).

Merritt, Russell. "Dixon, Griffith and the Southern Legend: A Cultural Analysis of *The Birth of a Nation.*" *Cinema Journal* XII (Fall 1972): 26–45.

Metz, Christian. *The Imaginary Signifier: Psychoanalysis and the Cinema.* Trans. Celia Britton, et al. Bloomington: Indiana University Press, 1982.

———. "Mirror Construction in Fellini's 8 1/2." In *Film Language,* trans. Michael Taylor, 228–34. New York: Oxford University Press, 1974.

———. "The Passion for Perceiving." In *The Imaginary Signifier: Psychoanalysis and the Cinema,* trans. Celia Britton, et al., 58–68. Bloomington: Indiana University Press, 1982.

Modleski, Tania. *The Women Who Knew Too Much: Hitchcock and Feminist Theory.* New York: Routledge, 1989.

Monaco, James. *The New Wave: Truffaut, Godard, Chabrol, Rohmer, Rivette.* New York: Oxford University Press, 1976.

Morris, Wesley. Review of *Sordid Lives. The San Francisco Chronicle.* June 15, 2001.

Mulvey, Laura. "Afterthoughts on 'Visual Pleasure and Narrative Cinema.'" In *Feminism and Film Theory,* ed. Constance Penley, 69–79. New York: Routledge, 1988. Originally published in *Screen* 16, no. 3 (Autumn 1975).

———. *Citizen Kane.* London: British Film Institute, 1992.

———. "Visual Pleasure and Narrative Cinema." In *Feminism and Film Theory,* ed. Constance Penley. New York: Routledge, 1988: 57–68.

Musser, Charles. "L-O-V-E AND H-A-T-E." *Cineaste* 17, no. 4 (1990): 37–8.

Nestrick, William. *Film Study Extract:* The Cabinet of Dr. Caligari. Mount Vernon, N.Y.: Macmillan Films, 1975.

Noble, Peter. "The Negro in *The Birth of a Nation.*" In *Focus on* The Birth of a Nation, ed. Fred Silva. Englewood Cliffs, N.J.: Prentice-Hall, Inc., 1971.

Perkins, V. F. *Film as Film: Understanding and Judging Movies.* Middlesex, England: Penguin Books, 1972.

Poe, Edgar Allan. "The Haunted Palace." In *Selected Writings of Edgar Allan Poe,* ed. Edward H. Davidson. Boston, Mass.: Houghton Mifflin Co., 1956.

Pogel, Nancy. *Woody Allen.* Boston, Mass.: Twayne, 1987.

Pudovkin, V. I. *Film Technique and Film Acting.* Ed. and trans. Ivor Montagu. New York: Grove Press, 1958.

Reisz, Karel, and Gavin Millar. *The Technique of Film Editing.* New York: Hastings House, 1968.

Rogin, Michael. "'The Sword Became a Flashing Vision': D. W. Griffith's *The Birth of a Nation.*" *Representations* 9 (Winter 1985): 150–195.

Rohmer, Eric, and Claude Chabrol. *Hitchcock.* Trans. Stanley Hochman. New York: Frederick Ungar Publishing Co., 1979.

Rosen, Marjorie. *Popcorn Venus: Women, Movies and the American Dream.* New York: Avon Books, 1973.

Ryall, Tom. *Alfred Hitchcock and the British Cinema.* London: Athlone, 1996.

Sarris, Andrew. *The American Cinema: Directors and Directions 1929–68.* New York: Dutton, 1969.

Schickel, Richard. *D. W. Griffith: An American Life.* New York: Simon and Schuster, 1984.

Seton, Marie. *Sergei M. Eisenstein.* New York: A. A. Wyn, 1952.

Silva, Fred, ed. *Focus on* The Birth of a Nation. Englewood Cliffs, N.J.: Prentice-Hall, Inc., 1971.

Sklar, Robert. "What Is the Right Thing? A Critical Symposium on Spike Lee's *Do the Right Thing.*" *Cineaste* 17, no. 4 (1990): 32–3.

Spoto, Donald. *The Dark Side of Genius: The Life of Alfred Hitchcock.* New York: Da Capo Press, 1993.

Stam, Robert. *Reflexivity in Film and Literature: From Don Quixote to Jean-Luc Godard.* New York: Columbia University Press, 1992.

Stam, Robert, and Louise Spence. "Colonialism, Racism and Representation: An Introduction." In *Movies and Methods,* vol. 2, ed. Bill Nichols, 632–49. Berkeley: University of California Press, 1985.

Studlar, Gaylyn. *In the Realm of Pleasure: Von Sternberg, Dietrich, and the Masochistic Aesthetic.* Urbana and Chicago: University of Illinois Press, 1988.

Taubin, Amy. "Fear of Black Cinema: *Do the Right Thing.*" *Sight and Sound* 17, no. 4 (2002): 26–8.

Thompson, Kristin, and David Bordwell. *Film History: An Introduction.* New York: McGraw-Hill, 1994.

Toland, Gregg. "How I Broke the Rules in *Citizen Kane.*" In *Focus on* Citizen Kane, ed. Ronald Gottesman, 73–7. Englewood Cliffs, N.J.: Prentice-Hall, Inc., 1971.

Truffaut, François. "A Certain Tendency of the French Cinema." In *Movies and Methods,* ed. Bill Nichols, 224–37. Berkeley: University of California Press, 1976.

Truffaut, François, with Helen G. Scott. *Hitchcock,* rev. ed. New York: Simon and Schuster, 1984.

Weis, Elisabeth, and John Belton, eds. *Film Sound: Theory and Practice.* New York: Columbia University Press, 1985.

Wollen, Peter. *Signs and Meaning in the Cinema.* Bloomington: Indiana University Press, 1969.

Index

All films are listed individually by title rather than under the filmmaker's name.
Page numbers in *italics* refer to figures.

Text:	10/13 Sabon
Display:	Akzidenz
Compositor:	Integrated Composition Systems
Printer and binder:	Thomson-Shore, Inc.